I am the
Reluctant Messiah
and So Are YOU

I am the Reluctant Messiah and So Are YOU

by
Rev. Robyn Accetturo, LCSW

Copyright © 2025, Rev. Robyn Accetturo, LCSW
All rights reserved. Printed in the U.S.A.

This book is a work of non-fiction. Except where permission was given, names have been changed to protect the privacy of all individuals. The events and situations are true. The dialogue contained within was not recorded at the time of occurrence, but after-the-fact, during the re-creation of the story.

No part of this book may be reproduced, stored in a retrieval system, or transmitted by any means, electronic, mechanical, photocopying, recording, or otherwise, without written permission from the author.

Quantity Purchases:
Companies, professional groups, clubs, and other organizations may qualify for special terms when ordering quantities of this title.
For information, email info@ebooks2go.net,
or call (847) 598-1150 ext. 4141.
www.ebooks2go.net

Published in the United States by eBooks2go, Inc.
1827 Walden Office Square, Suite 260,
Schaumburg, IL 60173

ISBN: 978-1-5457-6322-3

Library of Congress Cataloging in Publication

Words of Praise for the Teachings of
I am the Reluctant Messiah and So Are YOU

"I highly recommend I am the Reluctant Messiah and So Are YOU. This book is for anyone who is looking to understand themselves, improve their health, and improve their relationships. Reverend Robyn Accetturo, L.C.S.W., so clearly and simply teaches us to learn how to become our true Self. She uses her own traumatic life experiences, educational background as a Licensed Clinical Social Worker, and her years of practical experience and combines that knowledge with her research into the metaphysical world. This combination of physical, mental, emotional, and spiritual knowledge that she shares is priceless. She elegantly articulates how to heal from the inside out. Her explanation and use of the 4-stroke cycle is a stroke of genius. As an integrative doctor, I have used the concepts and tools she teaches in this book to help me work not only on a physical level with my patients but also on a mental, emotional, and spiritual level. I am a spiritual being in a human body. Raising my vibration with Robyn's help has brought me insight into myself, my family, and my patients. Thank you, Robyn, for this gift."

Anju Usman Singh, M.D., True Health Medical Center

"Reading through this awe-inspiring book, I am the Reluctant Messiah and So Are YOU, I experienced so many "God Bumps" as the author, Robyn Accetturo, L.C.S.W., refers to them. I felt my heart being busted wide open. This is a real-life story of survival, breaking traumatic family cycles, addiction, hope, resilience, transformative love, and much more. Robyn shares her spiritual journey including her life experiences that led her to "the 4-stroke cycle" for healing and beyond. This book reminds us of our innate Divine connection to our Spirit, heart, and Soul. It lays out many mental health and spiritual practices which are available passionately

and clearly for all to pursue. Robyn teaches and shares her Divine wisdom and message story after story that we can all genuinely relate to. This powerful book will change the world at a critical time in humanity for those seeking more spiritual connection, knowledge in consciousness, and making a positive difference in our lives and the world!! I am honored to give my blessings to Robyn and her healing book I am the Reluctant Messiah and So Are YOU. Much gratitude. Godspeed."

Patty Heatherly O.T.R./L, C.P.C. Behavioral Health Services – Holistic Occupational Therapist and Certified Life Coach

"Robyn Accetturo, L.C.S.W. has opened her heart and shared her mind to tell of her psychological and spiritual journey. From codependency as a child and abuse as a young spouse to insight, support and love as a devoted helper and healer, she learns to develop and bring forth her best self, her spirit in human form. In so doing, she enriches her life, the lives of others often in great need, and ours. A most constructive understanding of human experience and possibilities! A book to treasure, with so much substance you may want to reread it again and again to grasp its meanings!!"

Christopher B. Keys, Professor Emeritus, Department of Psychology, DePaul University

"As I read, I am the Reluctant Messiah and So Are YOU, it brought every emotion to the surface, from deep sorrow to pure elation. It is a book that will leave you craving to know more. I did not want to set it down. The author, Reverend Robyn Accetturo L.C.S.W. shares a riveting detailed account of embracing and opening to her spiritual gifts, which is utterly awe inspiring and empowering. What truly made me fall in love was the raw authenticity and vulnerability in which this book is written. This book is heartfelt through and through. I was immediately captivated by the real-life circumstances that were so intimately shared yet rarely acknowledged aloud in the 1980's. It allows you to feel as if you are right there in the story with her. Robyn's courageous openness and dedication to continuously give unconditional love despite the monstrosities she endured gives hope to us all. Robyn walks in faith and not fear while shining her love light on

everyone she touches in this book and beyond. She is blessed with the gift of unconditional love. This book reveals how what happens to you does not have to define you."

Deshawna Bentley, Spiritual Advisor, Psychic/Medium

"I have known Reverend Robyn Accetturo, L.C.S.W. for over 20 years. Her knowledge and deep spiritual wisdom have been such an inspiration. Her teachings are direct and so valuable. Her love, kindness, and integrity are second to none!

Robyn taught me to meditate, look within, and trust myself for answers to any questions I may have about myself. We are all learning! We all have the ability to look within for answers.

I am grateful for Robyn's inspiration, teaching, knowledge and friendship."

Rita Vogel, Vogel Hair Design

"In 2007, I had my first Reiki session in Fair Haven, New Jersey. My reaction to the session was unlike anything I had ever experienced, and I knew I needed to find a Reiki Healer in Illinois. Once I returned home and googled Reiki Healers near me, I found Reverend Robyn Accetturo, L.C.S.W. I was raised in Brooklyn, New York, in a rough area called Bedford Stuyvesant and was taught very early in life how to protect myself and to be cautious. So, calling someone on the phone based upon their name appearing on the Internet did not go along with the rules I had been taught. But, for some reason without skipping a beat, I picked up the phone and called Robyn. Although I didn't know it then, I was divinely guided to her.

Robyn came to my home for my first Reiki healing session. This night was a truly life-changing event. I was in awe! Through her gifts, I was reunited with my family and friends who had passed away, and I was introduced to my Angels and Spirit Guides. Thanks to Robyn's gifts, I discovered my faith in a new way. Robyn has become my friend, confidante and teacher. She has never-ending compassion for friend or stranger. Robyn is an everyday Earth Angel, and I treasure having her in my life."

Laurel Fisher, M.S. in Counselling, L.P.C., Licensed Professional Counselor, Grief Counselor

"In her book *I am the Reluctant Messiah and so are YOU*, Robyn Accetturo, L.C.S.W. weaves the mystical and the practical together in a way that keeps the reader enthralled. At times, the book almost reads like a fantasy, but in sharing the extraordinary nature of her personal experiences, there is no denying the truth Robyn expresses in telling her story.

No matter where you are on your spiritual journey, whether you are just starting to acknowledge unseen possibilities, or you are further along the path, this book provides valuable insights and down-to-earth suggestions, which anyone can use. The author presents specific tools leading to deeper and deeper spiritual awareness. The reader can choose tools that feel like psychology or ones that are more esoteric. Whatever resonates, this book provides a wealth of information.

Ultimately, it is a Self-help book, self with a capital S. It is a book to lead us within, to our true Divine nature, which is love. It also shows us the recognition that we are spirit fundamentally having a human experience. Knowing we are a spirit operating a human body, and acting from this space, will change your life. Let this book be your guide."

Ronni Weiss, M.S.W., Master's in Social Work

"Robyn Accetturo, L.C.S.W.'s part memoir and part lessons from spiritual guidance is a must read especially for those of us in the practice of the healing arts. As we follow our spiritual guidance and soul path, we open ourselves to the possibilities of seeing the miracles all around us, especially in what presents as pain and suffering in this world. Robyn does a masterful job of weaving these truths in her book and sharing from her heart the lessons from Spirit, with the ultimate lesson of knowing we are all connected both on this planet and in the space of spirit energy when we no longer inhabit out earthly bodies. Robyn's courage to share these fundamental truths despite those who aren't able to embrace it is one of the tenets of those who are called prophets. I am deeply grateful she is willing to have courageous authenticity and share deeply from her heart and soul."

Rita Lampe, L.C.S.W., Licensed Clinical Social Worker, Advanced Eden Energy Medicine Practitioner – In Harmony Energy Balancing and Healing, LLC

"If you have ever questioned why you were compelled to do something that you just couldn't explain, or wondered how you ended up being in the right place at exactly the right time, then Reverend Robyn Accetturo L.C.S.W.'s book, I am the Reluctant Messiah, and so are YOU is a definite must read! This beautifully written story is a call to action that implores the reader to recognize that we are all meant to be here, we all have gifts, and if we can just let go of the negative thoughts and feelings that are holding us back, we can share those gifts with those around us for the greater good of humanity. This book is uplifting and encouraging, and I implore every reader to open their hearts and minds to allow Robyn to teach you how to implement your own God given talents and gifts so you can be your true authentic self and the person God intended you to be."

Paula Bruce, B.A., Q.I.D.P., I.S.S.A., Social Services Advocate

"I met Robyn Accetturo, L.C.S.W. during a pivotal moment in my life. I signed up for Reiki training and Robyn was assisting with the training. Our connection was instant, and I was amazed at her vast spiritual knowledge and understanding. Growing up as a Catholic, I knew a great deal about religious teachings but something always seemed to be standing in the way of my connection to God. When my spiritual journey began, I started to understand that what I'd been searching for the whole time and missing from my life required a slight shift and opening to ideas that were different from what I learned in church. Robyn was the spiritual teacher and mentor who showed up as soon as I was ready to learn! She patiently listened to every question and fear I had, and she explained concepts and ideas that made sense to me. I ended up taking many meditation training classes from Robyn which were the turning point in my life. For the first time, I understood that God and my spirit were intimately connected, and I could feel that connection more and more strongly as my meditation and spiritual practice became a daily part of my life. I can't recommend Robyn and her book highly enough. Robyn was a true Angel in my life who appeared at just the right moment and helped my life to grow in ways that I only imagined possible. Robyn's spiritual

knowledge, connection, and understanding surpass anyone's I've ever met. If you want to change your life and learn how to feel happy, fulfilled, and excited about fulfilling your life's purpose, Robyn's book can help you get there."

Serafina Sharpe, M.S., C.C.-S.L.P., Speech Language Pathologist

"Thought provoking and beautiful, I Am the Reluctant Messiah and So Are YOU is a guide to understanding we are spiritual beings having a human experience. Robyn Accetturo L.C.S.W.'s "Spiritual Operations Manual" gives holistic guidance on healing from personal traumas and the importance of facing and releasing our emotions. A must for everyone. At the same time, this is a beautiful yet heart breaking story of someone who dug deep within herself to heal her own traumas. It shows Robyn's unwavering faith in a Higher Power and the miracles that happen when we operate as spiritual beings. I am grateful for her wisdom and courage to share."

Donna Ohman, P.T.A., C-I.A.Y.T., Physical Therapist Assistant and Certified Yoga Therapist

DEDICATION

I dedicate this book with my deepest appreciation for all their support, encouragement, love, and Light, to all my loved ones in Spirit, my Spirit Guides, Master Teachers, and Angels, and to my beloved family. I could not have accomplished this without my husband James, our daughter Kathryn, her husband Alan, our son Stephen, and our grandsons James and Levi.

ACKNOWLEDGEMENTS

I am so grateful to my beloved husband James, and my circle of Soul Sisters, Anju Usman-Singh, Ronni Weiss, and Patty Heatherly for their support with my manuscript. Much gratitude to Kathryn, Alan, and Stephen, for their assistance and feedback also. Grateful for all of my endorsements from my sacred Soul Sisters.

A special thank you to my editor, Heather Allen at 2 Doodles Consulting, my literary attorney, Steve Baron, of Baron - Harris - Healey law firm, and to Lawyers for the Creative Arts in Chicago. Another special thank you to Benedict Gierl, M.D., for appearing in my first prophetic dream that started my husband and I on our exquisite spiritual journey and for writing my foreword. Thanks to Professor Chris Keys for all your academic support at a time in my life when I needed it most. So much gratitude to all of you. Thank you from the bottom of my heart.

CONTENTS

Foreword xv
Introduction xvi
Chapter 1: A Life Changing Connection. 1
Chapter 2: Inward Journey to Knowing 7
Chapter 3: Prophetic Dreams and Spirit 21
Chapter 4: The Universe's Intention 32
Chapter 5: Seeking Spiritual Answers 37
Chapter 6: Camp Chesterfield 45
Chapter 7: No More Fear 56
Chapter 8: Oops, I Spilled the Beans! 62
Chapter 9: We Are Spiritual Beings 65
Chapter 10: Feelings are the Key. 74
Chapter 11: Hurt/Loss, Anger, Anxiety, Guilt and Depression. . 77
Chapter 12: Josie Figures Out Her Stinking Thinking. 83
Chapter 13: Completion 90
Chapter 14: The 4–Stroke Cycle Engine. 93
Chapter 15: Spiritual Operations Manual 98
Chapter 16: Sickening the Cycle 107

Chapter 17: Conflict between Our Mind and Spirit 111
Chapter 18: Following My Heart 116
Chapter 19: Life Skill Tools for our Well-Being 120
Chapter 20: More Tools for Our Physical, Mental, and Emotional Health. 135
Chapter 21: Using My Life Skills Tools with a Child Abuser. . . 144
Chapter 22: Many Spiritual Tools for our Self-Growth 147
Chapter 23 Prayer and Meditation 154
Chapter 24: Manifesting, the Law of Attraction, Affirmations, Visualization, and the Pendulum 162
Chapter 25: The Importance of Color Vibration as a Spiritual Tool 170
Chapter 26: Essential/Anointing Oils and Divination Cards. . . 176
Chapter 27: Clairvoyant Readings, Astrology, and Crystals . . . 186
Chapter 28: Reiki Healing. 191
Chapter 29: Numerology, Medical Qigong, Sound Healing, Masaru Emoto, and Chakras 194
Chapter 30: Jeremy's Healing 203
Chapter 31: Carolyn's Diagnosis and Proof of Her Healing . . . 207
Chapter 32: My Beloved James Accetturo 210
Chapter 33: Epilogue 221
About the Author 226

* Note from the author: I capitalize words that reference God, the Divine, Earth, Spirit, Spirit Guides, Master Teachers, Angels, Highest Good, Soul and more.

FOREWORD

It is truly a pleasure to read and closely study *I am the Reluctant Messiah and So Are YOU*. Robyn Accetturo has been incredibly open about her trauma and spiritual growth. With the help she has sought from many others who are remarkably gifted, she has created a powerful story of spiritual development. Robyn has been able to heal others miraculously by connecting with them spiritually.

Given the mental health crises of overdosing and suicide among young people, Robyn offers help for others. She unveils avenues to open their hearts and minds to the world of spirit. What a much richer world we will have when people gain spiritual knowledge and learn to listen for guidance through prayer and meditation. This is a much-needed story that is both inspirational and supportive to those who have experienced trauma. This book offers multiple pathways to pursue healing and spiritual expansion as one is so inclined.

I must disclose that I was the Psychiatrist in her prophetic dream in 1987.

Benedict Gierl, M.D., Retired Assistant Professor Department of Psychiatry and Behavioral Sciences, Rush Medical College, Chicago, Illinois

INTRODUCTION

*B*laze the new trail. Be in the world but not of the world. We are born here on Earth after choosing to come here from the world of Spirit, where our Soul resides. We take form in a human body that we chose to inhabit at this time. Each of us is a Spirit expressing ourselves as a human. Four years ago, a medium told me that some of us come here as Earth Angels, yet most of us come for karmic reasons to learn for our Soul's growth. She shared that my husband and I are Earth Angels who came here to do a specific thing that we agreed to do before we got here. We received the request to serve here on Earth, as instruments for the Greatest Good of All. So here we are. The title of this book came to me over 25 years ago when our children were small. Yet, both my husband and I had more lessons to complete in our own lives in order to honor our Divine timing of this book. It has not been an easy journey.

Using my deeply messed up life as a real example, the reader will learn specific mental health tools which I needed to learn to heal my heart filled with trauma, so I could become a mentally healthy adult. After growing up in an alcoholic family and moving in with my boyfriend at 17, I experienced six years of domestic violence until I had the courage to flee in 1983, at the age of 23. Therapy changed my life and set me on a course to becoming who I am today. I graduated with my master's degree in social work in 1989 and became a Licensed Clinical Social Worker in 1991. I was ordained in 2008 at the First

Temple of Universal Law in Chicago as a Minister and a Healer. I am also a Certified Reiki Master Healer and Teacher.

We are born as a Spirit into a human body. We have learned how to operate as humans but have forgotten who we really are. We have learned to listen to our thoughts and our stinking thinking, which are thoughts we think that do not serve our Highest Good. We have come to believe we are these thoughts. Truth is, we are the Observer who knows we have these thoughts. Our feelings hold the key to healing our trauma. We have forgotten how to feel. Too many of us have defended ourselves against our feelings for so long, we have become numb. We treat our depression, anxiety, PTSD, grief, and more using alcohol, drugs, risky behaviors, and even guns to act out our anger and rage buried for much of our lives.

We are individual sparks of God, Infinite Intelligence, Source Energy, whatever you want to call It, expressing Itself as us! I feel most comfortable calling It, Father, Mother God. We are each unique Divine Connectors between Heaven and Earth, here for a specific purpose. Yet we feel stuck, trapped inside the trauma of our own hearts. So much of our daily energy focuses on defending ourselves from feeling the stored-up trauma lying deep within, that we do not feel anything. Hurt and loss is always at its core.

Our trials, traumas, and tribulations hold the key to unlocking the real us, our Spirit within. Once we learn how to operate in a mentally healthy way, using the viable tools shown here, we can delve into learning how to operate our body from our Spirit using a 4-stroke cycle combustion engine as our model. We each have our own Divine Guidance System. We came here with Spiritual Senses that assist us in powerful ways. Once we can name them, we can claim them and change our life and our world. Our spiritual senses are our connectors to our loved ones in Spirit, our Spirit Guides, Master Teachers, and our Angels. This book will teach how to connect and experience our own Spirit and how we can connect with the world of Spirit.

We have chosen to be here now on the Earth Plane. It is time we learn how to operate these bodies from our Spirit. We are on a Spiritual Mission, individually and collectively to usher in the fifth dimension:

the Age of Aquarius, harmony and understanding. We are on a journey to find our way back home to our individual spark of God within, our Spirit. We are the instruments through which Divine Ideas manifest heaven on Earth, here and now. So, let's do this fellow Spiritual Beings. We are One Spiritual Community who CAN heal the world, beginning with our own heart. Let us dig in using both the mental health and spiritual tools given here and do this together. The world is waiting.

Chapter 1

A LIFE CHANGING CONNECTION

"In order to write about life, you must first live it." Ernest Hemingway

———•••———

As I knocked on the patient's door before stepping into his room, I instantly felt my heart start to race and got a feeling of nervous anticipation in my gut. I had completed many psychosocial assessments on this very same adult inpatient psychiatric unit, yet I had never gotten these sensations before. I introduced myself to the elderly man and invited him to my office so we could have more privacy. He introduced himself as Billy, looked me in the eyes, extended his hand with a firm grip, and stated valiantly, "I've been waiting my whole life to meet you, Robyn." I did have my ID badge on with my name on it, yet his tone and words sent shivers down my spine. The hairs on both of my arms stood straight up. I call them "God Bumps." I get them when I am receiving confirmation from my Higher Self.

Billy's chart revealed a diagnosis of bipolar disorder with psychosis and multiple hospitalizations in this same psychiatric unit over many years. This was my first time assessing him, since his assignment to my caseload for individual counselling and group therapy. I was the new psychiatric social worker on the unit. I had just graduated with my master's degree in social work with a specialty in both psychiatric and medical social work.

I showed Billy to the office I shared with my supervisor, who was the other therapist on the unit. I closed the door behind us and pulled my chair out from behind my desk, so there was less space between us. Here I am, a 29-year-old white female social worker interviewing, according to his face sheet, a psychotic, black, 77-year-old bipolar patient who tells me he has been waiting to meet me his whole life. Yet, Billy felt familiar, almost comfortable.

Billy sat somewhat sideways, spilling over the chair, so he could look directly into my eyes. His grey sweatsuit, which matched his hair color, was a bit too small for his large frame. He reminded me of a laughing Buddha, with his big belly, irresistible deep chuckle, and his palpable smile. I asked Billy to describe the reason for his psychiatric admission. His response: "So I could meet you, Robyn."

"Well, Billy, I have to admit, I have never started an assessment with a patient who tells me they're in the psychiatric hospital so they could meet me," I chuckled uncomfortably.

"That's because they are not ME. This is MY mission," he replied unwaveringly.

"All right then. Tell me more, please," I responded, feeling curious, yet restrained.

"Yes, yes, we have all the time in the world right now. Now holds the key." Billy shifted his weight to gaze out the sunny window in our office. "I grew up in one of the poorest towns in Illinois. I owned my own business as a master auto mechanic," he asserted, pointing his left thumb at his chest. "I raised my kids and gave them the best parts of me. I have an open heart, but it's selective. Few people in this world are as open-hearted as you are, Robyn." Billy turned and looked me straight in the eyes again. "You would run into a burning building without a thought, if you heard a child crying inside. Many would never even try."

Before I could speak up, Billy stood and walked over to the window, gazing into the sunshine with his back to me. He continued telling me my own life story, "The youngest child of a brilliant set of parents. Your mom became an alcoholic after your first decade of life. Your dad became an angry man who coped by working and sleeping too much. You were bright as a kid; you even skipped a grade. Your mom was a rebel who courageously defended the Black kids bussed to your grade school in 1967, when it was the first desegregated public school in Chicago. However, once her mom died when you were ten, your mother abused alcohol. Frankly, you did not seem to matter much anymore. You could have walked on water and only your mom would have noticed. But she was too under the influence to acknowledge."

I felt like I was in a movie scene with Clarence, the Angel earning his wings, in *It's a Wonderful Life*. My mouth hung open. I found it hard to form words. This was leaving me feeling quite vulnerable yet intrigued. Who in the world was this man? Why had the Universe brought us together like this? Why NOW? Was Billy truly psychotic? Why wasn't I spooked by his knowing about my life and me? But his "reading" of me was 100% on target!

I checked the clock and shifted the energy by asking Billy to sit back down so we could focus on my assessment questions. Billy cooperated and stated his reason for admission was mania. I gathered what I needed enough for my preliminary report. Our time was up. I would see Billy in group therapy in 15 minutes. However, Billy was not quite finished yet. Looking me directly in the eyes once more, he held out his hand to pat mine. "You are stronger than you know, Robyn. I have a few more things I need to say. I need to prove my validity as to why God has put us together. What our mission is ahead…"

I stood behind my desk, feeling intimidated. I was not surprised Billy did not feel his message thus far was enough, as I sensed his restlessness. Billy continued.

"One would never know that you moved from the frying pan into the fire at a mere 17 years of age. You survived six years of domestic violence when most people your age were out having fun discovering life and themselves. You eventually learned your boyfriend was an IV drug addict, after you moved in with him to seek a permanent respite from your alcoholic family system."

Billy continued, "What you experienced, Robyn, led you to right NOW, with you sharing your experiential knowledge of feelings and how to heal them. It is time you help others to do the same. You not only escaped, but you took action to heal from six years of domestic violence and growing up in an alcoholic family. You learned how to love yourself and those we deem unlovable. You escaped in Divine time, and you know it! The timing of your receipt of spiritual gifts and our meeting, none of this is by chance, Robyn," he said with passion. I had to sit down at my desk. My heart was galloping. I needed to catch my breath. A total stranger knew my life with 100% accuracy. The power of the truth of his words and knowledge about me felt eerie since they were coming from a psychiatric patient, yet his accuracy told me he was directly communicating with Spirit, just like a clairvoyant medium does.

Billy walked back toward my desk and stood beside me. A ray of sun shined through the window, illuminating his face. He turned to look me right in the eyes. "You KNOW as you've figured it out personally, you cannot rescue someone. We each must save ourselves."

"Yes, Billy, that is accurate. Life is an inside job. We each are responsible to save ourselves," I confirmed.

"I hope you're aware of the buzz on the unit about your therapy group, Robyn. Your patients are getting excited about themselves again. You and I both know that you learned incredible lessons from every part of your life – the good, the bad, even the horrifying. These lessons were key for you and are vital for all of us to help unlock our authentic Spiritual selves. You are doing the honorable thing by passing along your wisdom."

"So, here's the deal: You must practice on us what you're thinking and receiving from the intuitive guidance within you. Our job is to help you KNOW you are on target through the outcome of your group treatment. People are going to get better in your group. There will be one-time inpatient admissions, and the suicidal repeats will go home and not return to any more psych units if they commit to using, in real life, the skills you are teaching us in group. Your tools work. They are basic to use once you get the hang of putting them into practice."

Wow! Billy had only been to my group once. He brought my attention back to the room when he asked, "Well, what do you think? Will you go out on a limb and try us? Let us help you as you help us. It is a win-win situation. While we're at it, keep this all private except for your husband. You are going to need his feedback. Amazing spiritual man, you married. And he's a social worker!" Billy smiled and patted the top of my hand perched on my desk. Before I could even respond, he walked out of my office.

I continued feeling quite vulnerable and needed to pull it together before starting group therapy with over 15 patients in just 10 minutes. I took a deep breath and exhaled, doing my best to digest what had just happened. As I glanced at the clock, I heard a knock on my door. Billy stuck his head in, stepping inside once again and closing the door behind him. "It is most urgent I tell you the plan, NOW, why we must work together. I cannot wait another minute." I remained silent, listening intently. "I've been in that same level of functioning therapy group in this same hospital for years. You are onto something big here, Robyn. I am here to encourage you and to teach you about how a 4-stroke cycle combustion engine operates, so I can help you figure it out and write down your theory about feelings. So many people will be helped, especially men," he stated emphatically. "Trust yourself. Trust me. Trust God. Just do it, please, so I can be finished."

"Auto mechanics? Theory about feelings? So, you can be finished?" My voice trailed off as I let out an awkward laugh, wondering what Billy knew about this and how he knew what I had been thinking.

"Yes. I need you to take this seriously. Buy the book, *Auto Repair for Dummies*. I am here to teach you the mechanics of a 4-stroke cycle combustion engine. Beginning next Monday, I expect you in the art room after the workday is over to study with me, 5 p.m. Monday through Friday. Make sure we're finished studying before I go to dinner at 6, please." And with that, Billy turned around and marched out of my office.

When I got home after work that night, my husband, Jim, felt excited for me as I shared my experience with Billy. He did provide words of caution, however. "Be very aware of other professionals on the unit. I trust you. I know you are on a spiritual quest. Not so sure about others, though. They might think you're psychotic and lock you up on your own unit if they find out!"

Although Jim was teasing me, I knew he was correct. I had to be overly cautious not to share the spiritual experiences I already had with patients on the unit, not only with Billy. I accidentally let the cat out of the bag to my social work supervisor one afternoon. I ended up unknowingly giving her a powerful clairvoyant message I received from Spirit, through a painting she hung on our office wall. It was a gift from Mark, a returning schizophrenic patient admitted for hallucinations. He had painted it for her in art therapy. Eventually, another patient, Josie, a first-time psychotic admission, attempted to wash my feet with her hair while we were in the middle of the hallway of the psychiatric unit. More on those two experiences later.

When I checked in with my Spirit, it felt right for me to accept and trust Billy and his message. I listened to my inner voice, and I acted on it. I purchased *Auto Repair for Dummies*, read the chapter on the 4-stroke cycle combustion engine, and felt eager to connect with Billy for an hour after each workday.

Chapter 2

INWARD JOURNEY TO KNOWING

"Until you make the unconscious conscious, it will direct your life and you will call it fate." Carl Jung

---

My magical journey into gaining understanding of mystical spirituality began during graduate school two years earlier, in 1987. Why? After Jim and I were married and I began my clinical internship, I began having prophetic dreams about one of my patients.

Jim was totally open and supportive of me throughout this entire spiritual journey as we began our search together to find answers as to the occurrence and meaning of these dreams. We were led on a spiritual path where ancient knowledge revealed mystical and magical palpable outcomes right before our eyes. The more we experienced it, the more we yearned for this spiritual knowledge. We could not get enough! We sought out formal spiritual teachers and mentors. There was so much to learn and uncover from the inside out. We learned about gnosis, which is having knowledge without knowing where it came from. Gnosis is uncovering universal truths hidden deep within us. Like that speech written by Marianne Williamson and spoken by Nelson Mandela: "Our deepest fear is not that we are inadequate. Our deepest fear is that we are powerful beyond measure. It is our Light, not our darkness that frightens us the most."

My prophetic dreams were frightening and I HAD to find answers through real, experiential knowledge in our three-dimensional reality. This feeling was so strong, I knew I had no choice but to dig deeper and fasten my seat belt! I was on a spiritual journey leading me to uncover more sacred mysteries in the here and now. I felt it deep within.

This discovery of Spirit in action begins with self-discovery on the inside, through healing our stored feelings and trauma. Once we work on ourselves to feel and release these stuck feelings, we make space in our heart for the Universe to fill us with our spiritual gifts. The dreams that unfolded for me transpired two years after therapy, where I worked to uncover why I allowed myself to stay in a six-year relationship rooted in domestic violence. Growing up in an alcoholic family, I did not learn about feelings, and I didn't know how to handle them in a healthy way. I also did not learn how to set and keep good boundaries or learn healthy communication skills.

Not only did I did not know how to say no as an adult, but I was also not comfortable expressing anger either. This was because some of my adult siblings and my dad's anger was palpable to me as a kid. I did not like how their anger made me feel. So, I mostly felt hurt as a child, not only my own, but everyone's hurt underneath their anger.

My mom was an extraordinary woman who came to America from Ireland with my oldest sister in tow, after marrying my dad during World War II while he was stationed in Ireland. He was in the U.S. Army Air Corp and loaded bombs onto bomber planes. My mom spoke perfect Queen's English. She read a minimum of three books each week, both fiction and nonfiction. By the time I was born, my mom was 36 years old, and my dad was 45. Mom volunteered often in her community. She participated in the PTA, was my sister's Girl Scout and my Brownie leader. She volunteered for our local precinct on voting day, and more. She always had dinner on the table, and we ate daily as a family. My mom did not become an alcoholic until I was 10 years old after her mom passed away, back in Ireland. My sense is that her grief turned into depression, and she used alcohol to treat herself.

I was the youngest of five, with a 14-year gap between the oldest and me, so Mom and I were the closest. I always tried to help. Seeing my mom in so much mental pain and anguish taught me a lot of empathy. When she did not cope well with her feelings, I felt them for her. This is enmeshment. My mom and I lacked emotional separation. Most of my childhood, I took it upon myself to do my best to take her pain away. She was a brilliant woman who cared deeply for others and stood up for injustices. Once she became an alcoholic, I set zero limits on my mom's behavior. I did not even know what a limit was.

Just before my 17th birthday, my parents moved from Illinois to a condominium on Clearwater Beach, Florida after my dad retired. Since I skipped a grade as a kid, I was the youngest senior in my class. I had to move with my parents, as I had no option for staying behind in order to finish out my senior year in Illinois. I attended my last semester at Clearwater High School taking only one class while working at a convenient store on Clearwater Beach. I began dating a pre-med student from the University of South Florida in Tampa, who frequented the store for a deli sandwich.

My mom's drinking continued to escalate after graduation, so I moved into my boyfriend's apartment, in Tampa, with my cat, Toby. I was 17 years old. Toby, who had been severely abused prior to my adopting her five years earlier, sensed the bad energy immediately. Upon entering the apartment, she took a dump on the rug and fled.

My live-in boyfriend was a disabled Vietnam Veteran and a drug addict. I knew he smoked pot, but I had no idea about the drugs. The abuser manipulated me into thinking he was all I had, and that my family did not care about me anymore. I felt trapped and alone. Over time, he isolated me from family and friends. I made it through two years of junior college and attended my third year of college at the University of South Florida. The abuse got so bad I had to drop out. It had become exceedingly difficult to work full-time, attend school, and deal with his explosiveness.

The abuse was more than physical. It was shaming and degrading, meant to tear me down. The most horrific thing he did and I agreed to, happened when my dad was dying at home, in hospice, from cancer.

By then I was 21 years old. My mom had learned to give my dad morphine shots, as the cancer had spread to his bones causing excruciating pain. The only way the abuser would allow me to say goodbye to my dad on his deathbed was if he could go with me. Why? His plan was to steal some of my dad's morphine and shoot up in my parent's bathroom. If I did not go along with his horrible plan, not only would I not see my dad for a final goodbye, but he also threatened me with physical consequences. I felt like a prisoner with nowhere to go.

At the time, my wages barely paid half of the rent, utilities, and food. I did not own a car, and I could not afford taxi fare from Tampa to Clearwater Beach. I was so weighed down by my shame. I had no choice but to agree.

The abuser's plan came to pass. He shot up some of my dad's morphine in my parent's bathroom, while I was saying my final goodbye to my dad. At 21, I felt deep shame and remorse. My dad died a few days after my visit.

My mom's drinking was at an all-time high to the point of her sometimes blacking out. I did not talk to any of my siblings. I had severed ties with my friends, dropped out of college completely, and was working full-time bussing tables and being the alternate cashier in a mall cafeteria. This is not where I imagined myself as I attended college as a pre-med biology major with stellar grades. Neither was it when I was in junior high reading *Sybil*, *David and Lisa*, and other nonfiction psychology books from one of my older siblings who was a psychology major in college. At this point in our living together, I believed, in my codependent mind, that if only the abuser would listen to me and get help, he would be able to stop doing drugs. I believed we could live happily ever after, and I actually hoped he would propose.

Over the six years we lived together, the abuser convinced me that no one cared about me except him. I was 23 years of age when he proposed to me and promised that if I married him, he would get help. I believed him. I accepted his proposal, and now I see this was exactly what the Universe and my Spirit wanted me to do. It finally gave me a light at the end of the tunnel.

I am grateful to have survived those first 30 days of marriage. The abuser's violence against me increased in frequency as well as severity. I literally felt him up the ante. I felt more trapped than ever. But my will to live was strong inside of me. My Spirit knew better. The increased threat level along with my cat Toby returning to me by showing up at the front door pregnant, gave me the courage to finally escape. I knew it was Toby immediately. If I had any doubts, I just had to check a scar that one of her abusers left. I made her a spot in the closet and that night Toby gave birth to a litter of three kittens.

The day Toby returned was approximately three weeks into the marriage. The day before her return, we were driving in his car, and I was looking out the window, daydreaming. Unexpectedly, at a stop light, he began a tirade and accused me of flirting out the car window with a guy standing at the bus stop. Before I could even speak up to defend myself, he took a high-heeled shoe, hit me over the head with the heel enough to draw blood, and then slammed my head into the passenger side window. This was the most violence I had experienced so far. At that moment, I knew better than to speak. I also felt strongly that this episode was not over. I had no idea whose stiletto it was.

Less than a week later, for the first time ever, he threatened to kill Toby, her three kittens, and me. I cannot even remember why. Honestly, he fabricated many reasons to harm me. When he pulled out a butcher knife and slammed it on the kitchen counter, it scared me to my core. His threat was real. I felt it. I knew I had better take him seriously. When he left for the grocery store, while the knife and my fear held me hostage, the part of me who warned me to take this seriously quickly kicked into high gear to protect me. Our Spirit always communicates to us a response for our Highest Good. Always. But do we listen? I most certainly did this time!

I called my mom. I shared that I was in danger from domestic abuse. She told me to grab whatever possessions I did not want to lose, including Toby and her three babies, and flee immediately. She called a taxi that picked me up from a location where I was hiding in the bushes. I managed to escape with my clothes in a paper bag, sandals on my feet, and the kitties. I moved in with my mom. She found and paid for a therapist, who helped me change my life. Her condo had a gate with a security guard, which helped me to feel safer staying there. I was so incredibly grateful for her help and support. She decreased her drinking to only after dinner while I lived with her to heal my life.

I began individual therapy with a male therapist the week I moved back home. Sometimes I attended therapy two or three times a week, depending on how much the abuser was stalking me during that time. My therapist recommended I read *The Language of Feelings* by David Viscott, MD, which I did. I would carry a copy of the book with me, and I considered it my "Feelings Bible." It helped me to make sense of my feelings, including hurt and loss, anger, anxiety, guilt, and depression. By understanding and naming my feelings, I could claim them, feel them, and give them a voice, which allowed me to release and free my innermost truths. The knowledge contained in that book has had a profound impact on both my personal and professional life, as I have incorporated its knowledge not only into who I am, but also into my repertoire of therapeutic tools I have used ever since I read it in 1983.

While living with my mom, I worked at a local bank in Clearwater. One day, when I was called to the lobby, the abuser was waiting for me and made a huge scene. He begged me to come back, claiming to have stopped using drugs. I managed to calm him down, keep myself safe, not go outside with him as he was attempting to manipulate me to do, and keep my job with my response. Even though I handled it, it shook me to my core. When I called my therapist who supported me by phone during every crisis, I fell apart. I was truly proud of myself for confronting the abuser in person and handling him on my own. The healthy communication skills I was learning in therapy to stand up for myself were so powerful. Prior to learning them, I had no idea how to set a boundary or a limit with people. I let people walk all over me. I did not know how to stick up for myself. I said yes, even when I wanted to say no. At this point in my life, I only knew how to enable an addict so they could keep drinking in order to stay alive. That meant I helped their addiction to continue with zero consequences. First my mom and then him.

I was so grateful to learn how to set boundaries, limits, and so much more from my therapist. He insisted I stay in treatment until I figured out WHY I would allow myself to be in that abusive situation, so I would never tolerate violence against myself ever in my life. After nine months of intensive therapy, I had figured out my why!

I was eager and enthusiastic to graduate from therapy to be the REAL me. I was ready to start my new life. The skills I learned in treatment have served me greatly, in life, and as a practicing social worker since 1989. It is interesting that it took nine months as this number means "completion" in numerology. Through the relationship formed with my male therapist, along with the skills he was teaching me, it became a healthy template for me to follow and put into practice what a mentally healthy human being looks like in a healthy relationship. Prior to therapy, I had not been able to clearly communicate my needs. I also did not know how to receive, only give. This is a classic trauma response. Do not expect anything from anyone, so we do not get hurt!

I read a fabulous book as part of my healing after I ended therapy entitled *Codependent No More* by Melody Beattie. She also has a workbook to go along with it. Both were incredibly powerful tools for me, which contributed to my healing and finding my Spirit within.

Allowing myself to feel my feelings in the moment as well as feel and heal those repressed feelings from my childhood was the beginning of my transformation into my Higher Self. Learning healthy boundaries and great communication skills were all mental health tools I had to gain an understanding of in therapy, as I did not learn them from my family as a kid. Neither did I acquire the knowledge at school, Girl Scouts, or church. I had to learn to name and claim my stuffed feelings. Only then was I able to connect the dots and piece my life together. For the first time as an adult, I felt excited and enthusiastic about myself and looked forward to my future. I got divorced from the abuser and asked for nothing but my maiden name back. To get the marriage annulled, I would have had to attend divorce counselling in his church and face him again. So, I did not get it annulled. Divorce, my maiden name back, and my safety were all I needed.

At the age of 24, I began life anew. I found homes for all three kittens, and Toby and I moved back to Illinois. I worked part-time and ended up finishing my bachelor's degree at the University of Illinois at Chicago (UIC) in Psychology, with distinction. I graduated with distinction because of my three years in pre-med. Since I spent so much of my life helping and serving others, and I was no longer codependent on another trying to fix them to prove to myself that I was lovable, I changed my mind and decided against becoming a physician. I wanted to pursue psychology or social work instead, having discovered that my true passion was in the service of others through mental health. I knew if I could get myself out of domestic violence, I could support others in changing their lives from the inside out, as well. I had risen from my own ashes like a Phoenix and was eager to show others how to do the same.

Before becoming a professional counselor, my first semester at UIC, I saw a flyer in the Behavioral Sciences Building offering training to become a crises intervention and telephone counselling hotline volunteer. The In-Touch hotline provided services for the city of Chicago and was run by the Student Counselling Service. Every hotline participant was a volunteer. Doctoral students in psychology and social work who provided mental health services to UIC students through the Student Counselling Service supervised us once we graduated from training and became full-fledged hotliners. I was having so much fun living and loving my life and myself. The first day attending training, I had no idea at the time that I was meeting my future husband, Jim. He was the Student Volunteer Hotline Director and Trainer. Our meeting was a Divine Intervention. I was working on myself to become the best me that I could be. A romantic relationship was the last thing on my mind.

The hotline application was very personal and in-depth. I was vulnerable and had shared my recent freedom from domestic violence. I also shared how my history led me to serve others through mental health counselling. Not every hotline volunteer graduated from the training.

The first day of gathering for our instruction, Jim was late. The Director of Student Counselling opened the meeting by speaking to the 75 hotline volunteers. When Jim, the tardy volunteer student Hotline Director for that fall 1985 semester walked in, we were all sitting on the main floor of the church near UIC where the training took place. Jim quietly snuck around the speaker and sat, of all places, right next to me. We were instructed to introduce ourselves to the person sitting next to us. I turned and introduced myself, not knowing who he would become to me. When I spoke my name, I noticed Jim had an interesting look on his face. Later, when we became good friends and began dating, he shared that he had picked out my hotline application and decided he wanted to get to know me, personally. Wow! My being vulnerable on the hotline application and Jim's effort in connecting with me is how the Universe brought us together. We dated while finishing our undergraduate degrees at UIC.

From the beginning, Jim and I began a beautiful spiritual journey together. We did our best to both come from an open heart and to purposely share our feelings and be vulnerable together on a deep inner level. Jim had also been through therapy before meeting me. We read books together on many Sunday mornings while lying on a blanket at North Avenue Beach in Chicago. Then I would drive to Glendale Heights for my weekend job as a food server for Chi Chi's Mexican Restaurant. Books like *Seth Speaks* by Jane Roberts, *The Aquarian Gospel of Jesus the Christ* by Levi, *You Can Heal Your Life* by Louise Hay, *Creative Visualization* by Shakti Gawain and *Love is Letting Go of Fear* by Gerald Jampolsky, MD, were some of our favorites.

In fact, when Jim proposed to me in October of 1986, we used many of the books mentioned to write our own wedding vows together. We felt strongly, deep in our hearts, the more time we spent with one another, we became convinced we were Soul Mates. Because of our mutual love of God, spirituality, and the Universe connecting us, we acknowledged that we were a pretty unique couple. Our spiritual power increased when we were together. We deeply felt our mission to accomplish something magnificent together. Life's magic began to unfold right before our eyes, even on our wedding day. As Jim was loading his car to get ready at his parents' house, he was so nervous and joked, "I may need an ambulance! I am so excited and nervous; I feel my heart pounding out of my chest." As we went to load the trunk, an ambulance literally turned into the alley behind our apartment. The ambulance driver parked for a minute behind our car and then backed out of the alley and left! We laughed aloud at the synchronicity of the moment of Jim's instant manifestation of an ambulance. At this point, our Higher Selves were planting seeds deep into the fertile soil of our unconditional love. We had decided the best route to give our love freely to the world was to become healers, social workers, parents, and conscious community members.

I am sharing our wedding vows here to show how deeply spiritual Jim and I were even before my prophetic dreams led us on a quest for the Holy Grail. I was so grateful to be meeting my spiritual life partner. We were married in the summer of 1987, almost two years after we met. During our wedding ceremony, we both cried happy tears reciting our beautiful and heartfelt wedding vows to each other. They felt so powerful:

> "I promise to have an open heart: to give and receive love freely, to share my feelings and to communicate freely.
> I promise to be honest; to be responsible for myself; to love, honor, obey and cherish my own being and your being; and to honor the connection I feel with you and maintain that connection.
> I promise to support and care for you, and I offer you my love and my support throughout all our lives.
> I will continue to find an intensity of love and learning with you as we change and grow.
> I will strive to achieve my potential as God's creature and will share with you in the same goal.
> I give myself as I am, and I will be. And I do it for all of life. I love you."

Together, we committed to growing our relationship as a couple and taking it to a new, sacred level. We set our intention and dedicated our time and energy to serving God and Humanity. The Christ Consciousness sits in the heart, as our heart carries the highest frequencies of unconditional love, joy, peace, compassion, grace, mercy, and more. We can prepare for the entrance of the Christ Consciousness by healing and releasing our stored trauma. This allows our heart to become open and filled with unconditional love, which is our original birthright. The promise and commitment of each wedding vow we spoke aloud became our template to follow to allow the Christ Consciousness to fill us and work through us. Our intention to serve God reached further than our family and ourselves. We both felt deeply that we had come to Earth to fulfill more than one Sacred Contract together that had not yet come into our awareness. We spoke together of the Divine Feminine and Divine Masculine and discussed how we had both experienced the Divine Feminine energies inside each of us helping us to break through the repressed feelings of our subconscious mind. Growing up, both Jim and I played similar roles in our family of origin. For both of us, attending individual therapy played such an important role in helping us to step into our power to become an unconditionally loving, open-hearted Spirit operating a human body.

Weeks after our wedding, I began graduate school while Jim worked on a locked psychiatric unit of a hospital. Within our first four years of marriage, we both graduated with master's degrees in social work (M.S.W.). We both also became Licensed Clinical Social Worker's, or L.C.S.W.'s.

During my first-year clinical internship in the fall of 1987, my prophetic dreams began. After spending nine months in intensive therapy, I learned how to become mentally and emotionally healthy by feeling and releasing my stored-up feelings and childhood traumas. Sometimes our body must decide to survive. Then later when we are safe, our Soul helps us pick up our broken pieces to help us HEAL.

In therapy, I learned healthy boundaries, great communication skills, and more. I began to heal myself on every level possible – physical, mental, emotional, and spiritual. Each traumatic event taught me so much about my inner Self and inner strength. Each experience became an opportunity to learn about my Spirit operating in a human body. The stuck energy of the old traumas was awaiting my love and attention. Once I gave that to myself in therapy, allowing my inner deepest feelings to be seen, heard, and felt, their energy and power moved out! Their hold on me had vanished. The little girl in me felt safe again. I felt amazingly lighter. Because of the Natural Law called the Law of the Vacuum, we know that nature will not allow a vacuum. Therefore, when energy moves out, the space it created must be filled with new energy.

In my case, when the old energy moved out, the incredible love and empathy in my heart for all people such as that shown by my mother prior to her alcoholism, filled me to the brim. Soon I felt the will to serve God and Humanity as never before. So, with an open heart, I declared daily, "Heavenly Father, Mother God, I wish to serve." The space made by releasing my stuck feelings filled me with the highest vibrational energy of unconditional love, which was in me all the time. I felt it since I was small. I needed to set it free. I began to use it to serve God by allowing myself to become an instrument for following Divine direction to help others. The more I served with a heart full of unconditional love, the more Divine Interventions occurred right before my eyes. This has been a lifetime endeavor, to follow my heart and live out my passion of teaching others how to heal their inner child in order to step into our spiritual power and become who we incarnated to be.

Daily, with an open heart, I would pray and set my intention, "Heavenly Father, Mother God, I wish to serve." And daily the Universe would respond and show me ways to do so. In John 14:12 Jesus the Christ teaches us that, "Verily, verily, I say unto you, he that believeth on me, the works that I do shall he do also; and greater works than these shall he do, because I go unto my Father." The energy that Jesus is speaking of is the Christ Consciousness. It is through this Christ Consciousness that we accomplish these greater works. Jesus was able to empty himself of his ego self to operate from his Christ Self 100% of the time. The Christ Consciousness is within. It is not just in some of us but in all of us. It sits at the HEART. When our vibration is high enough in our thoughts, words, and deeds, we too can become a vessel for the Christ Consciousness to shine through us. By opening our hearts, we reach our higher frequencies of unconditional love, joy, peace, compassion, grace, mercy, and more. The only way to open our hearts fully and allow ourselves to fill with Christ's Consciousness is to feel our pain so we can empty our past hurts from our hearts. Our healed and open heart contains the KEY to unlocking the Christ Consciousness within. That key is LOVE. In Matthew 22:37-39, Jesus teaches us to love God with all our heart, mind, and Soul and to love our neighbor as ourselves.

I healed my heart by attending therapy and learning to become the best me. Feeling, releasing, and learning about ourselves from our feelings is the exact ticket we all need to heal our wounded hearts and continue to grow and allow this Christ Consciousness to work through us. Each of us MUST uncover our Light within and begin to recover from our past to reveal our Spirit and our specific SOUL'S purpose for being here in this lifetime. We owe it to ourselves. The world is awaiting the unique talents and gifts we agreed to share before we came here. The time is NOW. If not us, WHO? If not now, WHEN? The world needs us to do our inner work and return to unconditional love for ourselves and for each other and our planet.

Loving ourselves by feeling our feelings and taking back our power is the answer to healing our heart. Albert Ellis, psychotherapist, coined the term "stinking thinking." Stinking thinking are thoughts we think that do not serve our Highest Good. Believing we will fail, thinking bad things are always going to happen to us, self-hatred, loathing, and the critical and unkind ways we talk to ourselves are all examples of our stinking thinking. These thoughts become our enemy. We come to believe we are our thoughts. No. We are the OBSERVER who knows we have thoughts. Stopping our stinking thinking is essential to healing our heart.

Our heart holds the vibration of pure unconditional love for all, with zero judgement. This is also the definition of the Christ Consciousness. When our own consciousness within is sufficiently high enough of a vibration to become a vessel to hold the Christ energy, and we keep our FAITH, we too can become a vessel for the Christ power to transmute matter into Angelic Light. Every one of us is a Spirit operating from inside a human body. We can raise our consciousness high enough to be a vessel to carry the Christ Consciousness. The same Christ Consciousness that filled Jesus and allowed him to transmute energy into Healing Light, unconditional love, and even physical matter is REAL. Healing is possible, as is Angelic transmutation and more.

Indeed, we are the Holy Grail. Our human body is the vessel that contains our Spirit. God expresses Itself through each of us. We are each a Divine spark of God. We are the instruments on Earth to carry out God's Divine Ideas and plans. When we can be empty enough to be filled with that highest vibration of the Christ Consciousness and sustain it, as Jesus did, we too, can do as Jesus the Christ did. And we can do even more as he tells us in John 14:12, King James version. "Verily, verily, I say unto you, he that believeth on me, the works that I do shall he do also; and greater works than these shall he do; because I go unto my Father."

These prophetic dreams, which I will detail in the next chapter, kickstarted me upward and inward into the unseen parts of myself and my world. It was no accident that intensive therapy pieced my heart and Spirit back together, allowing my spirituality to open. To this day, it continues to blossom and grow. When we set our intention to serve God and the Universe from pure unconditional love, the Universe gives us spiritual gifts and power to serve with.

So, back in 1989, Billy, live, standing in front of me, in my office on the psychiatric unit was a beautiful awakening and just the beginning of my most powerful spiritual journey toward allowing the Christ Consciousness to work through me.

Chapter 3

PROPHETIC DREAMS AND SPIRIT

"Experience is not what happens to you; it is what you do with what happens to you." Aldous Huxley

———•·•———

How on earth could I feel so excited yet stay incredibly calm after meeting with Billy? Indeed, this meeting was extraordinary. My bipolar patient gave me a perfectly accurate clairvoyant Soul reading of my life, and we had never even met. Following Billy's instructions and learning the 4-stroke cycle combustion engine, both felt right for me to do. For some reason, I trusted Billy and I trusted my own instincts. After all, we were on a locked psych unit. What could go wrong?

I was counting on everything going right. I was learning to trust more than my path and myself. Spirit was simultaneously giving me a crash course on trusting them. It felt exhilarating on so many levels. Jim was excited for me and for us. He took every step with me that he could and encouraged my curiosity, trusting myself, and trusting Spirit. I was so incredibly grateful for my husband's support.

Two years before meeting Billy, I had my first ever, vivid, prophetic dream one night that literally played out right before my eyes. It happened the day I had a powerful counselling session with an elderly female patient at my clinical internship for my master's degree in social work. This dream and another, about the same patient, came true within a week and a few days of me dreaming them. The power of the whole experience shook me to my core. It led my husband and me on a life-changing journey for our future children, our community, and ourselves. It resulted in us taking spiritual development and meditation classes at a seminary/metaphysical Spiritualist center in Indiana, called Camp Chesterfield. It is part of the NSAC or National Spiritualist Association of Churches. We eventually found and studied under a wonderful spiritual mentor and teacher living in Chicago, Reverend Sally Wales. She resided at Camp Chesterfield from Memorial Day through Labor Day and taught classes from her home in Chicago the rest of the year. I felt such a strong push inside and knew I had to follow my instincts to discern the meaning and purpose of my experiences. The power of the bursting open of my Soul, which began as a series of dreams and then real-life experiences in the flesh, frightened me to my core. Even though it was life affirming and life changing, it felt too overwhelming. I needed a guide. I needed someone to educate and show me, us, how to navigate through the new awareness I was experiencing. This metaphysical, spiritual side of life is not religion. It is what Jesus the Christ taught. It is what many other Master Teachers who have walked on Earth have taught. Spirituality is metaphysical, which means more than the physical or transcending physical matter. It is who we are.

The power of my dreams coming to fruition right before my eyes felt daunting and intimidating. I wanted to tell the Universe to pick someone else. It felt like an incredible amount of responsibility, and not just personally. It felt heavier than that. It felt like the weight of a worldly responsibility.

Jim was incredibly supportive, grounded, and openhearted about my spiritual experiences since the prophetic dreams began. The day following the first dream, Spirit continued to get my attention. Neither my husband, nor I, had any clue what Universal Truths we were about to uncover. Sometimes, without us thinking about it, something moves us. Whether through our dreams, insights, songs on the radio, or a force that keeps us from making that left turn, we must heed the message. This is the Spirit of our loved ones, Angels, Spirit Guides, and Master Teachers communicating with us from the other side. They do not have a physical body, so there is no physical voice box of their own from which to communicate in our 3D world. Therefore, we must learn HOW to communicate with them through our OWN capabilities, and by practicing as we figure out each other's energy language.

We learn to decipher the intended message from Spirit through symbols, colors, sensing, listening with our spiritual ears, and more. Every physical sense we own has a corresponding spiritual sense as well. More details will follow. Through the relationship we eventually form with Spirit, we work out our dance of communication with them. Knowing God and experiencing the power of the Universe is so different from "believing" in God, which is what most religions teach. Spirituality beckons us to go within to uncover and find the "God spark" inside of us. It is not just in some of us; Source Energy resides in us all. When we clear out trauma from our heart so we can let go of the old stuck energy we have stored there, we learn to love ourselves. When we love ourselves AND our neighbor as ourselves, we step into our own unique spiritual power. It is through the study and practice of Natural Law, prayer, and meditation that we learn to communicate with our Spirit Guides, Master Teachers, loved ones in Spirit, and our Angels. Each of us chose to be here right now on the Earth Plane to learn how to be a Spirit in a human body and shift the vibration of the world to LOVE. We have the capacity to send love out to the world with every breath by setting our intention and following up with conscious action in the moment. Imagine how we can change the entire energy of the cosmos by each loving heart consciously sending out love and healing to the Universe on each exhalation. Unity. We are One Spiritual Community.

For Jim and me, both individually and as a couple, our lives changed tremendously one Thursday afternoon in 1987. It happened after I had finished a powerful counselling session with a 72-year-old white female patient. This patient had been admitted to the inpatient rehabilitation unit of the Chicago geriatric hospital, the Johnston R. Bowman Health

Center for the Elderly at Rush University Medical Center, where I was a social work intern. She came back to life in the ambulance, with a defibrillator, after she suffered a massive heart attack at home alone. She had two living sons, both in their late forties.

I met "Arlene," a retired statistician, after her admission. I introduced myself as her social worker and before I was able to explain my reason for visiting her, she said, "Why don't you go help someone who needs you. I'm an independent woman," and she threw me out of her room. However, within two weeks, Arlene's situation began to change, so I approached her again. After a complete cardiac workup, which ruled out many things, Arlene's blood pressure medications were changed. At the end of the week, Arlene was given the go ahead to be discharged, where she would be home alone. Her two sons made her discharge plan without her input. She mysteriously began experiencing physical symptoms as her discharge date came near.

Arlene had many other tests as her physicians attempted to ascertain the cause of her latest symptoms. All diagnostic testing came back negative. I learned that Arlene's orders included a psychiatric consultation. This meant she would be moved to the locked psychiatric unit in the same hospital if her symptoms continued and prevented her from returning home. I asked my supervisor if I could try something with Arlene before the psychiatric consult occurred. She agreed it was a good idea.

I knocked on Arlene's door and asked her if she would like a session with me. She reluctantly said yes. That morning, she came across as softer and more vulnerable. She shared details of her heart attack. Being brought back to life in the ambulance, via defibrillator, had traumatized her. During our counselling session, she was able to connect with her feelings of not wanting to live. She was not suicidal, but instead keenly aware she needed to do more planning of her wishes around her own death. She wanted to choose what she wanted done to her physical body if her heart stopped beating again. Arlene was a highly intelligent, left-brained woman, who had not yet come to terms with getting in touch with her anger about being "paddled back to life."

I became aware that perhaps the reason Arlene did not want to return home was that she did not want to live. I intuitively made up an exercise to get her in touch with her feelings. There was much under the surface. I asked Arlene whom she was closest to in her life. She answered her deceased mother.

I had Arlene visualize her mom sitting in the chair at the side of her hospital bed. Together, we explored Arlene's feelings about life and death and included her mom in the circle of conversation. Arlene began to cry, as she told her mom, "I want to join you in heaven. I wish to have never been brought back to life." Helping Arlene express more of her feelings allowed a dam to break, flooding Arlene's heart with her truth. Powerful sobbing filled the room. We continued in the moment, using Gestalt Therapy, to allow Arlene access to her feelings in the now, by having a powerful conversation with her mom. Gestalt is a form of psychotherapy that focuses on the present moment and uses our current experience to get in touch with our stored feelings. By the end of our session, Arlene was more in alignment with her whole Self, and stated she felt emotional and mental relief like she had never experienced before. She admitted she had not been able to cry or share her feelings since she was a small girl.

Expressing our feelings in a safe space is a natural response to honoring our Self and healing our Soul. I use a capital S, in Self, to represent our Higher Self, the Observer, which is our Spirit inhabiting our own human body. This whole experience took Arlene about 30 minutes to express and naturally allow her feelings a place to be heard and felt. Feeling and releasing one's feelings allows for the output, or the releasing of the exhaust, ultimately allowing our old stuck energy to become peacefulness and dignity.

That same Thursday night of my session in Arlene's hospital room with her mom, I had my first prophetic dream before I awakened the next morning. I dreamed I walked into my office at the Bowman Center to answer my ringing telephone. The Attending MD, Dr. Ben Gierl, from the inpatient geriatric psychiatric unit on the ninth floor, was on the other line. He shared that Arlene's CT scan and other tests came back normal, pointing to a mental or emotional cause for her symptoms. He took the opportunity to assess her to be admitted to the inpatient psychiatric unit. The outcome of this assessment was that Arlene was going to die, and soon. He did not share how he came to that conclusion. I felt stunned as these words exited his mouth. "Your role, Robyn, on this team, is to notify Arlene's family of her impending death while I share the news with Arlene herself."

I froze. Every ounce of my being revolted. Who did this physician think he was? God? I woke feeling infuriated by his response to Arlene, her family, and by his request of me. My heart felt extra heavy that morning. I did not have my clinicals until the following Tuesday, so I would have to wait and see what this dream, if anything, had to do with reality. I continued to pray for Arlene's Highest Good to be served and for Divine Order to reign over her life and affairs. Divine Order means "God's will."

As I walked onto the rehab unit at the Bowman Center the following Tuesday morning, my supervisor, Donna, shouted she would meet me in my office in a minute. She had something urgent to tell me. My heart began to race, and my palms got sweaty.

Donna walked into my office, closed the door, and sat down. "Arlene had a heart attack the evening after your session last Thursday. She's in the cardiac unit at the Rush Medical Center side of our building. She's confused. The only thing she is oriented to is your name, which I find fascinating. Normally, the hospital would not allow this, however, I trust you. So, I've gotten permission for you to follow her inpatient at Rush. I hope you are okay with that?" I answered in the affirmative. "Okay then, so go, go, go! Your patient awaits your help."

My heart raced as I walked to the other side of the hospital. I prayed for Arlene's Highest Good to be served, and for Divine Order to reign over our session. The dream I just had about Arlene and the psych consult to share her impending supposed death flooded my awareness. My hand shook as I stepped closer and knocked on her door. Before my speaking, Arlene seemingly sprang to life as soon as she saw me. She blurted out my name as I stepped inside her room.

"Robyn!" she said clearly, "Where have you been? I need you to help me talk to my mom!" I liked her excited tone, and her energy rose as soon as I got near. Her face flushed as she pulled herself up to a sitting position.

"Well, Arlene, let's do it!" I answered. "How are you feeling?"

"Better, now that you're here."

"Do you know why you've been moved here since last Thursday?"

Seemingly ignoring my question, Arlene blurted out, "I saw my mom again! We were together when I had my second heart attack after my first session with you! Seeing her was lovely. Please, help me. I MUST visit her again."

"You want to do the exercise again and talk to her?"

"Now, please!"

"Okay then. We shall connect with your mom again, together."

"Let's do this, thank you!!" Arlene straightened her posture expectantly awaiting to speak with her mother in Spirit.

I supported Arlene by doing Gestalt Therapy again. She spoke to her mom, whom she imagined was sitting next to her on her hospital bed. This time with Arlene so present, it truly felt like her mom was sitting with us having a cup of tea. Arlene processed her feelings. She was able to connect the dots to articulate that being in touch with her feelings and communicating with her mom made her 100% sure she did not want to be resuscitated again. Arlene wished to die with dignity on her own terms. We discussed the use of hospice care when it was time for her physical body to let go. She asked me if I could help her to communicate her wishes to her sons. Back in 1987, social workers did not offer forms to patients in the hospital as we do now, such as a Do Not Resuscitate (DNR) form, Living Will, or Power of Attorney for Health Care. All our paperwork was done manually as we did not have internet access yet. Arlene wanted both sons to be included in her important decision. She felt an urgency to communicate with them directly and honestly.

I suggested a family meeting where Arlene could speak her truth and convey her end-of-life needs with her children. I offered to obtain these forms so she could sign them before meeting with her family in case something happened to her heart prior to our session. She adamantly refused and stated emphatically she needed to tell them face-to-face. She did ask me to obtain these legal forms and present them at their family session as soon as possible. A Living Will would specifically state Arlene's wishes for the end of her life. Arlene refused to sign a DNR form and have it witnessed without her sons' permission. I explained to her she was taking a risk of coding and having the paddles used on her one more time, her worst nightmare, if she waited until her children were included. She still chose to wait so she could speak directly to them. She desperately needed them to support her decision. Arlene thanked me and threw me out of her room once more, asking me to call her sons NOW to get the ball rolling. Her feistiness and determination were refreshing. Our exercise helped her to gain back her awareness of person, place, and time.

I returned to my office and called both sons. I scheduled their family session for my next internship day, that coming Thursday. I sat for a minute and said a prayer of thanks. Arlene had pulled it together enough mentally and spiritually to make an autonomous decision about the most important thing in her life right now. Sharing her feelings and desires for a Living Will and DNR with her adult sons was scary for her yet liberating. Arlene was allowing herself to become vulnerable. Telling our truth and being vulnerable is not always easy. Yet, it is life-affirming. As for my dream about Arlene, I hoped it was just a coincidence that it predicted Arlene's death now that she had survived another heart attack. And this time, she certainly made an internal shift. With support, she was ready to tell her sons what she wanted, a huge step for her self-growth. I hoped my prophetic dreams about Arlene were over. I prayed for Arlene's Highest Good to be served, every night before I went to sleep.

At home after dinner, Jim asked about my experience with Arlene. I shared and felt comforted by Jim validating my feelings of still not feeling worthy of the power of my dreams and my spiritual power within. "I support you and your spiritual gifts, Robyn, however they unfold," was his response. "Trust yourself."

Hearing Jim's words sent "God-bumps" down my entire spine and arms. God-bumps are literally our body's way of confirming our truth. Something was up here. I was not sure what it was just yet. It felt powerful and life changing, though. However, the kid inside of me, who always shined yet was not noticed, was still there. I was passionate about shining my Light in acts of serving God and the Universe as a social worker but felt equally strong about remaining invisible and standing in my humility. I knew one thing for certain – this growing, erupting, powerful Light within was beginning to increase in its totality. It felt like just the beginning.

I awakened early Wednesday for my core first year social work classes. First year classes were held Monday, Wednesday, and Friday, while our clinical internship days were every Tuesday and Thursday. I felt good about my work with Arlene. A day of classes was just the break I needed. I was also looking forward to watching "St. Elsewhere," a television show about medical students practicing in a hospital. Jim and I watched it on Wednesday nights before bed.

I got to class in time for a coffee. Social Welfare Policy was usually very thought-provoking and challenged our critical thinking. I needed a jolt of caffeine to verbally spar with the professor. My heart sank, however, once he shared our topic of discussion - The legal aspects of withholding and withdrawing life support. Really, Universe? Okay, I surrender. Powerful laws govern these aspects of life. Right class, difficult timing. Or was it Divine?

My next class was Human Behavior in the Social Environment. Are you kidding me, Universe? No way, this was not happening. Topic today - Counselling a family to take their loved one off a ventilator.

At lunch. I had to go to my car to gather myself. I continued to feel so overwhelmed by the pressure I felt from the heaviness of my cumulative experiences of the past few days. I felt deep inside that something huge was about to happen, a powerful internal and external transformation. As it continued to unfold before my eyes, I was sure I would begin to see more clearly. I sat in my car and pulled it together before returning to class.

I walked slowly back to class, listening to the birds singing while consciously taking nice deep belly breaths. I was a few minutes late for Social Work Ethics. This class always brought powerful discussions. Today's topic - The ethics of taking a patient off a ventilator. I felt sick to my stomach and had a hard time catching my breath. The focus of my last class of the day, General Practice with Individuals, Families, and Groups was - Counselling an individual and their family regarding end of life wishes. Death of a loved one has a profound impact on the entire family.

I walked to my car at the end of my long day of classes, unable to drive home just yet. I felt drained. It did not take long for me to get in touch with my tears, so I sat in my car until I felt all my feelings. Beyond my tears was a layer of fear, and under the fear was so much excitement and possibility! The power of the day's topic showed me the Universe was not letting up anytime soon. I pulled it together enough to drive home. I was walking in unchartered spiritual territory. I certainly had not expected the Universe to continue placing powerful mystical and magical experiences directly on my path. As exciting and intriguing as it was, I still felt I needed to pull in the reins a bit.

I smelled garlic as soon as I walked into our apartment. Jim made stir-fry for dinner. I put my backpack on the couch and walked into the kitchen. Jim grabbed me, wrapped his arms around me and whispered, "Tough day, huh?"

In the calm of his embrace, I was able to allow and breathe through more tears. Jim gently let go of me, turned, and shut off the stove. "Let's go sit and talk." He poured us each a glass of wine and got me the box of tissues. We sat at the kitchen table. "Whenever you're ready, I'm right here ready to listen." I shared the content of all my classes and how overwhelmed I felt. "After your dream about Arlene, seems the Universe needs your attention. You are being given knowledge about death and about ventilators, specifically. Must be the Universe wants you to know the laws, rights, and responsibilities of all the levels necessary to be in a human body and from many different perspectives.

Also, to know the rights and responsibilities of having a loved one on a ventilator, and perhaps even how to help them when they are unable to speak for themselves."

"That feels comforting and grounding. Thanks Sweetie," I responded. "It still feels scary to me, though. Feels too heavy and way too much responsibility."

"I get it," Jim replied. "It is an incredible amount of responsibility. Obviously, the Universe is handing this responsibility for knowing and learning this knowledge of death and dying, to YOU. You are being prepared for something life-changing, *that* we can say for certain!" Deep down, I felt Jim was right. He had such a calming and reassuring aura and a way of being grounded and supportive to all who graced his beautiful presence. Whatever was unfolding through these experiences felt like it was something formal and that I could not stop it even if I wanted to. Jim's response was, "Trust yourself and trust the Universe. These are powerful Divine Interventions." This became my mantra from Jim, which I repeated when I felt overwhelmed by the spiritual power working from within me.

Chapter 4

THE UNIVERSE'S INTENTION

"Today is a gift. That's why we call it the 'Present'." Eleanor Roosevelt

———•••———

After dinner, Jim set us up in the living room to relax, cuddle, and watch "St. Elsewhere" with our three cats. He even popped real popcorn for us on the stove. "St. Elsewhere" was a television show that aired from 1982 to 1988 about a dilapidated teaching hospital, St. Eligius, in a poor neighborhood of Boston. Howie Mandel played the emergency room MD (fellow) Dr. Fiscus, on the show. We began to settle in as the story unfolded.

The show on this exact day showed Dr. Fiscus treating a young woman, 21 years of age, diagnosed with cystic fibrosis. She was admitted to the hospital for coughing up blood, and her oxygen levels were far below normal. Her boyfriend accompanied her and was committed to, and clearly aware of, his role in ensuring that he met her end-of-life wishes. She wished to allow the space to surrender to death, and to let go of life, naturally. As their story gets deeper into the plot, we see a young woman who does not want any heroic measures done to her, or for her, on her behalf. She said no to a bronchoscopy and to a blood transfusion. Dr. Fiscus reminds the couple that a ventilator is available, and if she does not choose intubation that night, he assures them both, she will not live to see the next morning. The boyfriend makes it clear to Dr. Fiscus that his girlfriend has chosen no treatment to prolong the inevitable. She came to the hospital to die with dignity, and he will support her wishes until the end.

The scene eventually switches to the patient's room late that same night. Her friend is playing music and having a dance party in her room while the young woman is lying in bed and has passed away. Dr. Fiscus enters her room with another physician, yelling and throwing her guests out. The other MD shares with Dr. Fiscus that other cultures hold different views that welcome death as a natural part of life. In response, Dr. Fiscus questions how the boyfriend or the patient herself could, "feel so little about their lives?"

At that moment, I became acutely aware that as a social worker, it was my job to honor and support the patient, no matter their view, if the person was not a harm to themselves or someone else. Choosing death, with forethought and discussion with a trusted confidante, IS a choice, after all. It is a beautiful and honest one filled with dignity and integrity. It certainly did not mean the individual felt so little about their life but said plenty about the dignity they desired at the end of their life.

Jim checked in with me once he realized the subject matter of the show. "Perhaps this episode and the dreams are meant to show you more of your future as a social worker. It is such a privilege to work with dying people. Stepping back and allowing the person you're working with to choose their path and destiny with respect to the end of their life is a big responsibility. Supporting folks in honoring their needs to choose death can be a beautiful and important part of our life's journey, just like the moment of our birth. But you know, it is often not how our medical professionals view death. Thus, enters, Robyn Accetturo to the patient's rescue, to speak their voice clearly and advocate for them. Wow!" Hearing Jim's words sent shivers down my spine. My God Bumps were back!

I was beginning to surrender to the fact that I was in for quite a ride ahead on my life's journey as a social worker. Not only with this patient at Rush, but I also felt I was on the fast track to learning, experientially, about God and healing, and perhaps even more. I continued to ask the Universe to slow it down, a bit, however. These accelerated lessons still felt a bit daunting.

The next day was my clinical internship. As far as I knew, Arlene was still on the cardiac unit. We had a family session scheduled with her two sons in the afternoon to discuss discharge planning, to create a Living Will with Arlene's desire for no ventilator, and to sign her DNR. This was an especially important part of Arlene's healing, to communicate her needs with her sons before it was too late.

I went to bed after a long and emotionally exhausting day. Tomorrow was a brand-new page in my book of life. I kissed Jim good night and quickly fell asleep.

I awakened early the next morning for my clinical internship and remembered I had another vivid dream about Arlene. I felt stunned and somewhat confused. I guessed the Universe had not finished my lessons yet. In the dream, I entered Arlene's hospital room at Rush Hospital only to find it empty. In fact, her room had been cleaned and made up for the next patient. My first thought was, "Did Arlene pass away?" I approached the nursing station to inquire. The nurse sent me to the Cardiac ICU. When I got there, I was stunned. Arlene was in a coma. Her ICU nurse filled me in on the events leading up to Arlene's intubation. She had suffered a massive heart attack the evening prior. After resuscitation, Arlene's oxygen level was too low, so she was on a ventilator to assist her breathing. I knew this was not what Arlene had wanted or planned. In my dream, her sons were doing everything possible to lengthen her life, without knowing their mom's wishes.

Today was my family meeting with Arlene and her sons. I knew Arlene was excited about her newly found assertiveness and sharing her wants and needs with them. Both Arlene and I had anticipated a positive response from her sons. Now, with my dream, I was not sure what was happening with Arlene. I would soon find out.

I got to my office early and looked for Arlene's chart. It was still missing, meaning she had not returned to our unit. It did not necessarily mean she had another heart attack or was in a coma, however. I walked to the Rush Medical Center side of the hospital to visit Arlene to remind her of the time of our family meeting later that afternoon.

My heart skipped a beat when I entered Arlene's empty, clean room. I approached the nurse's station with trepidation and inquired about Arlene's whereabouts. The entire day began to weigh heavily on my heart.

What was the Universe trying to communicate to me? It felt powerful beyond measure, yet also very overwhelming. It felt like the Universe was sitting on my heart with heavy responsibility. I was feeling a lot of sensory overload. I hoped my dream the previous evening would not unfold before my eyes.

Arlene's nurse shared Arlene had indeed suffered another massive heart attack the night before. She was in the Cardiac ICU after her sons gave permission for her to be in an induced coma, so she would not fight the ventilator supporting her life. In fact, she suffered her heart attack while Jim and I watched "St. Elsewhere" the evening before I dreamed the exact scenario.

Now that Arlene was unable to respond for herself, I was her only voice. I needed to prepare myself to enter her room. I felt somewhat nervous and heartbroken. Not only was Arlene nearing death, but she absolutely did NOT want to be in the exact position she was in, on a ventilator. Her worst nightmare had come true.

I said my prayer of protection and intention before gowning up and entering Arlene's room. As I pulled the only chair in the room closer to her bed, I felt saddened by her current state of being. She had grown a lot over the past several days and was excited to be vulnerable and speak her truth with her sons after working through her own feelings regarding her death. Now her sons may never know the person into whom she had quickly transformed. So instead of a family meeting for Arlene to share her feelings about never wanting to be placed on a ventilator, our discussion would turn to making a choice to follow her wishes and take her off the ventilator, allowing her desires to be heard, through me, so she could rest in peace.

Instead of an in-person meeting, I rescheduled a conference call with both sons. During our call, I shared Arlene's end-of-life decisions and how well their mom opened her heart and felt her way through to become clear on what she genuinely wanted, to make a Living Will today with them. After discussing the details of her wishes, each son voiced support of their mom's position. They discussed their plan to go to the ICU with their families that afternoon, say their goodbyes, and take Arlene off the ventilator. They thanked me for helping her to feel so empowered that she was able to express her feelings, and they promised to honor her desires.

I felt pleased by their response. Later that afternoon, the oldest son called me back to share Arlene had passed with both families holding hands and praying around her body. He commented on how peaceful her expression was, and that he would even go so far as to say she looked happy, which she rarely showed to them! Her sons were very appreciative that I had shared their mom's decision. They, too, were at peace.

I felt incredibly grateful to have been a part of introducing Arlene to her feelings again, as an adult. She had ignored them most of her life. Now that she had been honored by her sons listening and following through with being taken off the ventilator, hopefully Arlene felt the power of her sons' love. I felt privileged to have been a part of the end of Arlene's life.

Chapter 5

SEEKING SPIRITUAL ANSWERS

"The Kingdom of God is within you." Leo Tolstoy

Later that same Thursday afternoon, after Arlene had passed away with dignity, I had my weekly social work student support group. Five female master's level social work students attended. We were from three different universities in Chicago. Each of us had selected our clinicals at the Johnston R. Bowman Health Center, one of the first geriatric hospitals in the country, operated by Rush University Medical Center. There was a social work intern stationed in each unit of the hospital. I was the intern in the skilled nursing unit. Jenny was the intern in the acute inpatient hospital unit. Jenny, who attended Loyola University, was in her mid-thirties and the oldest student.

As it was my turn to share, I surprised myself when my voice cracked in speaking about Arlene's death by being taken off the ventilator. I rather shocked myself when I found myself sharing my prophetic dreams about Arlene with the group. As I did, tears began to flow. In fact, I could not stop crying. I could not help myself. The death of my patient, shown to me in two dreams, and the weight of its responsibility, had become extremely heavy. I needed an outlet. I had to express my feelings to keep going and was hoping for some answers and direction. Being that vulnerable with the group was a risk, yet I trusted everyone present.

The supervisor leading the group was "intrigued" by my experience. Although supportive, she offered no direction to help me and wished me well with figuring it all out. She had no experience with my situation. It was not until group was over, did I realize my vulnerability had paid off. Jenny asked to walk me back to my unit. I accepted.

"You're so weird, Robyn."

"Huh?" I felt a bit uncomfortable and faked a smile at her.

Jenny responded with a mischievous smile on her face. "Good, weird. I watch the books you read during lunch. I own many of the same titles. *Creative Visualization*, by Shakti Gawain, or *Your Word is Your Wand*, by Florence Scoville Shinn. I have information and direction for you. Would you and your husband like to come over for dinner Saturday night? We can discuss all of it in private and relax."

"That'd be lovely, thanks," I said, kind of loudly, feeling both excited and thankful. "Let's exchange phone numbers, and I'll get back to you after I check our calendar. I'm sure we can make it. I'll rearrange whatever is there to make it work. I'm grateful that you know something to help me. Thanks, Jenny."

"Absolutely! I love to share this stuff," she responded.

I was not quite sure to what "stuff" Jenny was referring. Hope and understanding are what I sought. I put my intention out to the Universe with gratitude.

"Have you seen Shirley MacLaine's mini-series, *Out on a Limb*?" Jenny asked.

"Yep, when it aired on TV," I responded.

"Terrific! This will be easy and fun." Jenny stopped and pulled a business card from her pocket. "Tell you what. Here's my card with my address and phone number. Call me if you can't make it. Otherwise, I'll see you both at my place at 6:30 Saturday evening."

I asked if we could bring anything. Jenny said simply to just bring an open mind and heart.

Saturday came around, and Jim and I drove to Jenny's condo in downtown Chicago. We had picked up a bouquet of flowers for Jenny. We were both excited about the possibilities ahead.

Jenny's condo was exquisite. A beautiful, shiny, black grand piano stood in front of her large living room window, overlooking a gorgeous view of Oak Street, with all of Chicago's lights and glamor of downtown. Jenny lived in an exclusive neighborhood called the Gold Coast. She had dinner prepared and poured us each a glass of wine.

We sat at her dining room table for the next 4 hours, sharing stories, food, drink, and experiences that were literally setting the stage for our future. Jenny had a large leather Bible on her piano and began the opening discussion by asking Jim to bring it to the table. She grabbed a family photo from the piano that was on display next to the Bible.

"Okay, this one will knock your socks off, just like in her movie, *Out on a Limb,* when Shirley MacLaine's friend had his Spirit Guides steer their truck and let go of the wheel. It takes FAITH and somewhat going out on a limb, as she suggests." Jenny elaborated further. "Jim, you carried my family's Bible here. Please open it. It holds a special picture inside. A picture on silk that I received during a séance."

"Séance?" I giggled. "Like the ones we'd have in Girl Scouts to scare each other?"

"Kind of, but not really," was Jenny's answer. "They are actually a format to reach Spirit, in a protected and controlled setting."

"Spirit? In a protected and controlled setting?" I asked, with just a hint of skepticism in my voice.

"Yes, Spirit. Our Spirit Guides and loved ones in Spirit," Jenny declared. "We say a prayer and set our intention to raise our vibration to meet Spirit. They hear us and lower their vibes so we can meet in the middle. It takes practice. But it sounds like you are experiencing a specific crash course in the present, Robyn! The power of it all can be intimidating. I am glad you came here tonight."

"As are we. Thanks, Jenny." I smiled and shifted my weight in my chair.

Jenny continued, "You may be wondering how I own all of this as a social work student." Jim and I glanced around at Jenny's beautiful apartment as Jenny continued speaking. "My parents were both physicians. My dad was a cardiac surgeon. My mom passed when I was born, and my dad passed when I was 17 years old. As you can imagine, I felt overcome with grief much of my life. Both my parents are dead. I, too, needed to find answers about death." Jenny turned to the framed photo she had moved from her piano.

"This is the last photo taken of my mom and dad prior to my mom's pregnancy with me and subsequent passing at my birth. Before I show you my picture on silk from Spirit, I'm going to share just a little more about the direction I'm headed, so you don't get freaked out by what you're about to see and experience."

Both Jim and I shifted in our seats. Jim squeezed my hand under the table and continued sipping his wine. I heard him take a deep breath.

"Years ago, a friend of mine introduced me to Spiritualism. To be blunt, it's the science, philosophy and religion of Spirit communication with dead people. It proves the continuity of life. We don't die, just our physical body dies. It's most popular in the United Kingdom, yet it originated in the U.S. We have three Spiritualist Camps here in the U.S. where folks can go and study Natural Laws, metaphysics, mediumship, healing and more. They offer seminary curriculum to become an ordained minister. One Spiritualist Center is in Cassadaga, Florida. Another is in Lily Dale, New York, close to where Spiritualism had its moment of inception in 1848. The third is near Anderson, Indiana, in the town of Chesterfield. It is only a three-and-a-half-hour drive from Chicago!"

Jenny took a sip of her wine and continued, "The ordained ministers are also clairvoyant mediums. Giving clairvoyant readings and messages from Spirit to prove to us our loved ones do not die, they simply change form, is an important part of what they do. Sharing knowledge from the highest vibration Master Teachers is also a large part of their ministry."

"Clairvoyant?" I asked. "Is that the same as a psychic? But they are ordained ministers?"

"To become ordained, one must study a specific seminary curriculum and pass each level of certification including healer, medium, and ordained minister. They also must practice and prove their gifts publicly. No, they are not psychics, they are clairvoyant mediums. Mediums reach higher with their intention whereas a psychic picks up information from the person's energy and doesn't necessarily reach a high enough vibration to connect to the Spirit World. You know, like in regular churches when they burn candles, incense, pray, and sing? All these rituals are intended to raise the vibration to be closer to God, also called Source Energy, and the entire world of Spirit, including the Angelic realm. A clairvoyant medium raises their vibration intentionally and seeks to connect with the highest vibration. They function as an instrument between the two worlds, like a telephone. They attune their body, mind, and Spirit to be able to communicate with Spirit. This produces the phenomenon called Spiritualism."

Jim and I remained silent; focusing on Jenny's every word. Jim took a gulp of his wine. His knee kept hitting mine intentionally from under the table.

Jenny asked if we were ready to have our socks knocked off by what was in her Bible. We were ready. She opened her Bible, and there was a piece of dark construction paper folded in half in one of its pages. "Jim, would you please grab the photo of my folks? I want both of you to come this way so you can see my Spirit pictures on silk more closely." Jim grabbed the photo, and we both got up and walked over to stand behind Jenny so we had a perfect view of the paper. She opened it carefully.

I gasped at the amazing colors of what appeared to be a replica of the exact photo of her parents. However, they were drawn as individuals with a replica of their torso and head. I had no idea with what it was painted.

"Oh, my goodness, what are we looking at?" I blurted out.

"Pictures on silk. I got these from a séance I attended by a medium who has many amazing spiritual gifts. This is a form of physical mediumship. There are other forms, too. Reverend Bill and Reverend Phyllis are my favorite mediums from which to get readings. Reverend Bill is the only medium I know of with the spiritual gift of pictures on silk. Many mediums offer other physical demonstrations of Spirit, as well. We can get into that later if you'd like. Both ministers are super powerfully gifted and trustworthy, with plenty of integrity to match. You'll be drawn to certain mediums and not interested in others. There are some folks who vibe higher with their desire to serve God and the Angels. Those are the mediums you want to connect with. They not only show the continuity of life, but they also serve humankind by giving forth higher knowledge and truths from the Master Teachers, Angels, and more."

"Phew. This is a lot to take in, Jenny. Holy Cow!" I needed a little breather to stop for a minute to digest our experience.

"Yep, it's incredible. Why don't we stretch and take a break? I'll fill our wine and bring out more goodies, so we can munch our way through the rest of the evening. Be back momentarily." Jim offered help in the kitchen, but Jenny told him to relax and keep me company.

When she left the room, Jim and I hugged. I felt our nervous anticipation. This felt exciting in a deep place inside each of us, yet we both were still on edge. We were ready to dive into the unknown at a new level of understanding, and we were grateful to Jenny for this opportunity.

Jenny came back into the room and filled the table with a beautiful array of finger foods and drinks. "You guys ready to learn more?"

I squeezed Jim's hand while we held hands under the table. Jim answered, "Absolutely!"

"So, let me explain how Spirit creates pictures on silk through the medium," Jenny continued. "Hmmm, where should I start? The color pigmentation we are seeing is hard to describe. In fact, many years ago, the Smithsonian Institute analyzed the Bangs sister's psychic artist 'precipitated portraits' hanging in the museum at Camp Chesterfield. Precipitated portraits are art which appears on the canvas of a medium without being painted by the medium. They are produced through the medium's physical mediumship abilities." (I will add here that currently, Wikipedia reports these two mediums as fraudulent. However, I suggest that before forming judgement, please visit the museum and discern the truth for yourself!)

Jenny continued, "It was found that the color was made from material similar to the powder of butterfly wings, yet not any substance they could specifically identify. The Bangs sisters were also physical mediums back in the early 1900's. Their paintings hang in the Lyceum Art Museum at Camp Chesterfield, in Indiana, where Reverend Bill and Reverend Phyllis reside. The materials which Reverend Bill's pictures on silk are created from look remarkably like the same materials as the Bang Sisters precipitated portraits. Pretty spectacular, right?"

"It's hard to fathom, and yet I see the colors with my own eyes! They do look like the powder of butterfly wings," blurted Jim as his mouth dropped open.

Jenny continued. "When one sits for pictures on silk, you sit in Reverend Bill's séance room with up to eight other people. With a red-light bulb on as the only light source, the medium walks around and hands each person a piece of blank construction paper. Then each person receives an empty white square of satin fabric from the medium. Instructions are given to place the fabric square on the center of the construction paper and then onto your lap. There is a table at the front of the room with a basket full of all different colored felt-tipped markers with the caps deliberately taken off." Jenny took a sip of wine and continued, "The medium then shares that as a group, it's the sitter's responsibility to keep the vibrations in the room as high as possible. This is accomplished just like in church, with prayer and song. The red-light bulb is turned off, and the vibrations build during this hour of intentional prayer and song. The laps of the participants remain covered with the paper and fabric. The séance room is pitch black while all this vibration raising and meeting with Spirit is going on. Although, if you too have the gift of clairvoyance, the room won't be pitch black when the lights are off. You will see shapes, colors, and figures with your eyes wide open in the darkness. After an hour, Spirit lets the medium know they are finished. The group is instructed to sit tight, while the medium finishes the process. It's important not to unroll the construction paper for 24 hours. A red light is turned back on, and the medium walks around and rolls each participant's fabric into a tube with the construction paper. The white fabric square and construction paper still look blank. Then the medium places that roll in a piece of black construction paper and slides a rubber band around it. When you unroll it the next day, you are flabbergasted, especially when they come out in color, like mine did."

Jim picked up Jenny's picture on silk and carefully looked it over. He handed it to me, and I did the same. Astounded does not begin to describe how I felt. It was hard to fathom. Part of me was also skeptical. I am an experiential learner. I hoped to experience it one day. Jenny concluded the evening with more experiences she had at Camp Chesterfield and wrote down the first and last names of Reverend Bill English and Reverend Philomena Harrison. Jim and I thanked Jenny for a powerfully informative evening and for her vulnerability in sharing her experience with us both. Many seeds were planted that evening for which Jim and I were so incredibly grateful. There are no words to describe how I felt after seeing Jenny's pictures on silk.

Still somewhat skeptical, though, I was walking ahead deliberating every step with gratitude and faith in the unseen world of Spirit.

Chapter 6

CAMP CHESTERFIELD

"I count him braver who overcomes his desires than him who conquers his enemies, for the hardest victory is over self." Aristotle

---

Jim and I took a year to get our courage to drive to Camp Chesterfield for our first clairvoyant readings from Reverend Bill and Reverend Phyllis. Frankly, neither of us was ready to talk to our dead relatives, if indeed it was even real. During the year after my prophetic dreams began, my father-in-law passed away in his sleep, unexpectedly, at the age of 54. I also had an aunt pass away. Jim and I were in our second year of marriage and my second year of graduate school. Jim continued working at a psychiatric hospital as a psychiatric technician on a locked adult unit.

In 1989, after I finished graduate school and before I met Billy, Jim and I drove to Camp Chesterfield. Camp Chesterfield, in Chesterfield, Indiana, opened in 1886. It is one of three Spiritualist communities in the United States, which demonstrates and teaches Spiritualism. A Spiritualist is one who has experienced communication with the Spirits of people who have passed away. Spiritualism is the science, philosophy, and religion of continuous life based upon the demonstrated fact of communication by means of mediumship with those who live in the Spirit World.

Modern Spiritualism came about originally in the home of the Fox sisters of Hydesville, New York on March 31, 1848. Two of the sisters heard rapping coming from their cellar. It took some ingenuity, but they eventually discerned that the rapping was coming from a Spirit who seemed to be behind a brick wall. They worked out a method of communicating the alphabet with this Spirit using rapping to tap the spelled-out answer to their questions. Public pressure eventually gave way from success to alcoholism and ridicule. Over time, the house came down and the remains of a man's skeleton were found behind a hidden brick wall. Thus, mediumship, communicating with Spirit, and modern-day Spiritualism began. Mary Baker Eddy, founder of The First Church of Christ Scientist, and Charles and Myrtle Fillmore, founders of Unity, began their churches without mediumship, but also as part of this New Thought Movement.

Camp Chesterfield had two hotels on the premises. Jim and I checked into the Sunflower Hotel, constructed in the late 1800's. It shared toilets and shower areas. Original furniture, now antique, filled the hotel. The place felt Spirit-filled. All around the grounds were homes where the mediums resided. There was a large church on the grounds and a smaller chapel, as well. A beautiful grotto called The Garden of Prayer, built of stone, is open to the public. It is a lovely place to meditate and commune with Spirit. As one walks from the grotto toward the Indigenous American totem pole, beautiful purple and pink larkspur, different colored cosmos, and snapdragons introduced the Trail of World Religions. In a semicircle are sculpted busts in memorial of the great religious founders in history. The arch begins with Osiris. Next is Zoroaster. Then Abraham, Mohammed, and Zeus, follow the semicircle. The Lao-Tse sculpture bears the words, "To understand and to proclaim." The arch continues with Vardhamana, the founder of Jainism. Next are Confucius and Buddha. Each bust gazes outward into the center of the circle looking toward the pedestal supporting the bust of the Christ looking up toward the heavens to the Creator.

On our walk to explore the grounds of Camp Chesterfield, we found the homes of both Reverend Bill and Reverend Phyllis. Reverend Phyllis owned the first cottage just past the administration building on the grounds, at the start of the long line of homes. Her sign-up book was out on her porch table. Jim grabbed it, handed it to me, and with a huge grin on his face asked, "Please, please, please would you go first for our readings?"

"Sure, Sweetie, I'll go first." I chuckled. "We're both brave for being here. It takes courage to step into the great unknown. We are blessed with faith and trust, and that we are stepping together. I'm so grateful to take this journey with you. Thank you." Jim and I both signed up for a reading with Reverend Phyllis for Saturday morning.

We went to bed early and left the next morning for the truck stop to eat breakfast. I, for one, was hungry. I was also nervous about my reading. I hoped I could take notes and would make sure to bring a notebook and pencil with me.

Time flew. After breakfast, Jim and I drove back to camp to prepare for our readings. We said a prayer together for our Highest Good to be served and for God's will to be done in our lives. When it was my turn, Reverend Phyllis opened her front door and called my name. I entered a quaint cottage-like room, with a desk that was facing me. She closed the door and walked around her desk. As she sat down, she commented that I seemed a little nervous and asked if this was my first clairvoyant reading. I answered in the affirmative. Reverend Phyllis handed me a piece of paper and asked me to write out a "billet."

I must have looked puzzled, as Reverend Phyllis explained, "A billet is a piece of paper that holds the vibration of your written word. Write down three questions you would like to ask Spirit. At the top of the same paper, print the names of your loved ones and pets in Spirit you'd like to connect with. List your Spirit Guides and Master Teachers if you know them by name. Then fold the paper in half and sign your full name on the outside of one of the halves. Go ahead and do that now. I will instruct you further upon completion."

I wrote Dad at the top of the billet, along with both of my grandmother's names, my patient, Arlene, and my mom's friend, Margaret. Margaret and my mom were both war brides from WWII.

They had been friends my whole life. My first billet question was to my dad, of course. I asked him if he could ever forgive me for the way I behaved when living with the abuser. I held such shame for it.

When Reverend Phyllis saw I had finished writing my billet, she continued speaking. "Now, take the folded paper and get your vibes all over it. Hold it to your forehead, between your palms, and on your heart and solar plexus. Say a prayer as you do that. Then when you're ready, hand it to me unopened, please. Oh yes, take the time to satisfy your curiosity. Look around for mirrors or whatever else you might suspect when one is cheating. Go ahead, it's okay."

I was a bit stunned that Reverend Phyllis knew I was skeptical and nervous! I took her up on her suggestion and glanced around the entire room. I found zero evidence of inauthenticity anywhere in the room. I let out a nervous chuckle. Reverend Phyllis lightened the mood by explaining what was going to happen.

"A medium is like a telephone between the two worlds – the world of Spirit and our human world. What happens if you're talking on the phone and the other person doesn't respond?"

"I might think we got disconnected," I said.

"Exactly! So, don't break the energy connection once we get going. If I say something that doesn't quite fit, don't say no, as a negative vibration makes it harder for Spirit to connect and keep going to give messages. Silence or no response can disconnect them. Nine times out of ten, the message will make sense to the receiver in a few days, as one's subconscious mind gives them more clarity. So, accept the information with grace, and know Spirit will help you make sense of it, even if it doesn't make sense at the time."

I responded, "Got it," and she continued.

"Okay. We open with a prayer, as in Matthew 7: 7-8 we know that as we, 'Ask and it shall be given to you; Seek and ye shall find; Knock and the door will be opened unto you. For everyone that asks, receives. Those that seek, shall find. And for those who knock, the door is opened.' That tells us that we must ask Spirit first in order to give permission for God, the Angels, and for Spirit to enter our lives. Prayer is opening that door and giving permission for them to answer."

Reverend Phyllis shifted in her chair and took my billet from her desk without unfolding it. She placed it on her third eye and stated, "Let us say the Lord's Prayer aloud together and then I will say a prayer of protection and we will begin. Shall we?" She did not wait for me to respond.

Then Reverend Phyllis recited a prayer of protection and called forth our Spirit Guides, Master Teachers, and my loved ones in Spirit. We began. I had my notebook and pencil ready. The first thing that came out of her mouth was the name, Bobby. "Would the name Bobby mean anything to you coming from a Sam?" I burst out crying. Reverend Phyllis continued, "I have a Sam here who feels like a father's energy."

I managed to squeak out that my dad's name was Sam and his nickname for me growing up was Bobby. I did NOT have either Sam or Bobby written on my billet. The only way the medium would know that was if my dad told her.

Once I regained my composure, Reverend Phyllis continued speaking. "Your father first wants to answer question number one on your billet. His answer is, 'I already did.'" I sobbed so hard I was heaving. Reverend Phyllis stopped and handed me a tissue and waited a minute so I could pull it together. The first question I had asked of my dad was whether he could ever forgive my shameful behavior when I was with the abuser days before he passed.

The next huge healing message came in the form of a memory. Reverend Phyllis went on to describe a traumatic argument my parents had when I was small, where I hid under the table because of their yelling. This was NOT on my billet. Yet, it was a 100% accurate description of my three-year-old's memory. After the explanation, I realized my trauma stemmed from this argument happening the same week as President Kennedy's assassination. It was not my parents' argument, after all, that had traumatized me. Seeing the president get shot on television had left its imprint.

This was not on my billet, yet my dad felt it so important for my healing, he brought it up anyway. Perhaps he did it to prove to me he was, beyond any reasonable doubt, the Spirit speaking to me through

Reverend Phyllis. He also showed me we can learn from our traumatic experiences through the spiritual knowledge of clairvoyance. Healing our feelings by feeling and releasing them is a powerful gift for us. Spirit can help us to remember!

My questions to my dad, from my billet, were all answered directly by my dad. There is no way the medium would have known any of dad's answers, NO WAY!

Then the medium asked, "Can you place the name Arlene in Spirit?"

"Yes, thank you!" I responded.

She continued, "Arlene wants you to know how grateful she is to you, Robyn, for teaching her about feelings and for helping her to get her needs met. As you know, she never did get discharged from the hospital. She died, just like in your dreams."

I was stunned to be hearing Arlene speak to me through the medium. I grabbed another tissue, as tears of joy streamed down my face.

Reverend Phyllis continued, as though Arlene was speaking directly to me. "You had a huge impact on me, my dear, and I had a powerful one on you. You will be doing this kind of work in the future, as a social worker, working with death and the dying. You must learn to detach. You have a huge heart. That's how you connect to people so easily, by extending your heart. You made me comfortable feeling vulnerable, probably for the first time in my entire life. I am grateful to you as my Soul will always remember feelings now and know them by name as they are felt. But you need to be able to let go easier at the time of your patient's death. I know you love deeply. So deeply, you even loved me. You loved me with that big heart of yours. Your heart helped my heart to heal. You have the ability to love the deemed unlovable, my dear, Robyn. And you are here to show others how to do the same. You just must learn to detach more at the end of the person's life, and allow them to go at their own pace, to the Light. Do not let your heart get in the way and be felt by the dying individual. Send them off with pure love and Light. Ahh, yes, much easier said than done. You will learn. Thank you again. Bye for now. All my love to you."

"Thank you, Arlene!" My heart was beating out of my chest!

Reverend Phyllis asked me a question. "Does your mom know you're here?"

"Yes, she does."

"Would she be open to receiving a message from a Margaret?"

"I'm sure she'd be delighted to hear from Margaret, thank you!"

The medium shifted in her chair and began talking. "Margaret tells us your mom was present at the time of her death. In fact, she was in the room with her."

"I had no idea," was my response, although a part of me did not believe my mom was present. At the time, my mom was a widow and lived in Florida. Nevertheless, I remembered Reverend Phyllis saying that even if a message does not fit I should still keep the vibe up. Therefore, I responded with, "Thank you, Margaret. I'll be sure to pass your message along to my mom."

Margaret continued, "Thank you, my dear Robyn, I knew you would! You will be doing the same kind of work that your mom did in the future. Your mom was a lovely woman. I loved her Irish brogue. I could listen to her talk for hours. Please thank her for me. It meant so very much to me that she made herself present for my death, so that I wasn't alone."

Both of my grandmothers also came through the medium by their first name. My paternal grandmother died before my birth. My mom's mom lived in Ireland. I met her once when I was three years old.

I did not want my reading to end. The hour went so very quickly. I thanked Reverend Phyllis and told her how grateful I was and how life changing this experience had been for me. "My husband is next for a reading. Thanks, again."

Reverend Phyllis let me out the front door where Jim had been waiting patiently. As soon as I came out, I started to cry. Jim reached for me and hugged me. He held me until I was ready to let go. We still had a few minutes before his reading began. I let go of our hug, took a deep breath, and said, "Oh my goodness, this is life changing in a HUGE WAY, my love!" With those words, Reverend Phyllis came to the door to retrieve him for his reading. I went to find the pay phone on the grounds. I needed to tell my mom what had just occurred in my reading and find out from her why Margaret made no sense in her message.

Mom picked up right away. "Hi there," she responded when she heard my hello. "I thought this was the weekend you guys were going to that camp to talk to dead people."

"Oh wow, you remembered! Yes, we're here right now. I'm calling from the pay phone after my first reading because I have a message for you, Mom."

"A message? What kind of message?" Mom inquired.

"A message from Spirit," I answered. "Specifically, from Margaret O'Neill. I printed her name on my billet, which is simply a piece of paper I printed the names of my dead relatives on along with three questions I wanted answered by Spirit."

"Okay…" Mom's voice trailed off.

"So, Margaret wanted to thank you for being present at the time of her death and for you to know how much it meant to her." Mom's silence was palpable. I gave her a minute to respond.

"That wasn't Margaret O'Neill, Robyn."

"I didn't think so; who was it then?" I asked.

I heard Mom take a long, deep breath. "This Margaret was my first hospice patient. I became a hospice volunteer, as I needed something to do with my time after your dad passed away. I never told anyone. It helped tremendously with my grief."

"Oh wow, Mom! That makes so much more sense. Amazing! Margaret said I was going to be doing the same kind of work you were doing. I'm so grateful for your discernment and that her message is clear to us both. Hospice work. Thank you, Margaret."

Mom and I ended our call, as Jim would be nearly finished with his reading. I wanted to be there when he came outside, so I walked over to Reverend Phyllis' cottage and sat on her front porch. The birds were singing as Jim opened the door and stepped out into the sunlight wiping his eyes with a tissue. Reverend Phyllis waved to me as she closed her front door.

"Let's go get some coffee in the cafeteria, shall we? I'm a bit shaken up at the moment." Jim and I walked hand in hand to the cafeteria and sat at a small table in an empty area.

Jim began sharing. "That was life changing. I am totally at a loss for words. If I didn't experience it myself, I'd have an extremely hard time believing any of this is real. Yet, I know it is. Just like you, I experienced truthful information through the medium, who had ZERO ways of knowing what she knew."

"And once you experience it," I replied, "it feels there's no turning back. I want to hire an airplane to write in the sky, 'THERE IS NO SUCH THING AS DEATH!'"

Jim continued shaking his head in the affirmative and wiping his tears. "My dad and my grandfather came through first. My dad talked specifically about my mom and an incident that occurred when we were kids up at my grandparents' cottage on Round Lake. The information the medium gave from my grandfather was not on my billet, yet it was 100% true! How can that be? I want to know more. Don't you?"

"Yes, I do. The power of it all still intimidates me, though." I felt a tap on my shoulder. Jim said hello to the person who did the tapping.

A polite female voice asked, "May I join you, please?"

Jim and I made eye contact, and I responded for us, "Please do."

"Good afternoon, I am Rita." She held out her hand to shake mine and asked, "And you are?"

"Robyn," I answered as I shook her hand. "And this is my husband, Jim."

"First timers?" Rita asked.

"Are we that obvious?" I chuckled nervously.

"No, I overheard your conversation. I'm a medium, healer, and an ordained minister."

I added, "We came seeking answers to my prophetic dreams I had about a patient of mine last year during graduate school. They came true in real life, twice, and the power of it is scaring me. Yet, I am in awe and feel a strong urge inside to keep trusting myself and moving forward, one foot in front of the other."

"So, here we are," said Jim.

Rita began, "Well you're most certainly in the right place! I've been taking classes here for a long time. Studied seminary for years and took the test to become ordained. So, may I ask, do you have a boy you are working with on the Earth Plane?" She asked us both yet seemed to be directing her question toward me.

"Neither of us work with children. Jim is in school full-time, and I work full-time on a locked adult psychiatric hospital unit," I replied.

Rita did not let that deter her. "Well, there is a dark-skinned little boy with huge almond shaped brown eyes and exceptionally long eyelashes. His Spirit is hanging around you right now, Robyn."

"How can that be? He's not in Spirit, he's alive?" I inquired.

"Yes. We are energetic beings – physical, mental, emotional, and spiritual. We have four bodies, you could say. This boy is so close to you spiritually, Robyn, his Spirit is hanging around both you and Jim. You will both eventually meet up with him. Robyn, you will be working with him for some time. A Sacred Contract. It will be a life-changing story for so many." Rita's voice trailed off as though she was seeing a vision off in the distance.

Jim and I shared a look of surprise, mixed with a tinge of excitement. I felt nervous yet still overwhelmed by the power behind these spiritual experiences. So, I asked, "Rita, is there anything I can do to slow this spiritual experience down? Can I back out all together? I don't really feel qualified to move forward with something that feels like so much responsibility that I know zero about."

"Back out? No way." Rita chuckled. "If you have been chosen for a Sacred Contract, God, your Spirit Guides, Master Teachers, and Angels will see you through to fruition of whatever that contract is, I promise. You are the instrument through which it will occur. God's Divine Ideas must be carried out here. We are the agents who take action to see Divine Ideas come through to fruition. God and your team of helpers are right there to assist you, every step of the way. They cannot interfere in Karma; however, they can put the right people on your path to help things along and in Divine Order. And they do it not just for you, Robyn. We each incarnate with our own team of Spirit helpers."

"Divine Order? We know that term. I'd appreciate if you'd please use your own words to explain what you are meaning." Jim requested, for which I was grateful.

"God's will. Divine Order means God's will be done, not thine own," she said.

"Yes!" Jim and I spoke in unison.

"So, Robyn, before you go to sleep tonight you can ask Spirit to allay your fears in a dream. Ask God, your Spirit Guides, and your Angel helpers to show you a dream to take away your fears. They will do it. There's really nothing to be afraid of as you will see when you begin your studies."

"Studies?" I questioned; since she already saw a little boy around us, I had a hunch that perhaps she was seeing more about us and not sharing.

"Yes, you both will be back more often. You will take seminary classes here at Camp Chesterfield. This is just the beginning for you both! Enjoy your journey. And know you are blessed as you are together walking this path. Such a gift for yourselves and the world. You'll see." We finished our coffee and excused ourselves from Rita as we were going to grab dinner in town.

Later that night, before bed, I said a prayer and asked God to show me in a dream how not to be afraid of these spiritual experiences. I soon fell fast asleep.

Chapter 7

NO MORE FEAR

"Knowing your own darkness is the best method for dealing with the darkness of other people." Carl Jung

---

I awakened in the early morning and snuck out for a walk so as not to wake Jim. I made sure to grab my journal. The sun shined brightly, and the birds' songs floating in the air helped my excitement build as I strolled to the cafeteria for a cup of coffee. I felt lighter as I sipped my first steamy sip. I allowed the tranquility from my dream to fill my entire being. I felt peaceful and calm, even in the cafeteria, with all kinds of buzz going on. I opened my journal and began writing. This is what I wrote:

I asked the Universe for a dream to help allay my fears around the power of my two prophetic dreams. And it worked. I had a beautiful dream, with no words, strictly experiential with powerful visuals and feeling. Here it goes and thank you, Universe!

I met up with a tribal man. A shaman. We stood in a one room mud hut with a thatched grass roof. The shaman wore a headdress woven with many colored crystals and feathers. His necklace was adorned with animal teeth and claws, seed pods, bones, ceramic beads, and more, as part of the embellishments on his body.

Both of us were covered in the white frothy material that covers a newborn's body at birth, called vernix caseosa. Underneath the vernix, ancient symbols adorned our naked bodies. The symbols were painted with some sort of white florescent paint; a texture and brightness I had not seen before. The shaman's skin was a deep shade of reddish dark brown. His belly made him look like the Buddha. His smile made me feel at ease.

The shaman softly took my hands in his and danced with me in a circle while looking directly in my eyes. I followed him as we made rhythmic movements to the beat of a powerful drum. They were repetitive movements to what sounded like a heartbeat, melding us together into One. We danced in every inch of space available to us. Twirling, swaying, always holding hands, I was led in a soulful dance of universal Light and love. Every breath felt powerful, as though each inhalation and exhalation became part of the sacred breath of the Earth herself. It felt intoxicating!

As we danced and connected on very deep Soul and Spirit-filled levels, I could feel my fear melting away through these repeated movements. Feelings of ecstasy filled me, turning to bliss. Peace, grace, mercy, joy, and unconditional love penetrated my entire being with a sort of new-found freedom and openness I find hard to describe. When I awakened from the dream, the fear was erased in waking reality, as well. The bliss remained steadfast. I felt grounded and expanded all at the same time.
Thank you, Universe!

I finished my journal entry and my coffee and returned to our room. I felt grateful for the tool of my dream as an opportunity to turn my fear around. Jim and I discussed it in detail over breakfast before we drove back to Chicago. We vowed to return the following weekend to experience more of Camp Chesterfield.

Jim and I enrolled in and attended a mini seminary for the next weekend. We felt excited to learn, in a formal setting, about the spiritual gifts and tools that lay buried deep inside of us. These tools bring us into a real working relationship with God and our team of Angels, Master Teachers, Spirit Guides and loved ones in Spirit who are present for us along life's journey. We only need to learn to ask for their help and support. Knock and the door will be opened, ask and ye shall receive, seek and ye shall find!

Jim and I took a class together to learn to meditate. We began a spiritual practice to meditate for 20 minutes a day with an intention to learn to communicate with Spirit. Learning to hear with your spiritual ears is called clairaudience. Over time, as we practice, we learn to listen and receive the answers and knowledge we seek. Prayer is talking to God. Meditation is listening. As we learned from Reverend Phyllis, Spirit lowers their vibes, we raise our vibes, and we set our intention to meet in the middle to communicate. It is important to set up an appointment with Spirit at the same time daily to meditate and to keep your commitment. That is exactly what both Jim and I began to practice daily.

I meditated in the evenings after getting home from work. Practicing quieting my mind and being the Observer in the space of my meditation was a great way to begin. Learning to trust Spirit, myself, and quieting my mind where I had zero self-judgement felt amazing. Getting to that space in between our breaths, the space in between our thoughts, is where we meet with Spirit during meditation when we set our intention to do so. I never begin meditation until I say my White Light of Christ prayer of protection when opening myself up. The Law of Attraction binds this spiritual practice. Like attracts like vibration. Thus, declaring the White Light of Christ for protection ensures that the Highest Vibration in the Universe not only surrounds me but also makes sure only to allow that same vibration to enter my space. Those teachers, Spirit Guides, loved ones in Spirit, and Angels I attract into my life for help and support only come through the White Light of Christ when this prayer of intention is set. Any energy not of the White Light of Christ is denied entrance. This prayer was originally channeled by Charlotte Bright Daising, the Founder of the First Temple of Universal

Law, where I was ordained in 2008. Her clairvoyant message was received from Nicodemus, who was her Master Teacher/Spirit Guide. The prayer follows:

> Heavenly Father, Mother God
> I wish to serve.
> Please surround me with the White Light of Christ for protection.
> I respectfully call forth my Master Teachers, Spirit Guides,
> loved ones in Spirit, and Angels to be present.
> (Speak their names aloud.)
> I ask for only the Highest Thoughts and Truths.
> And I, (speak your name aloud,)
> respectfully surrender and open my channel to Spirit.
> Thank you, Amen.

Jim and I continued taking seminary classes all summer and studied Spiritualism on the weekends. The more we kept our commitment to prayer, meditation, studying, and putting into practice what we had learned, my work as a social worker in the psychiatric unit brought me some extraordinary happenings between patients and myself. I was grateful not to be fear-filled any longer but filled with awe. The classes Jim and I took furthered our spiritual knowledge on our journey to serve God and learn all we could about the Christ Consciousness.

Our spiritual power within is the Christ Consciousness. I was beginning to surrender more and more and allow it to come through me with each spiritual experience placed in front of me once my Soul broke open. I continue to do so even today, as I type these words on this page. Remember, this Christ energy has the potential to fill all of us. We are meant to discover and use it to help Self and others and usher in the 5th dimension to create HEAVEN ON EARTH, here and now.

By feeling and releasing our stuck feelings of past traumas, we also let go of our old ways of coping. We stop defending our hearts against who we really are as a spiritual being inhabiting a human body. The anchor of the stuck feelings and their energetic hold on us ends, allowing healing to occur. We are set free. The more we give our held-in feelings a voice and release them, the more sacred space we create within our heart. This allows that perfect power within each one of us, the Christ Consciousness, to fill our heart.

Hence, the title of this book, *I Am the Reluctant Messiah and So Are YOU*, is true. Stepping into and allowing this power to shine through me has not been an easy journey. Since 1987, when my spiritual awakening began, I have walked my talk in humility. The families, couples, and individuals God has helped through me are aware of their own healing that has taken place. My husband and children are also aware. I am a humble servant of God. I do not brag about having this power. I am simply an instrument through which God and Spirit performs healing of some kind for the outcome of the Highest Good. We all have the potential to become an instrument through which healing occurs. Yet, to fulfill this Sacred Contract of sharing my heart and Spirit by authoring this book to completion, I feel pushed beyond my comfort zone in order to share my experiences, yet here we are. And so it is, Amen.

As Spirits in human bodies, it is important to work on feeling our stuck feelings that we swallowed completely and did not allow ourselves to feel as we grew up. Many of us sensed that if we did share our truth, we would not be loved anymore. We learned to survive by holding our feelings in check. And now, as adults, those feelings are simply blocked energy awaiting a voice to express their truth. Whose voice? Our voice. Honoring and releasing our feelings opens our spiritual centers and removes blocked energy.

As Jim and I progressed in our seminary studies and spiritual practices, a whole other world opened up for us. We took some phenomenal metaphysical classes including Natural Law, Meditation, Communication with Spirit, Death and Dying, Mediumship, and more.

In a class called The Study of Chakras, we learned that in Sanskrit, Chakra means disk or wheel. Each chakra is a spinning center of energy, which corresponds with specific nerves and organs. Stuck unfelt feelings block our chakras. We have seven main chakras that help our body to operate. If we have a stiff neck, for example, our throat chakra is out of balance. The remedy is to speak our truth aloud. Louise Hay's book, *You Can Heal Your Life*, is a great resource for helping with affirmations to counteract our stinking thinking for specific dis-eases.

With all our back and forth taking seminary classes, I was super careful not to share my mystical ways of being with staff on the psych unit, especially my lessons with Billy, my master mechanic patient. Then one day, I opened the veil between the worlds for my supervisor, Joan, inadvertently. I could not help myself. I was only sharing what I literally saw with my own eyes.

Chapter 8

OOPS, I SPILLED THE BEANS!

"Taking responsibility for oneself is by definition an act of kindness."
Sharon Salzberg

Joan was my Clinical Supervisor. We shared an office in the locked adult psychiatric unit. We were the psychiatric social workers who provided all the therapy on the unit, including individual, couples, family, and group therapy. There were three levels of functioning therapy groups, which met twice a week. I led the middle level, and Joan led the highest and the lowest level groups. Joan and I had gotten together socially with the art therapist, Deanne, several times, and I had shared some of my inner Self with them both. They knew a little about my spiritual experiences, until one fateful day.

Mark was a schizophrenic who had returned to our unit many times due to his hallucinations. He was Joan's patient in her lower-level therapy group. He was a gentle soul, incredibly soft spoken. I did not realize his spiritual gift for painting with watercolors until one afternoon. After attending Deanne's group, Mark knocked on our office door looking for Joan. She was at a meeting. I asked if I could help him. He responded by asking me to give Joan a painting he had made for her. Of course, I said yes. With that, he handed me the rather large rolled up paper, bound by a rubber band, for Joan. I thanked him and shared I would send Joan to speak with him upon her return.

Later, Joan came back and found Mark's gift sitting on her chair, where I placed it. "Do you know where this came from?" she asked.

"Mm hmm," I answered. "Mark dropped it off for you after art therapy this morning. He said he made it just for you. He'd like you to stop by his room after you open it."

Joan unrolled the large painting and held it up to tape it to our wall. It was beautifully colorful and flowing, painted with turquoise, purples, blues, greens, pinks, in a runny, wavy pattern. It looked like the flow of a calm river current. She began to examine it closely, deciding which way was up. I joined her. "There's something about this painting," she spoke quietly. Joan touched its surface with her hand.

Just then, I saw the entire painting as an abstract outline of a man's face. His nose and jawline were very distinctive. It was not obvious, however, that these wavy paint lines could form the outline of a face. I took a chance and shared what I saw aloud.

"Oh, my goodness, flip the painting over so that the shorter side is at the top. Do you see the outline of the face here?" I got up from my chair, walked over to the painting, and traced what I saw.

Suddenly Joan yelled, "Oh my God, Robyn. It's my DAD! It's the silhouette of my Dad." Her voice trailed off as tears streamed down her face. I grabbed a box of tissues and handed it to her. I asked if she would like a hug, and without answering, Joan put her arms around me. We held each other until she let go. "How can this be?" She continued to mumble while pulling herself together, wiping her eyes as she stared at the painting. It was the silhouette of a man. His jawline and nose were especially characteristic. "My Dad committed suicide when I was only 13 years old. He was so very handsome. He had some Native American blood as you can see by his nose and jaw! How did Mark see him? How is it that he painted his exact silhouette, Robyn?"

"Well, since I've been taking classes to understand and get further in touch with my own spiritual gifts as has my husband, I have to say I am questioning everything. At the place we're studying, I pay a minister, who is a clairvoyant medium, to talk to dead people. It's changed my life. I have received 100% accurate information from the Spirit World, from either my Spirit Guides, my Master Teachers or loved ones in Spirit."

"If I didn't know you, Robyn, I'd say you've lost it!" Joan whispered.

"I know, Joan, it's challenging all we are taught in school. Mental illness, hallucinations, psychosis, and seeing things others do not see? There has to be a connection. Especially now with this latest piece from Mark! My goodness, he must have connected to a spiritual opening in the Universe to be able to see and paint your Dad's silhouette for you as a specific gift! And your Dad's Spirit must have connected with him for him to see so clearly."

"Holy cow, Robyn, this is phenomenal. Please teach me more about all of this. It's mind blowing for me."

"It is for me, too, Joan! The more I learn, the more eager I am to learn and experience more."

Certainly, now, the cat was out of the bag; I was thrilled by Joan's openness. I just needed to keep my relationship with Billy, the bipolar master mechanic, still under wraps. Disclosing my studies of the 4-stroke cycle combustion engine would be too much for anyone else to fathom. At this point, it was still hard for me to fathom. I sure felt grateful for Joan's curiosity. I felt myself shifting and allowing so much gratitude for these spiritual experiences and knowledge, which, a short time ago, I wanted to run from.

Chapter 9

WE ARE SPIRITUAL BEINGS

"Think nothing else but that God ordains all, and where there is no love, put love, and you will draw out love." St John of the Cross

We are Spirits operating human bodies. We come to earth for our Soul to learn from our Spirit as it inhabits our human body. We grow, evolve, and experience opportunities in life, so we can discover our Light within. We come hardwired with a specific individual purpose – to discover we are the gift for which we are searching. It is time we figure out how to operate as a Spirit in a body.

We have four bodies that comprise our whole instrument: physical, mental, emotional, and spiritual. When we come here to incarnate, our Spirit inhabits this instrument, our physical body, like a hand fitting into a glove. When we die, our Spirit leaves the glove and rejoins our Soul in the Spirit World. Most of us become human out of our karmic cycle of past lifetimes. I received in a reading recently, that some of us come here as Earth Angels, chosen by God for a specific purpose to help the masses. No matter if we are here for karmic reasons, or we are an Earth Angel, we are EACH human and Divine.

Prior to our incarnation, our Soul chooses the major players for each earthly life including our parents. We come here to fulfill a mission that only we can accomplish. We travel in Soul groups. Someone in our Soul group steps forward to accomplish the important role they agreed to become on our life's journey, to assist us in learning the most about ourselves and our world that is of our choosing! For example, we may have chosen to grow up with an alcoholic mom for our Soul to learn empathy. Once we choose our major life experiences including our own time of birth and death, our Soul family steps in to incarnate with us to fulfill our Soul's destiny. For some of us, we are here to serve the greater good of all. All of this is for our Soul to experience living on Earth as a Spirit operating a human body and to fulfill our life's purpose while here. The world is awaiting our arrival as we learn to step into our Light. The earthly conditions we set into motion before we incarnated into this current body intentionally create plenty of opportunities for Self-growth.

Our Soul learning never ends, here or hereafter. But we have forgotten who we are. We have learned to identify with being human as all we are. The truth is that we are powerful spiritual beings operating from inside a physical body. Our body is our Spirit's instrument of perception that communicates through our physical, mental, emotional, and spiritual senses to our Spirit within. Our Spirit within is the Observer part of us who KNOWS we have a body. Sit back a minute and let us begin to observe our thoughts. Now let us observe our breath. Our Spirit is the Observer who KNOWS we have thoughts and a breath. We are our Observer.

If we think of the 4-stroke cycle of a combustion engine and how it literally is the reason a physical object can operate as a motorized transport, we can compare ourselves as a Spirit inhabiting a human body using this model. Our life's purpose is to discover the Divine within ourselves and all others, through love and authenticity, by walking our talk. Our life's journey is to figure out how we want to share our inner Light for the greater good. Especially important is our ability to learn to love those who are judged as unlovable on this Earth Plane. We forget what we know about our mission when we are born. We forget who we are. We come here to play the game of life.

Let us consider this concept of a 4-stroke cycle combustion engine as our Spiritual Operations Manual, which shows us how to operate the land transport of our human body. Let us learn how to discern our God-given spiritual senses and use them to better our world and ourselves. Let us refer to this Spiritual Operations Manual often, especially during challenging times.

The four strokes to make an engine run are intake, compression, firing, and exhaust. Without all four cycles functioning properly, an engine will not run correctly and can even die. The same applies to our human instrument. Most of us do not let out our exhaust in a healthy way, if at all. What is our exhaust? It is our output. The sharing of our specific truth. It can also be a change we make in our behavior, based upon our truth. All those years of holding in our exhaust, in the form of our feelings and truths, creates dis-ease in any one or more of our four bodies. Thus, to heal the wounds and trauma of childhood, it is essential to give voice to and hear our little boy or girl inside. How? By taking the time to listen and to feel our feelings, thereby releasing the stuck energy of our swallowed, unexpressed feelings.

Most of us are not taught about feelings by the people who raised us, whether a parent, guardian, or the child welfare system. After all, feelings are, in many ways, a journey into the unknown. Feelings can only be felt. They cannot be seen or measured. Yet it is our feelings that are our Spirit's way of measuring the safety of the environment from which those feelings came into existence.

We come from our mother's womb and instinctively strive to become independent adults and fly our wings from the day we are born. We are shown how to handle our feelings by sensing, observing, and being a part of our family system. Most of us do not learn how to be healthy in our physical, mental, emotional, or spiritual bodies of existence. We imitate our primary caregivers, who imitated their primary caregivers and so on. Life is an inside job. We are equipped to heal our wounds and to become the person we agreed to be before we chose to incarnate here this lifetime. Self-discovery, love, and authenticity hold the key.

When we are born, we depend upon our caregivers for our every need. From our first breath, we begin our journey of Self-growth to becoming independent adults. We are thrust into this world and immediately start to form impressions. Can we trust? Are we safe? How much can we open up? Every day thereafter, we learn to adjust internally as we sense and experience our environment.

Our core identity forms from birth to age three. Even as early as these developmental ages, many of us learn to give up pieces of ourselves to meet the needs and earn the love of those who raised us. It is an automatic survival mechanism.

Let us specifically look at how unhealthy behavior patterns can develop. Take for example, the origin of a person described as having borderline personality disorder. From birth, this infant is born into a family where the primary caregiver, often the mother, implicitly and explicitly communicates to this specific child that the child is here to serve the needs of this primary caregiver. Period. From this moment forward, the child cannot take steps toward their own autonomy and becoming the independent person we all innately seek. Instead, these Spirits operating their human bodies receive the message that if they step too far from the caregiver to meet their own needs, they are dead to the caregiver. Their supply of love from this primary caregiver will be cutoff. We develop ways to cope with this reality to protect ourselves. We create many mentally and emotionally unhealthy behaviors that become our way of being. Why? These behaviors help us to defend ourselves from our feelings of rage at having to give up our own identity to receive love from our primary caregiver. Our mind creates black-and-white thinking with little to no gray areas in between. When we grow up with these strict and unhealthy boundaries, we think of the world in terms of good or bad, as that is the way we view the caregiver who has set these detrimental boundaries with us.

To survive, we form the belief that the perpetrator loves us so much they cannot let us go. This is where the good and bad thinking come in. We feel both honor for receiving love in such a manner, and we feel rage at them for not allowing us the support and freedom to become our own autonomous selves. As a result, we do not allow people to get close to us in future relationships unless their love is proven to us through some dramatic and often unhealthy ways. For some of us, we are giving parts of ourselves up at inception before we have an awareness of Self.

Another example of a cluster of behaviors one might use to cope from birth to age three is the development of narcissistic personality disorder. There is also an implicit and explicit message from the primary caregiver that the child chosen is there to be a perfect object. Why? So the entire world can see how great the caregiver is. That is the child's identity, as an object only, just like the story of Narcissus. His core trait was his beauty and how much others could admire him. A person raised as such learns to give up their identity, so they will continue to please the caregiver and receive their conditional love. This caregiver displays extreme praise and extreme criticism toward this chosen child. Growing up as an object can cause feelings of internal superiority and an inflated sense of self. It also causes us to be deeply self-critical. When our caregiver does not mirror us and they are not capable of reflecting back to us our feelings, we do not learn empathy toward others. In fact, we may have difficulty regulating our emotions in general. We may only feel lovable when we are being "perfect." We grow up seeking excessive attention and admiration from outside of ourselves.

Being raised this way can cause us to be short-fused in our adult relationships. We can feel easily slighted, react with contempt, and belittle others to feel more important. Another defense is to act conceited and boastful and to insist on having the best of everything. All these behaviors are ways we defend ourselves against our feelings of objectification by the ones supposed to love us unconditionally. Loss of impulse control is inevitable, as our rage toward this type of love has a profound impact on us. Domestic abusers often suffer from this cluster of coping mechanisms, called narcissistic personality disorder.

I am not blaming or judging parents here, or the people who raised us. We all do the best we can with what we know. Evolution shows us that when we know better, we do better. I am saying we teach what we know. As children, we learn what we live. Our experience is the best teacher. Most parent based on the example set by their own parents and so on and so on. Still, as conscious parents, none of us are perfect. Even on our best days, we can screw up. We are wired to remember the negative more than the positive experiences of our lives. We learn empathy toward one another when we understand what it feels like to stand in one another's shoes, with loving compassion.

Feelings are our universal language of the heart. They are the parts of ourselves most of us have stuffed inside, as a way to cope and not feel them. Now these stuffed feelings are interfering with our lives. Too many of us never felt safe enough to express our feelings honestly in the moment, while growing up. Perhaps we grew up feeling as if we were an object, or told we were stupid, or we were physically or sexually abused. Whatever our experience and reason for not expressing them, our feelings await our attention. Others can easily trigger our unfelt feelings. Instead of working on healing them, plenty of us cope when feeling triggered, by projecting our held-in feelings onto the one who triggered us, instead of owning our old traumas and repressed feelings.

We may also pick on others by criticizing and judging them, instead of feeling and healing our own trauma. Projecting our feelings or nitpicking onto another person for something we dislike or feel unhappy about in them, provides us with perfect opportunity to get in touch with our old trauma. We often pick on another because we have those same parts that we judge harshly in ourselves, including the feelings and parts of us we do not want to acknowledge. We can stop our projection behavior and instead use it as an opportunity to feel our repressed feelings, which cause our nitpicking, projecting, and criticism.

Learning to communicate our truths to another by expressing our feelings in the moment using "I" statements allows us to feel acknowledged and safe. Sharing our feelings in the now allows us to come back to our natural center of love and trust. The energy of the current hurt is, in the moment, eliminated because our truth was set free. We feel heard and acknowledged, and we can return to center… to love. This is the basis of a mentally healthy relationship.

Feelings produce chemicals in our body and brain. Expressing our feelings in the moment allows these chemicals to return to balance.

When we stuff them, the chemicals remain off-balance, and so do we. Let us use the example of coming home late from an evening out as a teen, knowing we are in big trouble and would be grounded. Full of adrenaline, we open the back door, ready to face our consequence, only to find our folks left us a note on the kitchen table. Once we learn that we are not in trouble because they went out themselves, our chemistry and physiology return to normal. We know we are safe.

As newborn babies, we are born sensing our physical, mental, emotional, and even spiritual environment immediately. Yet, we are helpless. We have no defenses yet. It is important to take a moment and remember we are born as a Spirit entering this tiny human body.

The fabulous news is that, at that point, we have not been gone long from the Spirit World. We remember love! Deep down inside, we KNOW our own innate Light. As Wordsworth so eloquently speaks of in a stanza of his poem, "Intimations of Immortality."

> Our birth is but a sleep and a forgetting;
> The Soul that rises with us, our life's Star,
> Hath had elsewhere its setting, and cometh from afar;
> Not in entire forgetfulness,
> And not in utter nakedness,
> But trailing clouds of glory do we come.
> From God who is our home:
> Heaven lies about us in our infancy!

We are love. We can use every single difficulty we have lived through as an opportunity for our own Soul's growth. To discover love within is to uncover our inner Divinity. This is why we are ultimately here. We can become conscious spiritual beings. We are capable and worthy of working with the Angelic realm and the highest spiritual teachings. We can heal ourselves. The more we practice, the more we can be the instrument through which others heal.

Let us talk more about how we help ourselves heal. We give up parts of ourselves even as children. The child in us has always loved us. It has gotten us through many injustices. That inner child found a way to keep us as safe as possible, no matter what the circumstance. When we began to sense and feel the truth of giving up parts of ourselves in order to fit into our dysfunctional family system, our little one within defends us from our own feelings of loss of love. We may even think, "Do I have to give up myself to be loved by you?"

The continuum of injustices we survived may not even have to do with an abuse. As children, we may perceive someone's intention incorrectly, for example. Let us say a conscientious mom who has self-awareness raises us, yet she is a single mom with four kids under 10 years of age. It may be unintentional, but mom does not have time to address the wants of each child as they arise. She must do her best to provide for the physical, mental, emotional, and spiritual needs of each of the four kids. She may be peeling potatoes while one of the kids wants her attention to show her the beautiful gift of their painting. If mom does not stop and give her undivided attention, this child can form the perception that mom does not care about them. With each perceived infraction, over time, that child's mind may form all kinds of conclusions as to what is wrong with them.

We may assign and internalize it is our fault mom does not love us the way that we need her. So, we mold our personality into someone we are not, to please our primary caregivers to gain their love. We do our best to get our perceived needs met within what they can give and within the parameters they have set, consciously or unconsciously. The saddest part is that most of us do not learn to love ourselves. We are taught to only receive love from others. Without feeling loved by another, we believe we are doomed. Our stinking thinking can convince us of many false narratives that we then live by. Some of us had more of our needs met than others. Some had to fend for ourselves for our own survival. We each know our own truth. Our feelings show us the way.

Depending upon the degree of mental and emotional dysfunction we experience and where we are developmentally when an infraction occurs, our mind and heart may receive this lack of unconditional love and acceptance as a personal assault on who we are. We may internalize it as an attack on our own character and identity and a betrayal of who we are and can become.

Plenty of us grow up unseen. We do not feel accepted, acknowledged, or validated for who we are. We gave up parts of ourselves and learned what we needed to do within to please our primary caregivers, so we would receive the love we needed from them to survive our childhood. As adults, we may continue the dysfunction by seeking out relationships that feel like the love we felt from our primary caregivers. Sometimes we sabotage healthy love because we have only known unhealthy love. We may even provoke the person in the relationship to try to cause them to react like our caregivers.

Why? Despite knowing that our spouse or whomever we provoked loves us, if we can get them to react like our abuser, it proves to our stinking thinking that we are indeed lovable. Oh, the games our mind plays until we begin to understand that we are not our stinking thinking, we are the "Observer" of our stinking thinking.

As adults, we use relationships to mirror our feelings that we never allowed ourselves to feel, express, and release. Unfelt feelings are energetic. They remain stuck in our body, causing our perception of life to skew. Our loss, hurt, anger, anxiety, guilt, and depression, including feelings of not being good enough, worthy enough, or smart enough, function as a magnet. They draw people to us who will mirror for us in our relationship with them, what parts of us need to heal. Self is waiting for our attention and love. We are awaiting to be reborn into wholeness and to be set free to know and become love. The unconditional love and attention we sought desperately from our parents is awaiting inside each one of us. It is US! Once we figure out how to operate as Spirits inside these human bodies that house us, life makes much more sense and becomes magical.

Life is an inside job.

Chapter 10

FEELINGS ARE THE KEY

"The privilege of a lifetime is to become who you truly are." Carl Jung

———◆◆◆———

Once I purchased *Auto Repair for Dummies*, I studied the chapter on the 4-stroke cycle combustion engine. I began my hourly visits with Billy on the psychiatric unit after my workday ended. My mantra became the words of his instruction, "Intake, Compression, Firing, and Exhaust." Billy's mantra became, "The engine purrs like a baby when all strokes work properly. When one or more are not, the engine will eventually die." Together we worked to apply my instincts and hypotheses about how we operate as spiritual beings in human bodies, using the 4-stroke cycle combustion engine as our model. Billy encouraged me to use it and teach it during every therapy group.

In my group therapy sessions, we would learn about ourselves as spiritual beings operating human bodies. Group members came to understand that honoring ourselves by feeling our feelings in the moment helps us to handle our present lives more healthily. Feelings are our most direct response to what we are "now" experiencing on our pain-to-pleasure continuum at any given moment. Feelings guide us to open our hearts, depending upon the perceived safety of our environment. When we cannot, or do not, express our negative feelings in a healthy way as they arise, their energy is stored in the body. Over time, if not expressed, they affect our present state of being and our energy levels. We create defenses to protect ourselves against feeling the unfelt feelings. This way of coping creates stagnant energy in us. If we do not give our feelings a voice and allow ourselves time and space to feel them, we can become completely numb and detached from ourselves and others. Over time, we become physically, mentally, emotionally, and/or spiritually ill.

There are universal patterns to our feelings that each of us can relate to. When we cannot express our feelings in a loving space, we create coping styles called defenses to deal with these perceived undesirable feelings. Inside each of us is our pain-to-pleasure continuum of feelings we have experienced. At the core of our pain are the feelings of hurt and loss. Hurt and loss feel painful. Painful feelings whack us out of balance, and we must respond to them for our survival, even though it is our brain's natural response to try to avoid them. Our body sets off a natural physiological response to the perceived injury or stimuli creating thoughts, feelings, and sensations.

Language is how we express ourselves, yet words can get in the way of us feeling our feelings. When we use words alone without integrating our feelings into the experience, we are using our words to manage "not" feeling our feelings. Feelings communicate our truth to the real us, our Spirit in a human body. They tell us if it is painful and hurts because we feel the hurt. Our I Am Presence, our Higher Self or Spirit within, our Observer in this body, "feels" the hurt. Our thoughts try to control and protect us by using words to explain the hurt. This stinking thinking only meddles with our energetic field by our defenses stepping in. Our words justify, rationalize, and try to explain our feelings. Our feelings simply need to be felt and acknowledged by none other than our Spirit - the real us.

Over time, as we do not allow expression of our feelings, feelings of similar vibration piggyback upon each other. We store their energy in our physical body. These energy blocks cause symptoms, be they physical, mental, emotional, or spiritual. Dis-ease starts at a spiritual level, then goes to emotional, mental, and lastly, physical manifestation of the energy. It takes incredible energy at all levels to stay protected from these painful feelings, to keep them buried deep down. The energy of the stuffed feelings must come out somewhere as we become unhappy with life because our outer world reflects our inner turmoil. We erroneously see through the lens of this created reality when we stuff our feelings. Daily, our energy is used up keeping these feelings in check, in control, not felt. We use anti-depressants, anti-anxiety meds, pain pills, drugs, food, sex, shopping and even alcohol to numb our feelings. Some of us will do anything to avoid those dreadful feelings. It is our "fear" of feeling the feeling now that frightens us as adults. We get to a point where our kettle is about to explode. We cannot take anything in, positive or negative. We have become numb, detached from our Spirit. It is important for us to connect again.

Spirit always conspires for our Highest Good.

Chapter 11

HURT/LOSS, ANGER, ANXIETY, GUILT AND DEPRESSION

"You have power over your mind...Realize this and you will find strength." Marcus Aurelius

---

When we experience the painful feelings of hurt and loss, our system demands an emotional and energetic outward response toward the origination of our pain. Innately, we do this to correct the situation and tell our truth that the experience is not okay for us. This sets a personal boundary to draw the line that tells the perpetrator, "The way I am being treated is unacceptable." Inherently, we do our best to communicate our needs to the person to prevent a repeat. And universally, the expression of this energetic response is anger. Anger is our attempt to correct the source of our painful feelings of hurt and loss.

However, sometimes outwardly expressing our anger toward its point of origin feels impossible. We each have experienced situations where we knew if we told our truth, we would make it even harder for ourselves, jeopardizing our safety. So, what do we do with the energy of all that unexpressed anger? When we hold our response to feeling hurt or loss inside, we can become anxiety ridden. We fear feeling these core feelings so much that we do our best to block them from our awareness. When we try to prevent feeling hurt or loss again by burying it inside, we become anxious because we fear we will feel them again. This is the opposite of what will help us through our experience of feeling hurt or loss. Simply, we must allow ourselves time and space to feel so we can let their energy go. It is our own stinking thinking that perpetuates our feelings of hurt and loss, real or imagined, by creating anxiety inside of us to defend against having these feelings in the first place. We think we can store these core feelings away and they will not harm us. This is incorrect.

Another response many have when we are unable to express our anger outwardly is to turn that anger originally meant for the perpetrator inward against ourselves. Anger turned toward self creates guilt. Then we feel guilty for getting angry at them in the first place. We blame ourselves for our angry response and begin to meddle in our own truth. How? By creating internal drama and confusion to convince ourselves it is our fault the situation occurred in the first place. Self-blame creates self-anger, which complicates our healthy coping. Our stinking thinking repeats this pattern of self-blame, which can quickly turn into self-loathing. Repeated over time, anger and guilt turned inward toward the self leads to depression. Depression sucks the energy out of us. We use so much energy to keep our feelings under wraps. Many of us beat ourselves up for even having them.

Experiencing hurt and loss are inevitable parts of life. Our ideal response is to express our anger toward its source and communicate through our anger how much the situation affected us. When we are unable to share our truth of anger outwardly, we use anxiety, guilt, and depression to cope inwardly with the original anger. It is our brain's natural response to avoid painful feelings, even though they are important learning tools and opportunities for Self-growth.

If we think of our deeper feelings like the layers of an onion, hurt, and loss, lie at its core. The more important the loss, the deeper we ache and feel anguish. We hurt when we feel a loss because losses are painful. All our other basic innate deeper feelings surround the core hurt and loss in layers. These include our initial anger, followed by anxiety, anger turned inward, guilt, and depression. As Spirits in human bodies, we can experience heartache and pain on all four levels of who we are: physical, mental, emotional, and even in our spiritual bodies.

We all experience three major forms of loss as Spirits here on Earth. These are the loss of love, the loss of our self-esteem, and the loss of self-control. Loss of love can be through the loss of a loved one, the loss of a loving relationship, or the loss of feeling lovable within. These three types of love losses can devastate us for the rest of our lives, due to our stinking thinking.

When we experience a loss during our childhood, depending upon where we are developmentally, our way of coping can influence us negatively for the rest of our lives. If we cannot express our feelings of this specific loss safely in the moment, as a child, we must develop certain defenses to cope with having these feelings. Depending upon our age when we first experience this loss, if we do not resolve our feelings in the moment, we become sensitive to certain specific types of loss even through adulthood. These defenses we must form to deny our feelings of the original loss cause us to begin to cope in an unhealthy manner. All subsequent losses, no matter how large or small, piggyback onto each other causing their stuck energy to color our world. We see life inaccurately through the lens of our stinking thinking.

Let us use self-esteem as an example of how this early loss can affect us as adults, causing us to see our world inaccurately through the lens of those experiences. Say that when we were seven years old, our dad repeatedly told us we were stupid and would not amount to anything. We obviously understood it was not safe to share with him how offended we felt and how much his words hurt our heart at the time. Soon we found out it was not safe to express our hurt and loss to our mom, either. Since most of us are not taught to allow ourselves the space and time to feel our feelings and express them even to ourselves, we don't express our feelings to anyone. Period. We swallow our pain whole without giving it a voice. Our stinking thinking believes these buried feelings will not impact us and that we can control this energy deep inside. Therefore, we defend ourselves against our own feelings that did their best to get us through the experiences that caused the hurt and loss in the first place. We add to our own internal drama and trauma each time we repeat this pattern of swallowing our feelings whole without expressing them. It takes an incredible amount of energy to keep these feelings down, buried deep within.

As a child, once our dad placed his "stupid" label on us, our stinking thinking digested it, believed it, and continued to harm us sometimes for the rest of our lives. Many of us became the label itself, even though it is a false belief. That little boy or girl in us still holds the energy of the abuse deep inside. Our feelings have not been felt yet and set free. We erroneously have perceived our world through this lens of low self-esteem, based upon a rage-filled statement our dad made that we perpetuated in our own thoughts. In error, we have convinced ourselves that no, we are not good enough. We are not worthy. We may even have become so self-destructive to hold onto the inner belief that we do not deserve love. Now WE have labeled ourselves as unlovable. Then we wonder why our relationships do not work out or why we attract a certain kind of partner. All of this because we swallowed the label put upon us, and we believed it.

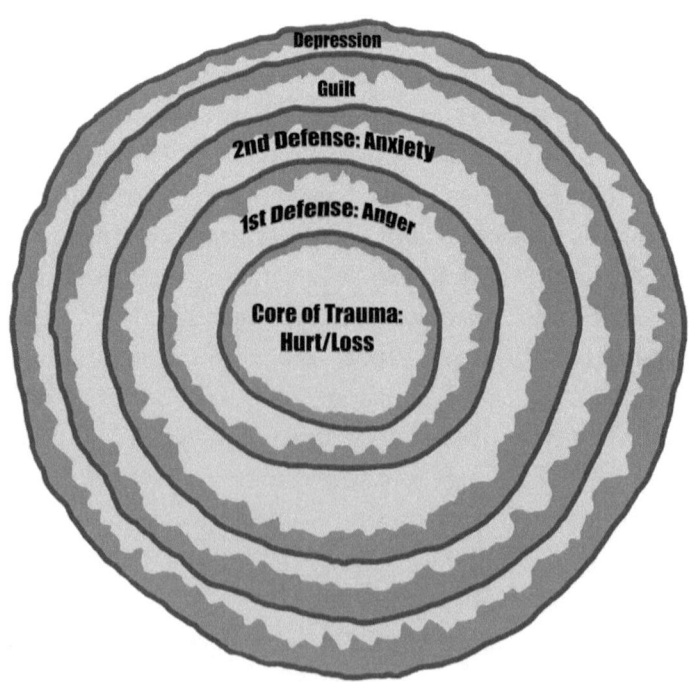

Earlier, I shared that I see our innate deeper feelings like the layers of an onion with hurt and loss as its core. Surrounding the core are the layers of anger, anxiety, guilt, and depression. Let us dissect each layer beginning with anger from the perspective of living as a spiritual being in a human body, and not as a mental health diagnostician.

Our human response to experiencing hurt or loss is to feel angry. Anger is our attempt to correct the source of our pain. But what do we do with that anger as a child? Anger is a powerful feeling. So many of us were shut down as children when we expressed anger openly. Anger can be scary to express or even own if we grew up with a lot of it when we were raised. Most of us did not learn healthy ways to handle anger. And what if the anger we needed to express was toward the perpetrator, who is often a family member? As children, we can learn incredibly early to turn our anger inward on ourselves. Over time, our way of coping beats the daylights out of us for feeling this way, even though feeling angry is a natural response to our experience.

Some of us have kept anger inside for so long, we are about to blow. Our anger has turned into rage. We have not felt our feelings or let out our exhaust. Acting out our rage is impulsive and dangerous. It is not the answer. There is a healthier way to deal with our rage inside. Feeling it and releasing it in a safe space is the key to not acting impulsively. Taking responsibility for ourselves by honoring and feeling our feelings is needed so badly in the world today. Doing our inner work will help prevent people from acting out their rage. We must stop using guns to express our rage in the United States. Being responsible for our own well-being is essential. It is urgent we heal our rage. We need to be able to bear an injustice without getting even. It is urgent we get help to express our anger before it becomes rage, and we do not harm self or others. Remember, our shadow simply means there is Light close by.

When we experience a hurt or a loss, and we are unable to express our anger toward its source in order to return to balance, our mind creates anxiety as the next layer of the onion surrounding our core feelings. Anxiety is the fear we hold onto of experiencing hurt and loss in the future. In fact, we fear feeling hurt and loss so much; our mind creates anxiety to protect ourselves from it as a defense. What's fascinating is that our body, mind, and emotions do not care if the perceived hurt or loss already occurred or if it has not taken place yet. By thinking it will, our stinking thinking creates our anxiety. When we listen only to our mind, we cause so many challenges for ourselves. Once we learn to feel our feelings and release them, we come to know we are our Spirit. When we shift to become the Observer operating our human body, life becomes so much more mystical and magical.

The next layer of the onion after anxiety is guilt. We create guilt when we turn our anger toward ourselves that is meant for the perpetrator. Anger turned inward creates guilt. We can blame ourselves and have the "If Only Disease." Our stinking thinking keeps us bound by the chains of our ongoing thoughts. It can cause us to accuse ourselves and take responsibility for things for which we are not responsible. For example, when we think, "If only I wouldn't have brushed my hair in front of him," we only do ourselves more harm.

We do not use our exhaust valve when we hold onto anger and guilt. We do not express or feel our deep inner trust when we play the "If only" game with ourselves; eventually the chemicals in our brain change and stay there as we continue this pattern of self-blame. This is when depression can set in. Anger turned inward leads to depression. Over time, it can turn to self-hatred and shame. We continue to punish ourselves and repeat this inner energetic imprint every single day by dragging this heavy burden with us like an old friend, re-stamping it onto our new page of life. Some of us have it down pat. Some go even further, blaming and even hating ourselves for feeling this way! This is a double whammy to punish ourselves. Depression sucks the life force energy right out of us. It takes all that energy and more to continually deny our truth to ourselves – the truth of our trauma and our swallowed feelings. All our feelings are asking for is a voice and to be set free.

We have the power to choose to heal our feelings. Giving my own feelings a voice is how I changed my life. It is also how I have touched and taught others along the way. We are all capable of turning our lives around. Still breathing? Inner healing is possible.

Chapter 12

JOSIE FIGURES OUT HER STINKING THINKING

"And one has to understand that braveness is not the absence of fear but rather the strength to keep on going despite the fear." Paulo Coelho

---

Earlier, I mentioned that I had to hide my experience with Billy from my colleagues on the inpatient psychiatric unit. I also had to hide my experiences with Josie, a first-time psychotic admission, who attempted to wash my feet with her hair in the middle of the hallway on the unit. Vibrations are palpable whether they are high or low. Have you ever found yourself drawn to a person when you walked into a room? Have you ever found that you cannot wait to get away from someone you just met?

Josie was in the lowest level of functioning group. She was a 21-year-old female from South America, and a strict Catholic. Although Josie was not my patient in group or individual therapy, one afternoon, while passing her in the hallway, she asked if she could talk with me. I agreed, so we went into the office.

"I know you are not my therapist, but I feel drawn to you," Josie looked down at the floor making zero eye contact.

"Normally, I'd have to refer you to Joan, your therapist, but she's off today. So, how can I help you, Josie?"

"I'm not sure. I just know I feel differently when I'm near you. Not as messed up. I feel the need to tell you why I had my first psychotic breakdown because I'm scheduled for ECT in two days."

ECT stands for electroconvulsive therapy which is a treatment often used when nothing else has worked for things like major depression, bipolar disorder, or other mental dis-eases.

"Tell me more," I said.

Josie began, "These God-awful visions won't stop! They are frightening! I hate to see my brother where he is, but it is God's will."

"Please tell me what you're talking about, Josie. What do you think is God's will that is so horrible? What is happening in these visions?" I asked.

"My whole family is deeply religious. My twin brother committed suicide two weeks ago. We have always been super close. We can even feel each other's feelings most of the time. I knew something was off the day it happened. But my family is Roman Catholic. Suicide is a serious crime against God. One must be punished. My visions show me every single day of his life in purgatory. Might as well be burning in hell for what he did to himself." Josie began to cry. I handed her some tissues.

"You must feel so devastated. Losing a twin is especially difficult. I'm so deeply sorry for your loss." Josie turned away, her long hair hiding her face from my view.

"Thank you. But the trouble is, these visions I see are of demons and gargoyles guarding my brother, holding him stuck in purgatory's darkest and most ominous of places." Josie's body shuddered as she sobbed onto her jet-black long hair, which muffled the sound of her grief and fear. I noticed her beautiful emerald, green eyes as she let out a deep sigh. "Do you have any idea how awful living every single day is in purgatory guarded by demons and gargoyles? I'd rather have these visions zapped out of my head with ECT by the end of this week. I can't take it anymore. It's so frightening. They won't stop."

"I'll answer your question if you give me a minute to explain. And thank you for sharing your experience with me. It takes a lot of courage to speak up about how we are feeling, and what visions we are seeing or hearing. I'm grateful to meet you. I am sorry to hear what you are going through. Now I'd like to answer your question, please, about how awful it must be to live in purgatory."

"Please, you can ask me anything you want, Robyn."

"My answer to your question about purgatory is that I didn't grow up Catholic. So honestly, I wasn't taught about it. Do you think the visions you are having, with gargoyles and demons guarding your brother in purgatory were taught to you by your religion?" I asked.

"What do you mean?"

"Do you know if purgatory is in the Bible, Josie?"

"No, I do not know," she responded.

I explained, "I do not either. Please do some research this evening when you get to your room. Ask your parents. Read your Bible here. Please show me purgatory in the Bible when you find it."

"That's a great idea, thank you. But what about my ECT coming up, Friday?"

"What's on your heart about it?" I asked.

"I was ready until just now," Josie responded. "You've given me hope. Thank you. I'd like to wait and see, with your help."

"You've got it, Josie. Let me know in the morning when I come in, what you find."

"I will. Believe it or not, I haven't had a hallucination since we began talking. Thank you, Robyn! I look forward to connecting in the morning."

When I arrived at the unit the next day at 8 a.m., Josie was waiting for me. "Please, may we talk now in confidence?"

I responded, "Yes. Let me see if Joan is here, yet."

"She's not," Josie said. "I checked. She is off again today."

"Let's go to the office, then. You seem excited, Josie." I hung up my coat. "So, what did you find in the Bible?"

"Nothing, Robyn, absolutely nothing in the Bible even mentions purgatory directly by name. My parents told me there are Bible passages that must be interpreted that show a place of becoming purified from our sins before we are worthy to enter heaven. I'm stunned! How can that be? What did they do? Make it up?"

"I can only imagine how much you really want to stop seeing these visions and stop feeling how scary you see it is in purgatory." I asked, "May we try something, Josie?"

Josie responded emphatically, "Oh my, yes! Yes, please."

"Please, make yourself comfortable in this chair." I instructed. "When we have a feeling, we also have sensations in our body to go along with the feeling. If you were to take a deep breath and focus on the sensations, where are they?"

"My gut," she affirmed.

"Good. Now please take a deep breath and put your attention on your gut. Focus on those body sensations. Let's take a few deep breaths together. What is your gut trying to communicate with you? Breathe from your diaphragm. Take your time," I said quietly.

Josie concentrated for some time in silence. "Something's not right!" Josie blurted out. She sounded panicky and opened her eyes. "My gut says this isn't right! But how can that be?"

"Tell me more," my voice trailed off.

"Catholic church teaches us purgatory is prison after death for those who committed suicide like my brother. It is punishment for the damned. We are taught that Souls stay there after death until they are purified to go to heaven. My hallucinations are of seeing my brother burning in purgatory because he took his own life, the most sacred gift we have for God. Suicide is one of the worst sins against God. In fact, it is a mortal sin. Many Catholics who have committed suicide cannot have a church funeral or be buried with the rest of their family in a Catholic cemetery. Will he be bound to spend the rest of eternity in this hellish purgatory? Literally, I see him with fire burning all around him, threatening him. There is no safety for him." Josie broke down sobbing. I allowed her the space to grieve, until she had no more tears.

"How are you feeling now, Josie?"

"Lighter," she said.

"Okay, now we're getting somewhere. Feeling our feelings helps us rid our body and our chakras of stuck energy," I explained.

"I know chakras! Our energetic centers."

"Great! Now, let's keep going," I responded with a new level of excitement. "I want you to go back and listen to your words I'm going to repeat. You are taught that Souls who committed suicide stay in purgatory after death as a punishment of their damnation, correct? And they aren't allowed in heaven until they've been punished enough for their sins, their wrongdoings, before they are considered worthy enough to enter?"

"Yes," she whispered.

"And since suicide is a mortal sin, he may not ever atone for that sin? He may stay in purgatory forever?"

Josie nodded in the affirmative.

"What if I told you this very well could be a belief taught by your church, of Souls rotting in purgatory?" I stayed silent, giving Josie time to respond. She remained motionless. So, I continued. "For me and millions of others, God is Love. Infinite, unconditional love. There is only one power in the Universe, God the Good, omnipotent, and omniscient. God is LOVE. Close your eyes, take another deep breath. Drink that in for a minute. Now how do you feel when you think of your brother's Soul?"

"Oh, my goodness, Robyn. So much relief. This feels right. The only truth is God is Love. Love is all there is. It could be I am creating those images in my mind, based upon my belief in purgatory by thinking and seeing him over and over again in that God-awful place. Wow! It IS my fearful repetitive thoughts that are causing my visions. Just wow, Robyn!" Josie's voice trailed off as the room filled with the ache of her grief. The loss of a twin is a powerful, especially because Josie was able to sense her brother's feelings. I allowed her more space to sob until she was ready to stop. I waited to speak until the silence was no longer helpful.

"Fear and our mind can create all kinds of illusions. And when we keep replaying the same thoughts repeatedly like a broken record, the chemicals change in our brains. Certain neurotransmitters can cause hallucinations. I am not doing clinical research here, yet it very well could be that your fear was so strong after the stress of your brother's suicide that your repeated thoughts became stuck like a broken record, causing you to see your brother trapped in purgatory as a hallucination. How are they now?"

"I haven't had one since yesterday after we talked. I feel different. More like me."

"Now, that is an example of what I call stinking thinking. It's a term from *Rational Emotive Behavior Therapy* by psychotherapist Albert Ellis. He defined it as, 'the tendency to persistently engage in THOUGHTS that do not serve us.' These irrational thoughts can lead to life-altering self-destructive behavior for the rest of our lives. Our own thoughts can continue to berate us as we swallow what others want us to think or believe about ourselves. If we are taught to think of ourselves in a false way, we carry that thought and live by it as though it were absolute truth. Why? Because our stinking thinking believed it and swallowed it whole, probably when we were young. And every day we continue to label ourselves in our thoughts and mind, we come to believe it as though it is the truth of who we are. So, Josie, the possibility exists that your stinking thinking caused your neurotransmitters to get out of whack, with the visions in your mind of him rotting in purgatory for eternity. I can't prove it, but it sure makes sense to me, especially if your visions have stopped as you managed to shift your stinking thinking!"

"Yes, that makes perfect sense. Dear God, thank you for showing me, Robyn. God loves my brother. He is not stuck in purgatory. I must go talk to my psychiatrist. I feel like my brain is back and my heart. I don't need ECT. I want to go home."

"Sounds beautiful, Josie. Please connect with your psychiatrist. Magnificent work these past couple of days. If you need me, you know how to find me. Take care."

"Can I hug you?" she asked.

"That'd be lovely." I walked toward Josie with outstretched arms. We embraced and she thanked me again for my help.

Later the following afternoon, Josie approached me in the hallway. She shared her news of discharge the following day, tears filling her eyes. Before I realized what was happening, Josie got on the ground and began to caress my feet with her long black hair, which gave off a heavenly scent. I asked her to stop and literally helped lift her from the floor. She was visibly shaking. I took her into an empty patient room, handed Josie a bunch of tissues, and remained silent.

Josie took a deep breath and began. "Robyn, you gave me my life back again. I can never repay you. I tried washing your feet with my hair wet from frankincense and myrrh essential oils my mom smuggled in her purse and gave to me yesterday. It was the only adequate way I knew to thank you. It is my gesture of gratitude. Just like Mary Magdalene did for Jesus the Christ. I am honored by your presence, Robyn. I feel the genuine unconditional love in your heart for me and for all. Thank you."

"I am honored, Josie. Thank you. Truly, I am grateful you are back to yourself again, as well! You're being discharged without electroconvulsive therapy. Congratulations, Josie. Fabulous work, young lady! You must be so proud of yourself."

"Hearing it now, I really am. Not seeing those visions anymore and knowing and feeling my brother is okay and God is love has shifted my hallucinations. I will always remember you. Good-bye, Robyn."

"I, too, will always remember you, Josie. Thanks for connecting with me. Take care of you. And always remember, God is LOVE."

We hugged again, and as I glanced toward the nurses' station, I saw Josie's parents wave to me. They were waiting to take Josie home. I ducked into the office and closed the door, grateful for Josie's gesture of gratitude and that no one saw her washing my feet. Such a beautifully powerful thank you!

Chapter 13

COMPLETION

"One does not become enlightened by imagining figures of Light, but by making the darkness conscious." Carl Jung

———•••———

*B*illy and I had our study time down remarkably well. I would meet him in the art room at 5 p.m. and we would study until 6 p.m. every weekday. Billy was adamant that I had to figure out how we as Spirit operate in our own human body similarly to a 4-stroke cycle combustion engine. He had an urgency about him and a determination that kept me going, even though a part of me knew I was taking a significant risk meeting with him. Billy believed we were constructing a Spiritual Operations Manual. He was confident that folks who applied it to their everyday way of being would feel hope for themselves again. What he loved most about our work together was the simplicity of seeing the results immediately in others in group therapy, who applied the knowledge coming together in my meetings with him.

Billy made a great point: "Relating to a car is something plenty of men do well. It has been drilled into many generations that boys don't cry. We were raised to believe strong males do not show our feelings. I want you to know that our 4-stroke cycle combustion engine gives all of us, but especially males, a way to understand ourselves differently. It gives us permission to feel our feelings and view how we operate in a new light. They will be great at using their inner knowledge of the mechanics of a combustion engine on themselves. Such a powerful tool we are sharing, my dear. Excellent! We must look inside and rediscover our own truths!"

Billy was not one for small talk. He took his role very seriously and stayed steadfast in his commitment. Two weeks into the process, I was sitting across from Billy, discussing the exhaust stroke and how important it is for our Spirit to have a say in our output. I looked up at Billy, in somewhat of a trance after a long day. As I stared off into space, my dream of the shaman during our first weekend at Camp Chesterfield floated into my awareness. I remembered our dance of rebirth and how much it relieved my fear. The shaman's round belly and beautiful dark skin decorated with crystals flooded my awareness as though I was dancing with him again, lost in the moment. I heard Billy shift his weight and came out of my trance. When I looked ahead at Billy sitting across from me, it dawned on me. He was the shaman in my dream!

The second I realized it, Billy, looking directly into my eyes with his impish smile, muttered, "I was wondering when you were going to figure it out." Then he let out a chuckle from the bottom of his round Buddha-like belly, got up, and hugged me. We sat in silence for a moment. I felt incredibly grateful for the Universe's Divine Intervention on my behalf. Meeting and working with Billy was a Sacred Contract we had both agreed to before we incarnated. Just now, we had come full circle in the present moment.

A Sacred Contract is an agreement made between two people and their Spirit Guide teams before they incarnate. The purpose is to meet up in Divine time to carry out something specific that only those two people can do here on the Earth Plane, often for the greater good of all. It is a commitment our Soul makes prior to our incarnation to carry out a human experience that will help Self and others to grow spiritually.

The entire process of understanding our Spiritual Operations Manual took three weeks of study and concentration. When we finished our work together and Billy could quiz me to his satisfaction, he was eager to be discharged to return home. In fact, his psychiatrist discharged him the following day. Saying good-bye was emotional for both of us. Deep down, Billy and I had a powerful spiritual connection that remains with us forever.

Four days after his discharge, Billy's family notified the unit administrator that Billy had passed away serenely in his sleep. Billy's son was emotional when he shared that he had never seen his dad look so peaceful.

I remembered the day Billy told me he had been waiting to meet me his whole life. This had been such a powerful experience from the Universe. Billy had completed our Sacred Contract to help allay the fears of my spiritual power. He taught me, as his Master Auto Mechanic Self, the 4-stroke cycle combustion engine, while gently nudging me to integrate feelings into this theory that was coming from me, and through me. When we finished, Billy went Home, literally, in his sleep four days later. Good for him for being able to surrender at the completion of a job well done!

Rest in peace, dear Billy! Thank you for every single ounce of love, courage, and support. I am forever changed. I am so incredibly grateful to have known you. I will always remember the power of your presence in my life.

Chapter 14

THE 4-STROKE CYCLE ENGINE

"We are not human beings having a spiritual experience. We are spiritual beings having a human experience." Pierre Teilhard de Chardin

---

Life shifts when we learn how to be a Spirit operating a human body. We can trust ourselves. We can trust the Universe. When we accept ourselves right where we are, messy feelings and all, and give ourselves the attention and nurturing we deserve, we learn to love ourselves. Loving ourselves and feeling our feelings are key to unlocking our spirituality. We begin to uncover and connect with our inner Spirit and its wisdom. Our Spirit, with study and practice, unites us with higher knowledge from the Spirit World. We can also learn to connect with our loved ones who have passed away, our Angels, Master Teachers, and our Spirit Guides. A band of five Spirit Guides chooses to be our team of helpers directing us for our Highest Good, throughout this lifetime. Our Spirit team helps us to connect to the people we are meant to meet in Divine Order in our lives.

All of us are born distinctive and exceptional individuals. How we look at things, how we do things is our unique talent and gift. In all the history of the world, there was never anyone exactly like us.

In all the infinity to come, there will never be another. We are not our bodies, our minds, our feelings, or whatever trauma we have had to survive in our life. We are not our suffering or our hurts. We are not victims. We are Spirit. We are energetic beings operating from inside a human body. We need our body to live on the Earth's Plane, yet our body is not the real us. It houses and is an instrument of perception for our Spirit.

Whether we chose to incarnate for karmic reasons, or we are here as an Earth Angel, our Spirit communicates to us readily and easily. But do we listen? Now is the time for us to awaken to this spiritual truth: we are Spirit living and operating a human body. Our Spirit is the true source of who we are, our I Am presence, our being. As I have worked with clients over the years, some call their Spirit their inner voice, their true Self, their Higher Self, their Soul, and even God within. This true source of our being communicates with us constantly. However, most of us gave up listening to it and trusting it a long time ago. Our Spirit is the REAL us, the *Observer* who knows we have feelings, thoughts, and a body. Our Spirit guides us on our individual path as nothing else can. It will not let us down. It can always be trusted. It is the real us that lives on into eternity, who chose to incarnate into the human body we are in now. Our Spirit knows why we are here this lifetime. It unlocks the keys to our inner happiness, unconditional love, peace, non-judgement, and so much more. Our Spirit reveals the channel for the Christ-Consciousness to use us if we are open enough to "become" unconditional love. When we vibrate high enough, we can embody the Christ-Consciousness to allow this vibration to flow through us. Unconditional love, compassion, non-judgement, and willingness to share these characteristics for the greater good hold the key.

How many times has our Spirit communicated with us and we did not listen? For example, we are driving our car and stop at an intersection with our left turn signal on. Suddenly, a thought we didn't consciously think tells us to not turn left. Some call this their first mind. The thought came to us. We turn left and a few minutes ahead, there is an accident, and we are late for our appointment. This is a spiritual gift called claircognizance, when a thought is given to us, yet we did not consciously think it. It comes from Spirit. Many of us are claircognizant. When we learn to listen and trust ourselves and Spirit, life becomes magical.

It is important that we understand the relationship our Spirit has with the other parts of ourselves, including our thoughts, feelings, and sensations and how we respond or react to life. What Billy and I worked on together for three weeks is a simple framework to help us understand and see ourselves as spiritual beings sharing a human experience. We used a 4-stroke cycle combustion engine as its model.

Before we sink into our 4-stroke cycle Spiritual Operations Manual, let us look at how an actual 4-stroke cycle combustion engine operates.

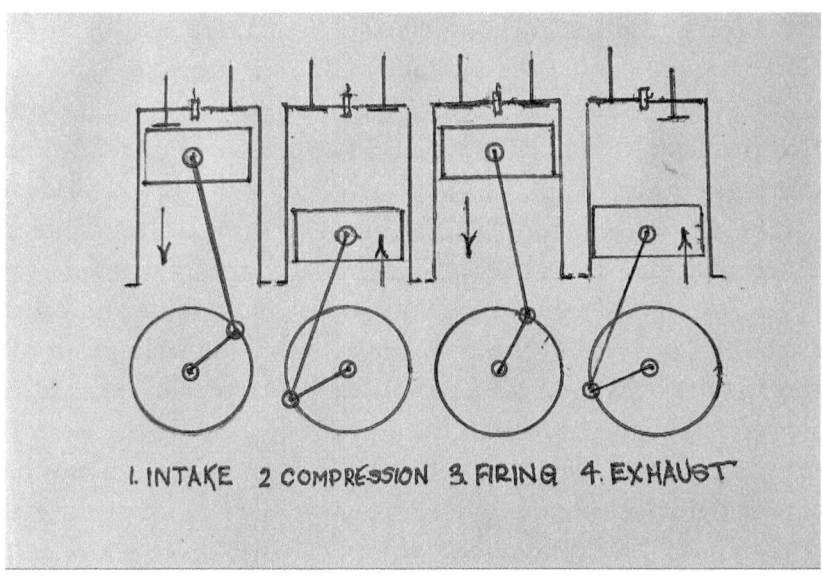

Artist: Ron Kane

An engine's operation requires all four distinct piston strokes. If one or more strokes are insufficient, the vehicle will run poorly or stop working altogether.

The intake valve is open at the beginning of the cycle. This is where the mixture of air and fuel feeds into the cylinder to fill it. The cylinder fills and the air-fuel mixture stays in the closed valve.

With the air-fuel mixture locked inside the cylinder, the compression stroke is next. Its job is to compress the air inside the cylinder in order to raise its charge for the ignition process. It does this by decreasing the volume of air inside the cylinder, in preparation for ignition. At this point in the cycle, both the intake and the exhaust valves are closed.

Both the intake and exhaust valves continue to remain closed as the power stroke begins. During the power/firing/ignition stroke, the hot forces of the gas expand the head of the piston to cause mechanical effort from the engine to turn the crankshaft.

The final stroke is the exhaust stroke, also known as the outlet or output. The exhaust valve opens and the spent air-fuel mixture is released into the air. Four-stroke cycle engines are the most common internal combustion engine for motorized land transport.

Now let us examine the 4-stroke cycle as it relates to our Spirit operating our human body, including our mind. Our mind and body are instruments of perception that our Spirit uses to receive and transmit information to us about what is happening outside of ourselves, in our environment, as our experience. Our thoughts, feelings, and the physical sensations that accompany them are very necessary parts of us, yet they are not us. So many think and believe we are only our thoughts and feelings. No. Our feelings are our automatic response to what we experience in our world. They are like our radar that tells the real us, the Observer, where on the pleasure-to-pain continuum the experience fell. Our thoughts, feelings, and sensations provide input to our Spirit to make us aware of the exact nature of our external situation. Using the 4-stroke cycle, our Spirit processes the information received and then transmits back to our mind, our resulting truths and knowledge.

This processing between our Spirit, mind, and body takes place automatically. Yet most of us gave up listening and trusting our inner voice while growing up. We believe that our mind, including our intellect, is in control of our life and affairs. We are leaving our Spirit out of the equation altogether. I am here to ask us to quit our stinking thinking. Our body, mind, thoughts, feelings, and intellect are all tools our Spirit uses to decipher what is best for us. We are our Spirit. We are the Observer, housed in a body. We are not the judge. We are not our thoughts. We are not our feelings. All of these are tools of perception for our Spirit, the real us.

It is time to pay attention to the processes that occur in us that connect us to our Spirit. We can start to trust ourselves again and "know" we are a Spirit operating a human body. When we become conscious of our Spirit and how all these parts of us work together for our Highest Good, we can change our outcome from a reaction to a response. Responding is a much more mentally healthy way to approach life than simply reacting. Responding comes from our Spirit, which always supports our Highest Good and gives us a peaceful knowing of our truths. We begin to view life as an opportunity for our Soul's growth. Even the most difficult challenges in life provide us with the opening we need within to learn the lessons our Soul agreed to experience before we arrived here.

The human body is designed to be mechanically perfect, just like a brand-new engine of a car. The 4-stroke of a combustion engine occurs within the engine block and consists of an intake, compression, firing, and an exhaust stroke. Of course, timing is the key to the whole cycle working properly and efficiently. Without a proper working engine, we know that our car can break down and stop running altogether. Same with us. Our Spirit uses our body as motorized transport with the 4-stroke cycle combustion engine operating us at our core. Breakdown occurs in the form of dis-ease and can affect any one of our bodies, physical, mental, emotional, or spiritual. Let us look at this 4-stroke model more thoroughly and see how simple it is to apply to ourselves as a Spirit operating our motorized transport. It can help us to understand ourselves more clearly, as the individual sparks of Source Energy that we are. Then we can figure out where we are sickening our cycle so we can do our internal work to heal ourselves and change our vibration and our life.

Chapter 15

SPIRITUAL OPERATIONS MANUAL

"There is but one cause of human failure. And that is man's lack of faith in his true Self." William James

---

We need to shift our viewpoint and come to know we are not our thoughts, feelings, mind, body, or our past traumas. We are a Spirit operating a human body. Our thoughts, feelings, and the sensations we feel in our body are instruments of perception used to communicate to our Spirit what is happening in our environment. Why? Because our Spirit, our innermost Self, is pure energy. Viewing ourselves as a Spirit that knows it has a body and a mind and deliberately using these parts to communicate with our inner Self, gives us a new clarity. Clarity helps us to heal by unblocking energy. Here we can create the life we want and deserve. Viewing ourselves as a 4-stroke cycle transport vehicle for our Spirit gives us room to expand and to heal. It allows us to get to know our inner being and connect to our own Spirit, and to our Spirit Guides, Master Teachers, Angels, and loved ones in Spirit as we learn and grow.

Let us relate this 4-stroke cycle to us, as Spirits in human bodies, with an example. Say we just interacted with another person, and we are left feeling angry over the way this person treated us. What internal process took place here that helped us to become aware we are feeling angry? Using our Spiritual Operations Manual as our guide, let us begin examining the 4-stroke cycle combustion engine as it pertains to functioning as a Spirit in a human body. Intake, compression, firing, and exhaust are the 4-strokes necessary to make our Spirit run at its highest level of functioning.

Intake Stroke
We have physical, mental, emotional, and spiritual tools of perception that absorb our raw environmental experience and provide this input to our Spirit. Our seeing, hearing, smelling, touching, and tasting take-in the truth of our physical experience. We also receive spiritual input to assist us. Our spiritual senses coincide with our physical ones. Our spiritual senses are clairvoyance, clairaudience, claircognizance, clairsentience, clairalience, and clairgustance. Many of us call these senses our intuition. I will share more about our spiritual senses shortly. Our total senses, physical and spiritual, complement one another to complete our *Intake Stroke*, or the taking-in of our environmental experience so our Spirit can understand what we have just encountered.

Compression Stroke
All input given by each tool of perception during the *Intake Stroke* is further assessed and expanded upon during the *Compression Stroke*. Each sense providing input expands its knowledge and communicates a more detailed truth of what was just experienced to our Spirit. Let us use our sense of smell as an example. Say we smell a particular odor as raw input during the *Intake Stroke*. During *Compression*, specifically we come to understand it is alcohol on the person's breath. The results of knowing the person we are dealing with is under the influence of alcohol comes as a thought communicated to our Spirit during the *Compression Stroke*. The input to and the outcome from the *Compression Stroke* create our thoughts, feelings, and sensations, which tell our Spirit our direct truth. We are sensing beings.

Firing Stroke
Once our Spirit receives our Direct Truth from our *Compression Stroke*, our cycle is at a momentary stopping point for our Spirit to integrate this information with our spiritual knowledge and past-life (Karmic or Earth Angel) knowledge base within. Connecting with our Soul always provides our highest vibrational response, which always comes from unconditional love, expansion, vulnerability, protection, and safety. Our Soul tells our Spirit our resulting personal truths and inner knowing, which fuels our *Firing Stroke* with our output. Spirit always provides for our Highest Good.

Exhaust Stroke
From this place of spiritual knowing, we understand our earthly experience more clearly. We discern our truth by connecting to our Spirit. The *Exhaust Stroke* gives our Spirit the direct expression of our truth. Yet, whether this is our exhaust depends upon our mind. Our mind may override our Spirit and decide it is best not to share our truth in every situation. If this is the case, we must exhaust in the safety of our own space and feel and release our feelings to allow for the output of our exhaust.

Let us expand on each stroke, beginning with the *Intake Stroke*. The *Intake Stroke* is about using all of our senses to take everything in that we just experienced. Our physical senses provide five different instruments of perception for our Spirit: seeing, hearing, touching, smelling, and tasting. The sight from our eyes takes in the person's body language. We see the expression on their face. We hear their words and the tone in which they are communicated. Touching, smelling, and tasting can also be involved, depending on what we experience. For all of us, an immediate physiological body response happens. Some of us feel like we were punched in the stomach or we may get a lump in our throat. Our heart may begin to race and our muscles tense. We can quickly set off our fight or flight response. If we are empathic, we can sense and feel the feelings of the person giving the message, even if they are not aware of them.

We also receive communication from Spirit through our spiritual senses or our clairs, which are similar to our physical senses, yet their origin is from Spirit. These messages from Spirit come through our clairvoyance (seeing,) clairaudience (hearing,) clairsentience (feeling,) clairalience (smelling,) clairgustance (tasting,) and even claircognizance (thinking.) When we are connected to Spirit, our clairs flood us with impressions from our Spirit Guides exchanging information to specifically assist each one of us personally. Many of us receive information from Spirit daily, but we do not realize its source. We call it our intuition. When we name it and claim it, it grows. It is not so important that we can differentiate specifically between clairs but that we get to know and discern what receiving communication from Spirit feels like. So, before we go any further, let us explore each spiritual gift in detail.

Spiritual information broadcasts around us in great waves. Yet it is an invisible energy. We humans often have difficulty accepting what we cannot see. That does not mean it is not real and palpable. It is. Animals see Spirit. My cat, Lucy, sees Spirit so much; sometimes her head moves quickly as if she is following a laser light on the wall next to me.

Clairvoyance is seeing clearly with our spiritual eyes. What does that mean? There are diverse ways we can experience this. For some of us, this happens during meditation as we shift our vibration to a higher frequency. Some of us may receive a movie-type scene in our mind's eye when working with our clairvoyance. This image comes to us; we are not thinking it up. Spirit uses many visuals, including colors, symbols, numbers, swirling or pulsating energy, and more. We see them inside our mind with our spiritual eyes when they are closed. These are ways Spirit communicates directly to us using our inner seeing. Another form of clairvoyance is the ability to see Spirit outside with eyes open in our 3-dimensional world that others do not see. In my 20's when my spirituality opened, I began to see a flash of the most beautiful blue light that would disappear as quickly as it came. I still do. Through spiritual discernment, I have come to know this blue light is Mother Mary. Her blue light always gives me confirmation of whatever I am speaking aloud at the time I see it.

Only once have I seen a Spirit as though they were a solid 3-dimensional human. It happened during a Reiki session I was performing on a client. My smoke alarm went off during the session, but when I opened my eyes, there was no smoke. However, I was so startled I screamed aloud when I literally saw a man standing looking in through my office window. The client looked out the same window and reported seeing no one. When I described the man to her, she broke down sobbing, telling me I had described her father who had recently passed away. I asked my Spirit Guides to please not scare me like that ever again. They have not, thank goodness. I am so grateful. We control our mediumship.

Clairaudience is hearing with our spiritual ears. The Archangel Gabriel announced aloud, so human ears could hear, the coming of the Christ. This is one example of clairaudience, a voice from Spirit on the outside for us to hear. This has happened twice in my life, where I heard a booming voice externally. I felt so uncomfortable; I asked my Spirit Guides to please stop. Our mediumship is very personal, and our Spirit Guides respect our boundaries and our power. The other form of clairaudience is when we receive a message by hearing another's voice in our mind. Like claircognizance, clairaudience comes to us as the thought in our head we did not think.

When we receive a message from Spirit, it always leaves us uplifted, no matter how dire the circumstances presented. Practicing spiritual discernment here is of the utmost importance. As one practices spiritual development and working out communication with their Spirit Guides, Master Teachers, loved ones in Spirit, and Angels, spiritual discernment becomes easier. It takes practice.

Clairsentience is sensing impressions from Spirit from our solar plexus chakra, our emotional center. Spirit steps so close to us, they impress upon our solar plexus the information they want us to receive through feeling and sensing. God Bumps, what I call the hair standing up on my arms, is another form of clairsentience. It gives us spiritual confirmation. When we say we are listening to our gut, we are really receiving a message clairsentiently from Spirit through the impressions we feel from them, literally from our solar plexus chakra area.

Claircognizance is when a thought comes to us, and we did not think the thought. It is definitely not our stinking thinking. All of us have experienced claircognizance but many of us do not take it seriously. How many times have we told ourselves, "If I had only listened to my first mind?" This is our claircognizance at work.

Clairalience or some call it clairolfactory is when Spirit puts a scent in the room, and only we can smell it. I know when I walk in a room and smell a cigar, and no one is smoking in the room, it is my dad saying hi! My father-in-law comes through with the smell of coffee. Why? So that the person intended for their message recognizes them. Clairgustance is similar, except it is taste. It is the ability to taste something when there is nothing physical in the mouth producing the taste. It comes from the spiritual realm. This form of mediumship is rare, yet I wanted to define all clairs.

Once we understand our spiritual senses and name them, just like feelings, it is important we claim them. When we do this, they intensify. Therefore, it is important to pay attention to all input we receive, as our life is infinitely enhanced and magical when we operate properly as a Spirit in the body that houses us. All information coming in from every single tool of perception (physical, mental, emotional, and spiritual) communicates to our Spirit during this important *Intake Stroke*. Our intake valve is open and receiving during this stroke of the cycle.

During the *Compression Stroke*, the information input from the *Intake Stroke* is further assessed and expanded upon. Each sense, both physical and spiritual, expands upon the raw data received by adding more knowledge. These resulting truths from our *Intake Stroke* create our thoughts, feelings, and sensations, which then communicate their truth to our Spirit during this *Compression Stroke* of the cycle. Both the intake and the exhaust valves are now closed.

Using our sense of smell as an example for the *Compression Stroke*, let us say we interact with our older sister and she makes a hurtful comment about us. We notice a particular smell on her breath as she spews her hateful comment during our *Intake Stroke*. During the *Compression Stroke*, we receive more knowledge, and we discern the smell from her breath is alcohol. We also remember that our sister is on medication, and she is not supposed to drink. These results of knowing she is on medication and under the influence of alcohol come as a thought communicated to our Spirit during the *Compression Stroke*. The outcome of the *Compression Stroke* creates more thoughts, feelings, and sensations, which tell our Spirit the direct truth of our experience.

The *Firing Stroke* is next. Our Observer, our Spirit and I Am presence, plugs into Source Energy, God. The *Firing Stroke* is a stopping point of integration where we connect with Source Energy. Through this integration, the knowledge received during the *Compression Stroke* combines with our access to our Soul's book of knowledge, the Akashic Record. Our personal truth becomes "One" with Universal Wisdom within, which always provides us with a loving response that comes from unconditional love, compassion, mercy, grace, expansion, vulnerability, protection, and safety. This connection with Universal Wisdom moves us into the fifth dimension - Ascension. Not only do we experience our present knowledge base of what we have learned and experienced in this life, when we connect to our Akashic Record, we gain access to universal knowledge, past-life knowledge, and we become more open to our Spirit helpers. During this *Firing Stroke*, we can take a deep breath and pause to allow our Spirit a moment to combine all our input with our repertoire of Soul experiences within, so we can discern how to best handle this encounter. We can respond and not react. Being aware of our spiritual nature as who we really are, we must take this stopping point as a pause, to serve our Highest Good. We get to choose and not be automatic. We can respond when we pay attention to our Spirit. Life becomes more magical and manageable when we learn to operate from this space. Our Spirit's response fuels the *Firing Stroke* with our resulting personal truths and inner wisdom. It always provides our highest vibrational answer. However, before we are ready to express the output of our truth during the *Exhaust Stroke*, our Spirit must share these deep inner truths with the mind, as language is how we communicate our *Exhaust Stroke*. Both the intake and exhaust valves remain closed during the *Firing Stroke*.

The final stroke of the cycle is the *Exhaust stroke* when our exhaust valve opens, and our output expressed. Our Spirit conveys its resulting knowledge, truth, and direction for our Highest Good to our mind. We can see and understand the experience clearly from this place of spiritual knowing. During our *Exhaust Stroke,* we make our needs known. Our mind controls language. Language is the primary tool our Spirit uses to communicate our exhaust. So, before we speak our truth, or not, the mind does its own processing. When we do not react and we respond by allowing ourselves to choose our words, tone, and body language as our output of the cycle, our life changes for the better. This stroke is our opportunity to open up and tell our truth.

The *Exhaust Stroke* doesn't get stopped up energetically with stuck emotions. However, if our mind decides to override our Spirit, we may not always choose to complete the exhaust the way our Spirit instructed in the *Firing Stroke*. Our exhaust protected us as children, and now as an adult, when we feel we are in danger. It always will. Yet to operate from this protected space repeatedly, as an adult, robs us of our joy and our birthright to be happy. It gets in the way of us becoming who we came here to be. We can experience joy and fulfillment if we learn to allow our Spirit to express our inner truths. We become free. We can heal others and ourselves.

Even if we choose to not tell our truth in the situation or walk away, our Spirit still gives us insight into the processing of what just occurred to cause our hurt and anger in the first place. Our Spirit always loves us through the entire four strokes of each cycle. Expression of our output is necessary for our well-being. So, even though we do not feel safe telling our truth to the person directly as our exhaust, we need to take the time to feel those feelings of anger and hurt and express our output anyway. It is important for our mental health to feel and express our feelings. We deserve to give them a voice. We need to allow ourselves the space to get angry and express our anger until the feeling dissipates. Please give Self the time and space needed to express anger, so it does not build up and turn into rage. This is an example of a healthy 4-stroke cycle of a Spirit operating a human body.

Chapter 16

SICKENING THE CYCLE

"Acceptance of what has happened is the first step to overcoming the consequences of any misfortune." William James

---

As children, many of us learned not to express our feelings. Explicitly, our family may have taught us certain rules by speaking to them directly, like boys do not cry, or it is not lady-like to get angry. Implicitly, we may have grown up with family rules that were enforced yet never spoken about. For instance, our family may have only honored intellect over showing our feelings, sensitivity, or vulnerability. Because of this unspoken rule, the child who shared from their heart was ridiculed as a sign of weakness in the family. As kids, we hold dark family secrets including drug addiction, alcoholism, and sexual abuse, among others. We survived dark places; our safety and security threatened if God forbid, we told. We each know our own story and what we have lived through. Plenty of us are still holding onto these dark parts of ourselves while keeping our family trauma deep inside. We continue to try to cope by denying our trauma exists, even as adults.

There are many ways our 4-stroke cycle can get stopped up and not work in a healthy way. Since the *Intake Stroke* includes us taking in information with all our senses including feelings, we first must understand feelings in our own personal knowledge base. Where do we learn about our feelings? Why is this important? Because we need to name our feelings to claim them.

Many of us become a storehouse for our negative feelings. As we shared earlier, at the core of our negative feelings is hurt and loss. Next layer is anger, and then anxiety, followed by a layer of guilt, which can turn to depression. Depression can lead to self-hatred and shame. Denying our Spirit and not stepping into our potential is painful. Feeling our feelings helps us take responsibility for ourselves. Our unique feelings inside make us the best possible Spirits in human bodies we can be. We must give up our need for perfection. Perfection is a cover for our truths - our real, raw feelings. No one can take away our feelings or negate them, as our feelings are unique to each one of us. We call these difficult to express feelings negative, but by no means should we consider negative, in this case, to be bad. All feelings are important. They show us when we tap into Source Energy, or we are resisting Source Energy. All emotions are our way-showers to ascertain our connection to our Spirit and to God. Our darkness within provides us with a space to choose to react out of fear or respond out of love. Fear shows us where we disconnect from Source Energy.

The more we push down our negative feelings from our awareness to try to keep them in check, the less we feel our positive feelings, as well. The further we bottle up our feelings, the stronger they become, and it takes extra energy to keep them buried. We become numb over time, as our energy defends us against feeling, which is a natural role of our emotional brain. We fight, fear, and can even feel hatred at our stuck feelings. The truth is that these feelings are what we need to begin to befriend and understand.

Our body, mind, and Spirit all honored us at the time of the dysfunction when it was not safe to express our truth. The decision for protection was to stuff our feelings. To heal, we must name the feeling to claim it. Then we must feel the feeling. When we allow space and give the feeling a voice, we can feel and then release its stuck energy. We honor ourselves by allowing and not resisting what is hidden inside. By making friends with our feelings and finishing our output and expressing our truth, our 4-stroke cycle will run smoothly and without resistance. The highest outcome over time is when we can fill our hearts with gratitude and allow recognition for how beautifully our body, mind, and Spirit have always protected us.

So, what happens to our Spirit in the 4-stroke cycle if the process does not flow in an open and healthy system? The locked-up feelings block us from being our true selves. They prevent us from consciously living from our Spirit. Think of the engine of a car that has not gotten an oil change or a tune up in many years. The engine of the car becomes blocked by sludge, and it does not run properly, or at all. Neither do we.

Our Spirit tried so hard to get us to pay attention to it and to show us how to step into our personal spiritual power. Sometimes this is accomplished through dis-ease. We can manifest dis-ease in our physical, mental, emotional, and spiritual body to signal to us that we are out of balance in one or more of them.

Our Spirit wants us to shine and to reach our potential for incarnating this and every lifetime. These lessons are all opportunities for our Soul to learn and grow. By expressing our feelings, loving ourselves through it all, and stopping our stinking thinking, our life becomes mystical and magical quickly. We begin to see the results in our outer world that immediately reflect our change in thinking and the energy shift within. By releasing the old feelings and experiences that caused them, our energy begins to balance. We are meant to achieve our potential individually and collectively, while here on the Earth Plane, for the greater good of all.

We can live our life coming from unconditional love, non-judgement, compassion, and authenticity and set our intention to hold space for the Christ-Consciousness to shine through as us. As we walk our talk, and maintain our vibrational alignment with Spirit, we know from Philippians 4:13 that, "I can do all things through Christ who strengthens me."

As children, we try so hard to protect ourselves from the painful truth of what we are experiencing in our caregiving family, explicitly or implicitly, when we are not loved unconditionally. We learn to get love from an outside source. We feel that without this love from others, we are doomed. Over time, our physical, mental, emotional, and spiritual bodies have a way of communicating to us when we have been listening and acting upon our stinking thinking, which is wrong for us. We are not loving and caring for ourselves for our Highest Good. We are caught in the dysfunction that we have lived through and the resulting feelings that accompanied those experiences. We think this is our fate.

The truth is we have not finished the 4-stroke cycle in a healthy way, by letting out our exhaust. Eventually, we can close our exhaust valve and feel like we are slowly dying inside. Each feeling we have swallowed completely has a chemical reaction that has not yet had the opportunity to return to normal. Honoring our feelings by naming, claiming, feeling, and releasing them is our route to returning home to our Spirit and God, and our brain chemicals returning to balance.

Chapter 17

CONFLICT BETWEEN OUR MIND AND SPIRIT

"Unexpressed emotions will never die. They are buried alive and will come forth later in uglier ways." Sigmund Freud

---

Thus far, we have addressed both a healthy and clogged 4-stroke cycle. Let us again use the example of an interaction with a family member where we were left feeling angry over the way this person treated us. Many factors help us to determine whether we complete the exhaust cycle by being vulnerable and speaking our truth freely, or we do not. What we say to the other person in response depends upon each situation and its participants. Is the person who needs to hear our output a parent, spouse, or a child? Can we put trust in ourselves and risk being vulnerable, or do we hold our response inside? The reason we speak our truth or choose to keep it to ourselves has much to do with our own painful past experiences and where we are in our response to seeing and treating them as opportunities for growth. Do we continue to keep our traumatic feelings still buried as adults? These experiences with their accompanying pain are what have clogged up our cycle in the first place and put us in our current awareness and life circumstances.

Our Spirit always tells us the truth about every situation we experience. Our mind, however, can override our Spirit and our truth. This can change the cycle to an unhealthy one if we do not allow our output to release. The exhaust valve instead closes and holds in the truth of our feelings from what we just experienced. The mind decides the truth is too painful, so it defends us by not allowing us to feel the pain in the present. We revert to the injured little boy or girl inside of us, who believes if we open up and tell our truth, "they" will not love us anymore, and we will be doomed.

Inner conflict occurs when our mind overrides our Spirit and takes over our output. Too many times, we gave up sharing our truth for protection from our own painful feelings. We continue to listen to our stinking thinking, and we give up our Spirit, allowing our mind to be in charge. When we do not listen to our first mind, that inner voice that gives us our unadulterated truth, we find repeatedly, had we listened, we would be much better off.

One cocaine addict who attended my therapy group had made a serious suicide attempt by slashing his wrists, described his mind/Spirit conflict beautifully. "I was lying in bed the night I tried to kill myself. My mind kept telling me to get up and get the drugs, man. F**k work tomorrow. It's 4 a.m. Something else kept telling me, don't do it! You have a family who loves you, an excellent job making decent money, and you have a lot to look forward to. And then my mind and my stinking thinking kicked in again and let me have it. My self-loathing came out. F**k it. Go get a knife and get it over with, you're just a worthless piece of s**t. I understand now that I listened to and acted on, my stinking thinking. I am grateful to be alive. Now I know I am not my mind or my thoughts. I am grateful to know I am so much more."

For many who are in so much physical, mental, emotional, or spiritual pain that they want to end their physical lives, there is also a place tucked away inside our Spirit that is a wish to live. This wish is to honor and fulfill our destiny as spiritual beings in human bodies. We are here to meet Sacred Contracts we agreed to before we incarnated here.

With every trauma that we survived, when our safety was at stake, our physical, mental, emotional, and spiritual bodies saved us from further pain. Our mind, which controls language, ended the 4-stroke cycle with its mind-altering output, and not with the truth from our Spirit. Over time, the defense mechanism that saved us, not expressing our feelings, makes us become numb to all our feelings, even the positive ones. We have become so accustomed to this unhealthy cycle of hiding and not allowing ourselves the time and space to heal, that we feel unsure which way to turn regarding our dis-eases and our dissatisfaction with life. We wonder why we are not happy and have no grasp of the internal processes that are literally occurring constantly to create our world.

Now as adults, we find that our 4-stroke cycle is clogged. Many of us are still walking around never having felt or released the feelings that we have stored inside for so long. These feelings are real and are awaiting our attention and love. Until we take the time to experience them and release them, we will need to continue to keep them in check. As Freud said, "…feelings buried alive will come forth in uglier ways."

Plenty of us use drugs, alcohol, food, sex, work, and every other addiction to try to keep our unexpressed feelings down. Now, especially since the COVID pandemic, people are using guns to act out their feelings, especially rage. This must end. It is essential we learn to feel our feelings in a healthy way. As we make friends with our shadow, we uncover our Light within. We can become depressed, anxiety ridden, and even worse if we continue to listen to our stinking thinking. We must understand that we are Spirits in human bodies and begin behaving as such.

Many of us remain so defended against our swallowed feelings that we act them out in unhealthy ways, often with those closest to us because we feel safe with them. We cause harm and add to our karmic debt by doing so. Projection is our easiest defense to avoid accountability for our own trauma and buried feelings of original hurt and loss. We project onto another by blaming them for how we feel, instead of looking within for an opportunity to heal our old hurt.

It is time for us to STOP ACTING OUT OUR FEELINGS. We MUST TAKE RESPONSIBILITY FOR OUR FEELINGS in a kinder fashion for our families, our nations, and ourselves. We owe it to ourselves to turn our hearts to love. Only we can bring world peace, beginning with our own heart. Peace begins with me. Peace begins with each of us.

There are many ways the mind can stop the output of our 4-stroke cycle. Since our mind controls language, it can alter our output during the *Exhaust Stroke*. One way is when our stinking thinking kicks in with fear. "If I tell them my truth, then _____." Fill in the blank with the greatest fear we store deep down inside, such as they will not love me anymore, they will make fun of me, or I feel like I will die.

A perfect quote by Anais Nin, a French-born American author, addresses projection beautifully. "We don't see things as they are, we see them as WE ARE." Until we have the courage to do our inner work to heal our emotional pain, we will continue to create more karma and cause pain and hurt to the people we project onto. Doing our inner work to feel and heal our stored feelings holds the key to stepping into our spiritual power.

The "should" syndrome is another way our mind keeps us stuck in the old energy patterns of our stuffed feelings. I have come to understand that "should" means "rules swallowed whole without ever being digested." Our stinking thinking keeps the rules actively going in our lives until we become conscious of our thoughts. Depending upon how we were raised, we may have heard many "should" and "shouldn't" statements. "I shouldn't talk to my parents that way." "I should never be rude to my boss." "I shouldn't speak my truth," for example. We each know what specific family rules were forced upon us. Our "should" game with ourselves is just another way we cause ourselves to feel guilty for having our feelings instead of expressing our output.

Another interference by the mind is rationalization, telling ourselves, "Who cares? I do not need them or their love." Reacting from our trauma with an "I can do it myself" attitude only alienates us more. Somewhere along the journey, we ended up closing ourselves off from the world, which causes us to lose opportunities to get close to other people. We think we are protecting ourselves from the hurt and pain when all we are doing is prolonging our own unhappiness. This old way of coping no longer serves our Highest Good. Deep down we know this. No matter what defense we are using to keep our feelings buried deep inside and our 4-stroke cycle a closed one, we deserve better. So do our relationships. There is a way out!

Chapter 18

FOLLOWING MY HEART

"...I can see no way out but through." Robert Frost

———•◦•———

Even with Billy's presence gone from our therapy group, many of the same patients still participated enthusiastically in our treatment time, mixed in with new patients who had just joined us. My heart felt overjoyed by the ownership each member took in learning about themselves as a Spirit in a human body. Group members learned tools of empowerment. These tools helped them with their stuck traumas while arming them with loving kindness and open-heartedness. They learned healthy ways to communicate, how to set boundaries and limits, and learned to name and claim their uncomfortable feelings. I was tickled to the brim when I overheard more than one group member teaching others on the unit who were not in my group, how to stand up for themselves and speak their truths easily and in a non-threatening way. The vibe on the unit was changing. Patients were interacting with one another more, and they seemed to be having fun communicating with their newfound strengths and skills.

Then one fateful Monday morning when I came into work, Joan quietly shared that I was in trouble with the unit administrator, and she was sorry, but I had to meet with him privately about an occurrence from the weekend. She could not give me any details. I wondered if somehow they found out about my studying with Billy after work.

I was confronted by the administrator and found out that the prior Friday evening, the patients in my therapy group had organized and staged a hunger strike for the entire unit. Why? To communicate their dissatisfaction with the nurses on the psychiatric unit. One of the members, who hung out with Billy when he was on the unit, was the leader. He shared the patients' demands for better treatment from the nursing staff. Their major complaint was that the nurses did not know how to handle the patients' feelings. Literally, nurses were telling patients to write out their feelings on paper, and to lock their paper in a drawer and not think about them. That was the exact opposite of what my patients were learning and becoming more comfortable with in both individual and group therapies. The patients in my therapy group were teaching the rest of the patients on the unit what they were learning from me that felt so empowering to them. I was profoundly grateful this was not about my meetings with Billy. I felt proud of my group members for organizing others on the unit and standing up for what they needed. This was huge progress for them!

The administrator and other unit staff had talked the patients into calling off their hunger strike and convinced them to eat again, because the nurses agreed to stop telling patients to lock their feelings in a drawer. Systemic change was happening, and it was good! However, the administration was not happy with me and blamed me for the uprising. I was thrilled to see the patients standing up for themselves. It was hard to imagine not being able to teach or share the way I had been in my therapy group, which was having such a powerful impact on its members.

My response? I knew I could not continue to work as a psychiatric social worker on this unit if I couldn't teach my life skills tools and how to operate as a Spirit in a human body. The administrator made himself clear whatever I did to "insight" this behavior from the patients had to be stopped. So, I looked for a new social work job. My heart fluttered with excitement when I read a small ad for a position serving Cook

County's DCFS Intact Families with AIDS. A university in Chicago had received a grant from the Illinois Department of Children and Family Services to provide counselling and case management services to these specific families. This meant the parents had been cited for child abuse and/or neglect, and one or more of the family members had HIV or AIDS. Intact meant that the abusive or neglectful parents still had custody of their children. This was back in 1990, when we did not know much about AIDS. I sent in my resume, interviewed, and got the job on the spot.

I called Joan, my supervisor, at home the day I got the job and shared my news. I would be giving my two weeks' notice at work the following day. As I explained a bit about what I would be doing, Joan interrupted, asking, "Are you out of your mind, Robyn? What possessed you to take this job? Why on earth would you go into Robert Taylor homes and Cabrini Green? Gang bangers shoot people there! What does Jim say?"

"Jim knows that even if I must go into some of Chicago's most dangerous housing projects, I will be safe and protected. He also knows that when I have a strong conviction about something, it is pretty hard to change my mind."

"You guys and your spirituality stuff. I don't know about you," Joan replied.

I said, "We rely a lot on our spirituality. If we didn't, I don't think I'd even consider this job."

"More power to you, sister. I'm happy for you, I think. You'll be greatly missed on the unit."

As I hung up, part of me wanted to shrug off her response. Another part of me understood where she was coming from. Even when I told my mom and my siblings, I sensed their concern and apprehension for my safety. I appreciated their respect for my decision, though. I had a strong belief, an internal knowing; this was the path I needed to take.

I anticipated remarkable things happening while serving these families. I hoped I would be able to reach people on a very deep level. I would be helping families through the most difficult crises of all, the death of one or more of its members. Not only that, but I also wanted to help make a significant difference in children's lives.

I gave my two week notice on the psychiatric unit to respond to the push I felt inside. Whatever drove me to make this lateral move, one thing was certain, the feeling inside of me was so strong; I could not live with myself if I did not take this job. I called it my spiritual calling. Jim shared my excitement and had as much faith and assurance that everything would work out for me and for us, as I began my new position. Perhaps my prophetic dreams were behind the internal push that was driving me to take this job. I knew there was something greater behind the strength and conviction of it. I was excited to continue teaching folks about operating as a Spirit in a human body, and the importance of feeling our feelings to unclutter and clear out our trauma from our protected hearts. I wondered going forward, how my life's work would touch folks I would be serving in my new position, along with Arlene's Spirit message about working with death and dying. I was excited to find out.

Chapter 19

LIFE SKILL TOOLS FOR OUR WELL-BEING

"The whole is greater than the sum of its parts." Aristotle

Besides teaching how to operate as a Spirit living in a human body, my therapy group also taught its members many life skill tools to become more mentally and emotionally healthy. I continue to use these exact same tools daily, both professionally and personally. They support us in becoming sure of ourselves, which helps us to step into our power and inner Light. The life skill tools listed here are what I needed to learn after fleeing the domestic violence marriage I had committed to as a codependent 23-year-old young woman. Why? I had not learned these pertinent life skill tools in my alcoholic family system. Neither had I been taught them in any other system, including school, church, or even Girl Scouts. We will discuss them in detail.

- Systems Theory
- Healthy Circles
- Healthy Boundaries
- Limit Setting

- I Statements
- Concept of Being Ready
- Mirroring

The first life skill I learned that helped me see myself more clearly was *systems theory*. Systems theory helps us to understand and see how we influence each system we are a part of and how that system affects us. It governs every system we are in including families, relationships, and organizations. The key concept of systems theory is that the whole is greater than the sum of its parts. These individual parts interact with each other within the system and influence each other over time, which allows the stability and solidity of the larger whole. Everybody plays a part as we fit into this whole system in order to survive. We often give up who we are to do our best to thrive within the environmental systems with which we belong.

To grasp the meaning and power of systems theory, I always use a simple model to explain this important concept. Let us look at a mobile, hanging over a baby's crib, as our example for learning about systems theory. No matter how many arms hang balanced, the unit works together, functioning as a whole. As the mobile moves, the entire system moves together. Each part attached to one another makes the whole. Now, imagine taking one of those arms of the mobile and pulling it up and out of its original position. What happens to the rest of the mobile? Well, it is lopsided now, as one arm is functioning differently. However, it still functions as a whole unit.

The same thing happens to us as we make different choices for ourselves within each of our own systems. When we make a decision that living within a specific system no longer serves us, we make personal changes in our behavior. When we return to the system, no matter what system it is, the entire system must change to accommodate the new way that we are behaving. The whole is greater than the sum of its parts.

Let us use my family as an example. We each played a certain role in our dysfunctional alcoholic family system. I was the "responsible one." I played the role of the "model child," and "the hero." I did my best not to cause any more difficulties within my family system. I did not get into trouble. I never received a spanking. I got mostly straight A's. I skipped a grade. I began working when I was 13 years old. I took everything very seriously. I needed to feel in control of my own life, as living in my family felt so out of control.

I tried to bring esteem to my family through my achievements. I put a lot of pressure on myself and kept my self-expectations high. My oldest sister nicknamed me "Grandma" when I was only 10, as I was so very responsible. I volunteered my time for greater causes with my next oldest sister, Sandy, and my closest friends. We "Hiked for Hunger," did our best to stop pollution by literally cleaning up garbage everywhere we went, and we would volunteer for a local animal shelter. One year we made over 500 catnip toys as kitty Christmas gifts.

I repeatedly played the family member who paid attention and took responsibility for my alcoholic mom. My mom and I were remarkably close before she became alcoholic. My three older siblings were already adults in 1969. Sandy and I were still minors. After our mom's drinking became a problem, our dad could leave for work at 4:30 in the morning without having to worry about mom. He avoided dealing with her by napping on his days off. He knew I would keep an eye on her and make sure to meet her needs. He came through in a clairvoyant reading I had in 2022, over 41 years after he had passed. The medium shared that my dad choked up when he literally apologized to me for slacking on his responsibilities toward my mom and toward me. The medium shared my dad was so angry with my mom for many years and felt unable to handle her being under the influence of alcohol daily. He admitted to using work, sleep, and plenty of anger to deal with her drinking. We did not go to Al-Anon, the recovery program for families of alcoholics, until I was a senior in high school, and we had moved to Florida.

During therapy, I decided with the help of my therapist, I no longer wanted to play the role of the responsible one. I desired to become more mentally and emotionally healthy and not be in charge of anyone besides myself. Nevertheless, I still lived in an unhealthy circle with my mom at the time, and she was still drinking daily. Her beverage of choice in the beginning of her alcoholism was beer, cases of it. As she got older, she used straight vodka. I did not know how to change and make different choices, as I held the belief my mom might suffer harm if I did not stay responsible for her. I would feel guilty for not rescuing her.

Systems theory teaches that my family would still function even if I was no longer fulfilling my role as the responsible one. It would adjust and remain a completely functioning system. Would it now be a healthy system? No. It was not a healthy system before. So, me changing to become healthy myself, did not make that system a healthy one. Yet, one part of a system making a change can be the catalyst for the whole system to get help, as the status quo is no longer working. The system itself must change. As it does, the members within the system change as well. However, there is a difference between health and wholeness when it comes to systems theory. Wholeness refers to the sum of the system's parts and not the wellness of the system. Yet, if every member of the system got help, as I chose to do, and began to understand themselves better and change their dysfunctional ways of coping, the whole system would become healthier.

Systems theory can help us to see that the role we assumed in our family does not serve our Highest Good. It teaches us it is permissible to make our own healthy changes within and not be concerned with what our change will do to our family system. We do not have to feel guilty for making a healthy decision for ourselves that changes how we behave within our unhealthy family system. In fact, over time, the changes we make within eventually have a positive impact on our unhealthy family system, when folks have to step up and take more responsibility for their behavior. The system must change in order to survive.

This leads us to our next life skill tool, *healthy circles vs. unhealthy circles*. Let us go back to our example of a mobile. We are the arm of the mobile that has set an intention to change something within ourselves we are unhappy with. Say we go out and seek mental health counselling for codependency. Codependency is when we put the needs of another before our own needs, except for parenting children, of course. Over time, in therapy, as we are learning how to heal from our codependency but are still living with the person we were rescuing, more responsibility is placed on the person themselves. As we change, and do not respond to the person in the same way, the person must decide how they need to handle things differently. As we continue getting more and more mentally and emotionally healthy, we find that this person who is choosing still to be unhealthy in our system is interfering with our satisfaction. Thus, we have a decision to face.

Do we want to remain healthy and live in this unhealthy circle? Or do we want to leave the circle and form a separate, new, healthier circle? The beautiful thing is we have a choice. These are our circles. We get to create them. We may choose to remain healthy in our unhealthy family system, or we may choose to form new, healthier circles. We may also do both. It is our choice. The best place to come from in making these choices is love. Even if we leave the unhealthy circle of our family system and form a new healthy one, we get to decide how much we want to limit our interaction with the people in the unhealthy circle.

It is okay to set limits and firm boundaries with what behaviors we will allow in our relationships. For example, after leaving an unhealthy alcoholic family system, a powerful limit would be to tell the alcoholic we would only speak with them if they were sober during the call. If it comes to a point where the alcoholic cannot call sober, then a firm boundary would be to call weekly on an agreed set day and time, where only sobriety is allowed. If they blow this boundary, we need to give ourselves permission to separate from them for a while. Even so, we may still maintain the connection by sending love from our heart to theirs, for their Highest Good. They do not need to know. Their Spirit will know.

Being able to set *healthy boundaries* and *healthy limits* are two super important life skill tools to understand how to establish. It is important to identify what we want and what we need. It is also important to discern what we do not want or need. A limit is a restriction, an invisible fence we build that communicates a bound beyond which one may not go with us. A boundary is stricter. It shows others where that line in the sand is drawn that says, "Do not cross here," and "If you cross it, there will be a consequence." We are the ones who choose where to draw that line. We are responsible for enforcing it and holding the person who crossed it accountable for their behavior toward us.

A boundary shows us where we end and someone else begins. It teaches others what we will tolerate from their behavior and what we will not tolerate. The opposite of an emotional boundary is enmeshment. During therapy, I had to learn how not to be enmeshed with another person. Enmeshment is a lack of emotional separation. My mom was not good at expressing her feelings under the influence of alcohol. Instead, I felt them for her. We lacked emotional separation. Once my mom became alcoholic, I took it upon myself to do my best to take her pain away. I set zero limits or restrictions on my mom's behavior. I did not even know what a limit was. I just tried to help her, no matter what, even when I did not feel up to the task.

For example, my mom used to visit my aunt and uncle and they would finish off several cases of beer while arguing politics, religion, and history from Saturday night until 3 a.m. every Sunday morning. Then she would drive home about 10 miles, totally drunk, with me in the car. I would visit every weekend with her and made sure I was awake and alert on the drive home, so she did not kill herself driving home drunk. Only once did I have to grab the wheel. This was the day she had set my aunt and uncle's kitchen curtains on fire accidentally with her cigarette, while they were discussing politics. Regardless of the curtain fire, my mom drove us home afterward. I remember vividly grabbing the steering wheel to save us from crashing into an orange construction sign. It would have hit the passenger side of the windshield, where I sat. Setting a limit with my mom at this point in my life felt impossible, since I had assigned myself the responsibility for keeping her safe. An example of a limit in this case would be if I asked her to let us sleep over at my aunt and uncle's house if she was going to drink a case of beer. A boundary would have been if I told her I was not getting in the car with her driving under the influence, period. I did not know how to set either, until my therapist taught me these life skill tools. I had to practice them daily to build them into my repertoire of behaviors. I also had to give myself permission to set limits and boundaries to avoid repeating old behavior patterns.

One of the most powerful tools we have in our tool chest of mentally and emotionally healthy behaviors is to speak in an *I statement*. Learning how to communicate with an *I statement* is of utmost importance for a healthy life. In many of our families we learn to triangulate and not speak directly to the person with whom we have the issue. We triangulate by speaking to another about how we feel about the person with whom we have the conflict instead of speaking to them directly. Triangulation is like gossip. It causes more drama and by no means does it solve anything.

Another unhealthy communication style is to communicate by blaming or projecting onto others. Some of us have the need to communicate and defend ourselves by proving we are right and someone else is wrong, and we do not hesitate to yield this truth over others during a conflict. Literally when we begin a sentence with the word "You_____," we begin the blame game. When we blame others and do not take responsibility for our feelings, we are projecting our negative traits, feelings, beliefs, and flaws onto someone else as a form of protection from our own unresolved inner conflicts. How many times have we said, "You hurt my feelings when you_____," or "You made me_____?" Beginning a sentence with the word "you," points one finger of blame at another and three fingers are curled around back pointing toward us. This blame game simply leads to more conflict and drama. Taking responsibility for our feelings sets us free. Freud called projection a "primitive defense mechanism," which we use unconsciously to protect ourselves from our own unresolved feelings. He used "primitive" because even small children initiate this defense early on in their development.

Feelings are the way-showers for us, the one feeling them. No one can take our feelings away from us. They are unique. They are our inner power and truth coming out to be seen and heard. Thus, we need not blame anyone for our feelings. Instead, ownership of our feelings gives us pure strength during a conflict. Let us use hurt as an example. "You hurt me when you called me lazy when I refused to pick up your mess." Speaking this way puts the responsibility for our hurt onto the person who called us a name. Now let us change that into an I statement. "I felt hurt when you called me lazy because I refused to clean up your garbage. I am not lazy. Please pick up your own garbage."

No one can take our feelings away from us. Stating our truth yields us power. It is our personal exhaust stroke, our truth of our output given to us by our Spirit. Using an I statement allows us to take responsibility for ourselves. It commands respect. "I" statements do not add to our stored trauma. They allow us to speak our truth so we can be heard, and our feelings can go back to balance.

Since I did not know how to say no or speak up for myself, I had to practice making I statements. I practiced them by writing out my I statement responses on a small piece of paper. I would carry the paper with me, just in case during the confrontation I got flustered while I spoke my truth. If I felt I would fall apart and cry, thus stopping the expression of my exhaust, I would pick up my cheat sheet and read it. I would literally shake when I needed to allow myself to feel and express my anger. Feeling hurt came much more naturally to me. Speaking our innermost truth, "I feel_____," is where our power lies. Stating, "You made me feel_____," gives away our power to the other person. I statements allow us to take responsibility for ourselves without blaming anyone, thus contributing to our Highest Good.

Another life skill tool is the concept of *readiness*. Being ready to heal our trauma and stuck feelings cannot be forced. When we decide we are ready to deal with our past by feeling our feelings, our physical, mental, emotional, AND spiritual bodies must all agree we can handle it. No matter how hard we try to retrieve a memory or feel our stuck feeling, we cannot access the energy if a part of us is not ready. Just like a small child who learns their alphabet and knows the letters d – o – g, until they are ready, the concept that it spells "dog" cannot be forced. It is the same with healing our trauma by feeling it.

When a situation triggers specific feelings such as anger, this gives us an opportunity to gain access to a past stuck feeling. We can access our stored-up anger by connecting our present anger to a past scenario. Instead of acting out our anger in the present with say, road rage, or projecting or nit-picking our feelings onto another through blame, we allow the anger to simply be until we can give ourselves the time and space to feel it. When we allow ourselves to get in touch with the first time we ever felt this exact same intense anger, we can gain access and give voice to what we have been holding onto since childhood. Depending upon how much trauma we have stored in our heart, we sometimes find there is more present than we expected. We may become frustrated with just how much we need to feel and release before we feel free. I like to envision our stored feelings as an iceberg that can be chipped away.

By feeling our feelings, we have access to some of them, yet others may still be lurking deeper within. Whittling away at our stored feelings and trauma by allowing ourselves the time and space to feel is crucial in uncovering our inner Light and stepping into our spiritual power. Becoming our authentic Self as a Spirit operating our human body, we come to know the purpose for our incarnation. It is vital we give ourselves permission to be exactly where we are in our healing journey and not beat ourselves up for not completing it yet. If we are still breathing, we are always works in progress toward becoming the Christ Consciousness 100% of the time, as Jesus did when he walked the Earth Plane. The Christ Consciousness is waiting patiently to fill us all. We are meant to discover it within and use it to help Self and others. It is our job to usher in the 5th dimension and to create Heaven on Earth, here and now.

For our heart to allow access to these past traumas, a fantastic exercise I use myself and with clients is to close our eyes and ask our unconscious mind to retrieve our first memory of ever feeling the same way when we were small. If all four of our bodies agree we can handle feeling the feeling, our unconscious mind will give us access to the original trauma that connects us to the current feeling. The energy of that first time we could not feel our truth and we had to swallow those exact feelings has been awaiting our attention, acknowledgement, and acceptance since it occurred.

We need to allow ourselves to feel our hurt, loss, and our anger that have been stored inside for so long. When we acknowledge them, their energy fizzles out in intensity. Seeing and remembering the memory now is different. We can see ourselves as a small child and have compassion for what we survived. We need to give ourselves permission to get angry with the person and situation as we revisit the experience from the age we are now. The experience looks different when we view ourselves as an adult and not from the perspective of that traumatized child inside of us. By not feeling the feeling, we hold that trauma in its original form. By going back to the traumatic memory and feeling our feelings, we can see the situation differently. We can let it go and release its energetic hold on us once we process our feelings to see more clearly. This is how we come to terms with it and heal.

Our body, mind, and Spirit are always watching out for our Highest Good. Each trauma becomes an opportunity for Self to grow spiritually. We can learn about ourselves from each painful situation that we have been afraid to face. Our friends, our feelings, are here to teach us about our innermost strengths and ourselves. Coming back to uncover our heart is so worth our investment of time and energy.

Mirroring is another important tool to put into use for our Highest Good. It serves multiple purposes. Our brain houses an area called our Mirror Neuron System (MNS). This is the same area of our brain that processes rewards. Our MNS activates when we implement a goal-directed action during our interaction with another person. It also activates when we observe another person executing similar actions that we just took. When we communicate, the MNS of both the giver and receiver of the communication activates. It helps us to convey our understanding of the other's output and shows our intentions of being present in the experience or not. It plays an important role in our social functioning every single day by helping us to understand the actions, intentions, and emotions of another. Let us more deeply dissect the experience of our MNS.

Physical mirroring is one aspect our MNS. This is like holding up a mirror to the person we are conversing with, crossing our legs during the conversation, or scratching our nose, and seeing the recipient respond by crossing *their* legs or even scratching *their* nose. Our brain mimicking the movement of the person communicating shows our intention of being present and stepping deeper into the moment by joining our movements to show we are in harmony.

Emotional mirroring is another function of our MNS. One kind of emotional mirroring is experienced when we hold up a figurative mirror to a person with whom we are experiencing conflict. We reflect back to them, using our "I" statements, how we received their words, tone, and body language, and how it impacted us. Reacting with blame and "You," statements, is NOT emotional mirroring, but a defense we use to avoid feeling our original repressed feelings inside. "You" statements add to our swallowed feelings and cause us additional self-inflicted trauma. Emotional mirroring is our way of communicating to another our truth of how we experienced their interaction.

Lack of mirroring by our primary caregiver is a big part of the reason some of us receive a narcissistic personality disorder diagnosis. Let us say our dad was not in a good mood and called us an "idiot" for not knowing how to change the air filter in the cabin of our car. Emotional mirroring would be to respond by reflecting back to Dad that just because we do not know how to replace the cabin filter does not mean that we are an idiot. Using "I" statements to communicate our feelings helps us to clarify our position and come back to balance. "Hey Dad, I feel hurt by your judging me as an idiot just because I don't know how to change the filter! I am not an idiot." By sharing and taking responsibility for our feelings, (that we felt hurt by his name-calling,) we build healthier relationships in the present. We mirror back to the originator of the communication how we received their message. Speaking this way doesn't add to our trauma, it helps bring us back to balance by allowing our exhaust valve to stay open and unclogged.

Another example of emotional mirroring is when we experience another's feelings without the person directly communicating to us how they feel, yet it is obvious to us. For example, a good friend snaps at us when we share that we had a tough day. Since that is not their normal response, we dig a bit deeper and reflect back to our friend that they seem angry with us. This is with the hope they trust us enough to be vulnerable and share what is happening by their response. This is where the term "empath" comes from. We sense what another is feeling before the other knows what they are feeling.

A fourth example of what I view as emotional mirroring is when we use the defense mechanism known as projection to avoid feeling our own painful swallowed feelings from our past. We project our feelings onto another subconsciously, and then we accuse the person we are projecting onto as the cause of our feeling. Merriam-Webster Dictionary says that projection is "the externalization of blame, guilt, or responsibility as a defense against anxiety." We know that anxiety is our way of protecting ourselves from a perceived hurt or loss, real or imagined. Projection is when we accuse our spouse of being angry, for example, when it is really us who is angry with them. Instead of owning our feelings directly and responsibly, we project onto the other person what we are feeling not only to avoid dealing with our present anger, but also to avoid getting to the root of our stored feelings of past trauma, conscious or otherwise. We may even provoke an argument to get in touch with our own anger in an unhealthy way, or not at all. When we know better, we do better.

Empathy is our super-power tool to help us to do better and be better humans. Empathy is the ability to reflect back, using our words, tone, and body language, to show another how we experience and feel what it is like to be standing in their shoes. It takes understanding from our heart to feel empathy and to be empathic toward another. Empathy is universal. The world is a better place because we have empathy. It makes us kinder and less judgmental people. The power of empathy lies in being present for someone without trying to fix anything. Our acceptance allows for acknowledgment of their truth. It shows we feel what another is going through, and it lets them know they are not alone. Knowing what someone feels because we have experienced the same or worse ourselves, gives us the most empathy. The world needs more empathy. Please, practice it often.

The famous 20th century psychologist, Carl Jung, devised the term "shadow" as the dark or unconscious parts of our personality that our ego does not want to recognize. Jung described it as the darker, shadow side of our personality because we tend to repress and hide it deep inside. Why? Because we judge our shadow as inferior, morally deficient, and counterintuitive to what we hope others perceive of us. This can include feelings of rage, jealousy, cruelty, and other personality characteristics that we do not want to acknowledge. Our swallowed feelings of not getting our needs met in our family can also become part of our shadow. All the parts of us we self-judge as unflattering, uncivilized, or unacceptable, we hide them deep within our shadow. Our shadow helps us to cope with having these parts, by protecting us from them within. Our stinking thinking believes these unacknowledged shadow parts will stay buried inside forever and not affect us. Our shadow can even include positive attributes that we judge to be unacceptable or that we are fearful of and want to hide. We may even push down our emotional sensitivity, our personal power, and even our Light, when we continue to deny them.

Jung found that we deal with our shadow by projecting our perceived shortcomings onto others. We can end up viewing the person we projected onto as being morally deficient. In this space, when we experience someone meeting their own needs, we react to them and project onto them our self-judgement, while also accusing them of judging us. Oh, the tangled webs we weave to not feel our feelings or take responsibility and move onward and upward in our lives. Too many of us use projection to cope against healing our own past traumas and swallowed feelings. When we choose to not feel our feelings and communicate them in a mentally healthy way using I statements, we can easily fall into blaming and projecting onto others what we do not want to own in ourselves.

There are several ways that these feelings, deep inside our shadow self, show themselves in our lives, when we do not operate from our Spirit. Have we not all experienced opposite feelings toward the same person, such as love *and* hate? We can feel both envious and yet disapproving of another person. This is a sign that our unmet childhood need is triggered inside. It provides a great opportunity for our Soul's growth when we allow ourselves to feel our way through and discover what that exact need is and then meet it for ourselves.

If our stinking thinking is judging another for their behavior it is more than likely because deep down, we are judging ourselves. This person is mirroring our deep self-judgement, yet we think it is they who are behaving badly enough that our ego feels the need to judge them. Judgement is also part of our shadow.

Spirit never judges. Ever. We are Spirit in a body. We get to choose. I choose no judgement, only love. The most difficult social work case I have taken on caused me to work hard on myself to come from a spiritual perspective and not a human one. I was dealing with a mom with borderline personality disorder, who was physically abusing her six-year-old son while he was dying from AIDS. I had to choose to love this mom through her abusiveness if I was going to help her to see her unhealthy ways of coping. It took 22 months of working with her until she changed her extreme behavior.

The Christ Consciousness is LOVE; thus, it always chooses and acts as LOVE. Empathy helps me to understand a human's way of behaving that society judges as wrong. I know this person did not become this way overnight. Bullies experienced bullying. Pedophiles likely experienced sexual molestation as children. Child abusers knew abuse as children themselves. We learn what we live. It is much easier to observe these denied parts of ourselves in another than to acknowledge that we have disowned these same parts within ourselves. Too many of us act out and become our shadow self out of ignorance of forgetting we are as a Spirit operating a human body. We are the Observer who houses this body. We are not the rage of our experiences, no matter how traumatic. Our rage is the unexpressed output of our experience. It needs to be felt and released in a safe space, which best happens with a licensed therapist.

The more we operate from our Spirit and become the Observer, the more we step into our spiritual power and shine as the Light we came here to be. When we feel our feelings, we open the channels of stagnant energy it took to keep them at bay. Feeling our feelings creates the opening inside to release that old energy, replacing it with new loving energy. We are set free, just like that. As we step into our spiritual power, we find our anger rarely becomes triggered. Others we used to find difficult, we do not even give them our attention. Where our attention goes, our energy flows. Operating as Spirit, we are Source Energy, which is always LOVE.

Let us focus our attention on being always the Observer, operating as our Spirit in full command. It is up to us to start a LOVE revolution, beginning with our own heart. Love outwardly toward others, toward all that is. For we are ONE HEART connected by LOVE.

Chapter 20

MORE TOOLS FOR OUR PHYSICAL, MENTAL, AND EMOTIONAL HEALTH

"The wound is the place where the Light enters you." Rumi

Learning and incorporating these life skill tools into my life has helped me tremendously personally and professionally. The ability to ask for what we want and need, and the ability to stand up for ourselves in a healthy way, are essential life skills that assist us in being as mentally and emotionally healthy as possible. I do my best to operate using the model of a 4-stroke cycle combustion engine and respond to life instead of reacting as I walk my talk. My hope is that these tools will help us respond to our lives more lovingly as we learn to operate as a Spirit in a human body.

Let us say I have a feeling I need to work on, yet I am not feeling it hot and heavy in the moment. However, I am in therapy, and I know I need access to this feeling to heal my stuck energy. I also know that allowing myself the time and space to work on my feelings is crucial for maintaining my health. It is also critical for healing in all four bodies -

physical, mental, emotional, and spiritual. So, when I want to work on myself, but do not have access in the now, I use these tools to help me gain entrance to my feelings, both past and present. I teach them as well. Let us discover how they can support us as we explore these tools in more detail.

Mental/Emotional Health Tools
- Letter Writing and Burning
- Journaling
- Foam Baseball Bat
- Forgiveness
- Gratitude
- Giving and Receiving
- Shower Ritual
- Calming Breath
- EFT – Emotional Freedom Techniques

These tools assist us in going deeper within to heal our heart by helping us to feel our feelings. To explore how these techniques can support us getting access to our past stuck feelings, let us use the example that we come home from work after an altercation with our boss, and we are still out of balance and upset about the experience. We could not express our truth about their behavior and words to them directly and held our feelings in. It is important we take the time to feel them anyway and let them out in a safe space once we are able. One way to connect with our feelings and allow us to not only feel them in the moment but also release them is to write a letter to our supervisor and then burn or shred it without rereading it when finished. The purpose of this letter is to express our output, our exhaust. Our truth is waiting to be acknowledged and then set free, so we can come back to balance.

Letter writing and burning serves several purposes. Telling the perpetrator how we feel about the way they treated us is a powerful experience. Even though we were not able to express our feelings in the present, it does not change the ability for us exercise our power by writing them a letter, now. This helps us to not clog up our exhaust with unexpressed feelings. While writing, we feel our feelings and are giving them a voice. We love ourselves through this experience, even though we were not able to do so with the perpetrator at the time. On a spiritual level, our Spirit is communicating with the Spirit of the perpetrator. Even though the letter will not be delivered physically, it is delivered energetically. After writing, if the person or feeling still gives us a sensation or charge somewhere in our body, then we write another letter, and another letter until the energy of its hold on us dissipates. And if it comes up again on another day, we write again. Burning safely or shredding each letter after writing it is also a powerful and symbolic part of this experience. We are telling the Universe and ourselves that we are letting go and releasing the energy imprinted on our heart so we can heal and return to balance.

As we let it go, this experience of letter writing to our boss can serve as a conduit for opening deeper feelings not easily accessed beneath our anger, such as hurt and loss. Remember the layers of our onion? Hurt and loss are at the core of most of our feelings. If we allow ourselves the space and time to connect the dots to the first memory of experiencing this exact same feeling, we can gain access to healing even deeper hurts. When we use our letter-writing tool, it allows us to get in touch with our feelings, which helps us know our truths. In this example with our supervisor, when we began feeling our unsettledness, we had no awareness what other feeling was lurking underneath that layer that needed our attention and love. Every time we chip away at our unexpressed feelings, we are that much closer to being a clearer vessel for the Christ Energy to express itself through us, as us. We are the vehicle through which the Christ Energy lives, breathes, and has its being in the here and now. Our body-mind-Spirit cares for us so beautifully. We are forever loved. We are LOVE.

Journaling is another tool to assist us on our journey to self-love and inner healing. We keep our journal, as opposed to extinguishing it like our letter writing. Writing in our personal journal is another way we can connect to express our feelings privately and in a safe space. Writing is a powerful way to find answers and gain insight into our heart, which connects us to our Soul. We can ask ourselves a question, as simple as, "How am I feeling today?" Over time, as we answer each journal entry, we will watch our growth on all levels - physical, mental, emotional, and spiritual. When we give ourselves the opportunity to surrender to our heart and honor ourselves by giving our feelings a voice, we transform from fear to love.

Another good writing entry is asking Self, "What do I need today?" The answers to both of those questions, when written from the heart, will allow our Spirit the outlet it needs to share its truths on paper, in our journal. Over time, we are creating a roadmap to fulfilling our unlimited potential and stepping into our personal power. We are raising our vibration and becoming who we committed to be while we are here. I love the exercise where I draw a line down the page in my journal. On half the page, I write my to-do list. On the other half of the page I write, "Things I am asking the Universe to do for me today."

I mentioned in an earlier chapter that anger is a tough feeling for some of us to express. Folks tend to act out their anger and do not know how to express it without raging at someone or losing control. One great therapeutic tool I have used, and encourage for others, is to use a *foam baseball bat*. It is a fabulous tool for expressing our anger, present or past. Hitting a hard surface like a mattress or couch to allow expression of our anger outwardly is powerful. Beginning to hit the couch with the foam bat may feel silly at first, especially if you are not feeling anger at that exact moment. When we start to speak aloud our exhaust of anger, we begin to feel our anger as we hear ourselves tell our truth and express it with physical force. The combination of actions opens our heart to allow our inner truth to flow. Again, do not be surprised if hurt, loss, and grief may be lurking underneath our anger. It is so important we allow the expression of whatever our heart desires to release, on an ongoing basis in our life. It helps bring us back to balance and back to love.

Forgiveness is an important tool we must learn how to utilize. It is an act of self-love. Most of us believe we must retaliate or be vengeful when another has caused harm to our loved one or us. We think that our ongoing rage and battle toward the unforgiving thing the perpetrator did will hurt them. We rage at the experience and keep the poison inside of us going by our continuing stinking thinking. Forgiveness does not mean that we forget the person and the harm they did to us. It also doesn't mean we have to make up with the person or include them in any part of our circle. It certainly does not mean we need to excuse the perpetrator, either.

The best definition for forgiveness I have integrated into who I am, and I have used professionally, is from Lisa Nichols, coauthor of *The Secret*, published in 2006. I learned her definition when I attended her conference in San Diego right after *The Secret* came out. She shared, "Forgiveness is the ability to thank the perpetrator of the experience for-giving us the opportunity to learn about ourselves." It is important to step back and consider how this hurtful incident has taken up our energy. We are the ones who continuously carry this trauma daily onto our blank new page in our book of life. It is imperative we let go of our betrayal, hurt, devastation, trauma, and loss. Over time, these feelings eat away, consume, and punish us, not the perpetrator. Forgiveness is an act of self-love. Forgiveness heals our heart and opens our Soul.

When we step back for a minute and become our Spirit, the Observer, we can see that the person who harmed us does not carry the baggage of poison for us each day, we do. Forgiveness allows us to use the experience as an opportunity to learn about ourselves and connect with our inner strengths and wisdom. As Lisa Nichols shared, it is when we can get to a place inside ourselves where we can thank the person for-giving us this incredible opportunity to learn about ourselves that deeper healing happens. We connect to our heart, our gratitude, and the Divine within when we can embrace the lesson.

Gratitude is an excellent attitude, which increases our vibration and helps us maintain it at a high point daily. Gratitude is like a magnet for us broadcasting to the Universe what is important to us. Making a gratitude list is a great journal entry to begin our day. It allows us to become more aware of even the smallest blessing in our life that we may take for granted. "I am so grateful for my sight." "Thank you for my breath." Thus, gratitude leads to us seeing ourselves more clearly and gets us out of our stinking thinking mode. It can help us keep a more balanced view of life by reminding us to stay grounded and humble. The Greek Philosopher, Epictus, who died in 138 A.D. wrote, "Men are disturbed not by things, but by the view which they take of them." Gratitude is a tool for lifting us up to a higher vibration. It helps us to have grace, manage our stress, and sleep better. We begin to appreciate ourselves and others more when we are grateful. We notice the little things that bring us joy. No matter how much we bring more gratitude into our lives, our world will be enhanced as we shift to a higher vibration for our physical, mental, emotional, and spiritual health. Gratitude shows the Universe what we are grateful for, and it attracts more gratitude in our lives.

Many of us allow our trauma response to kick in when it comes to depending upon others. As a result, gratitude may be incredibly difficult for us to receive. We may not have had someone whom we could depend on while growing up. Without someone we could ask for help or support, and receive it with no strings attached, we learned to stop asking. Sometimes we stopped expecting things from others, as we learned at a young age that asking was not answered reliably. Over time, plenty of us stopped receiving and only gave to others. Giving became one of our coping mechanisms and does not allow time and space for one to receive. Codependency allows us to be the strong one, the giver, the rescuer who fixes everything. As we heal from our trauma, we can learn to receive. *Giving and receiving* is an important part of our life.

My husband, Jim, took me on our first date on my birthday in 1985, approximately two years after I fled domestic violence and two years before we were married. I had a meltdown in the car on the drive home. So much so, Jim pulled over to help me process my feelings, as they were raw. He began his support with a question. "What kind of tears are they?"

"Overwhelmed by all of your gifts today," I shared.

"A good overwhelmed? Or not so good?" Jim asked with compassion.

"Both. We had an amazing day! You took me shopping, bought me a beautiful dress, shoes, and had a belt made for me that cost more than the shoes! We had lunch out, dinner and drinks, and then jazz music afterward. I have never had anyone give so much to me, never mind all in one day. I can see you appreciated me enjoying your generosity as much as I appreciated your generosity. Who are you?" I asked.

"I'm me," Jim said. "I just wanted to make you feel love and joy on your birthday."

I interrupted Jim. "I feel your love and our connection so strongly; my heart is overflowing. I have learned to be a giver. I love giving. It makes me feel good to help others. I truly don't know how to receive. Or perhaps I should say I don't allow myself to receive. I mostly only give."

"Giving and receiving is the circle of life," Jim responded. "I know how awesome it feels to give with no strings attached, as I too, am a giver. But I also know how important it is to receive. Receiving completes the circle."

"What do you mean?" Jim's passion was palpable.

"As much as you love to give, can you think about what it feels like when you want to give someone something, but they refuse to accept your gift?" he asked.

"What?" I asked, "It feels icky. Like they are denying me my opportunity to give."

Jim affirmed, "Yes, that is correct. They are. And it doesn't feel good, right?"

"Right." I nodded.

"So, you need to learn how to receive, so you don't sell your giver short and deny them the joy of giving to you. Giving and receiving are the circle of life. We need to know how to do both to keep the energy of our lives flowing."

With that beautiful definition of giving and receiving from my beloved Jim, I began to allow myself to receive. My hope is that we all allow ourselves to receive, so we can complete the circle of life by giving and receiving and allowing joy.

The *Shower Ritual* is a tool I began using daily in 1991. My new social work job serving intact families with AIDS was very intense and caused a lot of stress. Serving DCFS Families did not increase my salary while the responsibility of this job felt incredibly heavy.

As soon as I met "Jeremy," a six-year-old boy with AIDS, I knew my second case was the reason for the push inside of me to take this new job. I could feel it intensely, deep in my heart. Jeremy fell through a canopy from a second story window, down to the sidewalk, and crushed both his legs. After three months, Jeremy's full body cast was removed. His mother received a citation from DCFS for lack of supervision. This entry into the child welfare system brought me into their lives as the family's social worker/case manager. My job, according to DCFS, was to support them every way possible while always keeping a watchful eye on the child for signs of abuse. Jeremy did not know he had AIDS. The mother demanded that no professional involved tell him the truth.

As I did my best to begin to get to know this family and build trust with them, I became acutely aware of the seriousness and urgency of their situation. To comprehend that a mom, with HIV, would even consider harming her child while he was dying from full-blown AIDS, absolutely had me on heightened alert. I found myself constantly praying for both the mom and the child. I made up a ritual to speak in the shower to the water and myself. I began to speak aloud once I stood under the flowing shower water:

> Heavenly Father Mother God, I wish to serve.
> I ask that this shower cleanse my body, mind, Soul,
> and Spirit of all negativity.
> And that it restores me to Perfect Health
> Perfect Light
> Perfect Love
> Perfect Truth
> Perfect Wisdom
> Perfect Me
> Perfect You
> Perfect…

Then I would speak the name of the people aloud who I wanted to receive healing energies. The first names I always prayed for were Jeremy and his mother, "Delilah." My list of names for healing was long. As a final outcome, I would give gratitude for the healing water and visualize all negative energy being sucked down the drain. I still perform this shower ritual daily. It is a good self-care habit to form.

Another technique to help us remain in the present and connect to Spirit is the *calming breath*. Some call it the 4-7-8 breath. This is where we inhale to the count of four, hold our inhale to the count of seven, and exhale to the count of eight. Conscious breath work can help us to process and release our trauma and stuck feelings. It helps us to alleviate stress, panic, and anxiety. It calms areas of our brain linked to emotion, attention, and body awareness. Breath work is a powerful tool to relieve stress in the now.

A brilliant tool we can use on our own or in therapy with a professional is *EFT or Emotional Freedom Techniques*. Gary Craig, a Stanford engineer who worked for the developer of Thought Field Therapy, Dr. Roger Callahan, developed it in the 1990's. EFT is also known as tapping. I have always gotten immediate relief from tapping. Tapping combines ancient acupressure with modern psychology. It uses specific meridian points in our body to access our feelings in the now. A gentle and loving approach helps us retrieve and make connections to our difficult and traumatic feelings that lie buried within, which cause our energy blocks. Emotions are energy in motion. EFT helps us to open and release this energy in a safe space. It helps restore our inner balance. It is calming and immediate in its response.

The physical, mental, and emotional tools taught here help give us access to our deepest feelings, so we can uncover their hold on us and work toward releasing them. There are plenty more tools out there to help us access our feelings in the now. The ones I have shared here specifically worked great for me and still do. Inner healing of Self is an ongoing process. We are so worth our own efforts.

Chapter 21

USING MY LIFE SKILLS TOOLS WITH A CHILD ABUSER

"Act as if what you do makes a difference. It does." William James

---

As I worked with DCFS Intact Families with AIDS, I soon discovered that sharing my life skills tools with my DCFS parents taught them real skills they could choose that would help them cope in a more positive way. Teaching the parents how to operate as a Spirit in a human body helped them to see themselves in a new way. However, I quickly became aware that Delilah, Jeremy's mother, suffered from borderline personality disorder (BPD,) which I have described in chapter eight. Personality disorders are challenging to treat, as the core identity and character of the person is impacted by these deeply dysfunctional inner ways of coping and being. Many studies show a 50% success rate of folks treated in therapy for BPD over a 10-year period. We did not have 10 years. So, over the next 22 months of which approximately six of the months were on my own time without any pay, I worked diligently at breaking through Delilah's defenses. She had to learn how to express her rage so she would stop lashing out mentally, emotionally, and physically, at her dying six-year-old son.

Together, Jeremy and I experienced many Divine Interventions along the way. Thank goodness, he was my only abuse case. My husband, Jim, was the glue that held me together while handling all this responsibility, especially working with Delilah and Jeremy. I have written about my 22-month journey with Jeremy in my 2003 book, *Dance with an Angel, the True Story of an Eight-Year-Old Hero*. My spiritual experiences with Jeremy continue to this day. Jeremy continues to watch over my family and me. *Dance with an Angel* begins:

> In the fall of 1992, Delilah Miller refrained from suffocating her two-year-old son, Simon, with a pillow. She then, for the first time in her life, signed herself into a psychiatric hospital. I can't help but think had I reached her sooner, the fate of her eight-year-old son, Jeremy, may have been different and I might not be telling you our story. Yet, every cell of my being knows that my journey with them was not by accident.

The day I met Delilah and Jeremy through their DCFS caseworker, my experience with the medium at Camp Chesterfield almost eight months prior flooded my awareness. When a boy with beautiful dark brown skin and huge almond eyes walked in Delilah's apartment after school during our introductory meeting, I immediately knew he was the child the medium had predicted. As I became more involved with Delilah and Jeremy, the seriousness of the entire situation weighed me down heavily. I absolutely needed to rely on assistance from God, the Universe, Spirit, the Angelic Realm, and my own spiritual gifts and tools for help with this one. A six-year-old boy's life was at stake.

So far, DCFS had only wanted me to keep these AIDS families together. The law in Illinois is focused on family preservation. Their intention is to keep children in their family homes when safe and possible. Unfortunately, the case workers have too many cases on their caseload, and in my experience, they lack clinical acumen. A bachelor's degree does not provide much clinical experience, knowledge, or training in psychopathology, or the scientific study of mental disorders. Both clinical acumen and time were necessary components of helping this family, and a DCFS caseworker has neither. Therefore, DCFS offered a private contract to a university in Chicago to support these families with AIDS. I was the first social worker to take on this difficult and intense position. I felt a push inside to take a job that I could not ignore.

I needed to apply all my knowledge to this case - clinical, mental, emotional, and especially spiritual. I invoked and used many spiritual tools to assist in Jeremy's Highest Good being served. I needed help from Spirit to execute Divine Order in a dying boy's life in order to fulfill our Sacred Contract together. Spiritual tools may not seem to be working immediately from a human perspective. Prayer and intention work as soon as we speak or think their invocation. Once we create, think, and speak them, the Universe receives them on a spiritual energetic level. In *Dance with an Angel, the True Story of an Eight-Year-Old Hero* we see powerful proof of our spiritual tools in action. And so it is, Amen.

Chapter 22

MANY SPIRITUAL TOOLS FOR OUR SELF-GROWTH

"Out of suffering have emerged the strongest Souls, the most massive characters are seared with scars." Khalil Gibran

---

Spiritual tools are another level of life skills that provide us with great benefits. We may or may not see the results immediately with our human eyes. Yet, as we use these tools, we will come to know they are powerfully fulfilling our requests and intentions in the unseen world of Spirit. A farmer would not plant a seed and expect a physical manifestation of an instant stalk of corn. We must trust that the seed will eventually grow and become a physical manifestation. By keeping the High Watch or constantly seeing each situation through the eyes of *faith* and not through fear or doubt, we keep our vibration and consciousness at our highest point. In doing so, we create what we are holding in faith. And so it is, Amen. Addressing our needs from a spiritual level, we facilitate our Self-growth as a spiritual being operating a human body. I will list the spiritual tools here that have been most influential in my life. We will discuss them in the next several chapters.

Spiritual Tools for Self-Growth
- Faith
- White Light of Christ
- Prayer
- Meditation
- Manifesting
- The Law of Attraction
- Affirmations
- Visualization/Vision Board
- Pendulum
- Color Therapy and Color Bubble Tool
- Essential Oils/Lilies of the Valley Anointing Balm
- Divination Cards
- Clairvoyant Readings
- Astrology
- Crystals
- Reiki Healing
- Numerology
- Conscious Chi Gong
- Vibrational Sound Healing
- Masaru Emoto – *The Hidden Messages in Water*
- Chakras

We are each responsible for our own spiritual growth and welfare. Our spiritual growth is attained by our own aspirations and striving to overcome our wrong thinking, wrongdoing, and our own unhappiness. Many religions have placed a veil between the words of God and our own heart in order to separate humanity from the kingdom within. It is up to each of us to lift the veil of mystery through spiritual understanding to grasp the kingdom of God IS within. Where we stand vibrationally creates our reality here and now. We can only see clearly that which our raised consciousness and vibrational frequency allows. As we heal our hurt and empty our trauma from our heart, we raise our consciousness and vibration. How? By allowing in LOVE, where there was once trauma and unfelt heavy painful feelings. When we fill our heart with love, we connect with the heart of Oneness. We become an empty vessel for the Christ energy to fill us.

Circumstances in our life do not create themselves. They come from our thought patterns and our inability to feel and express our feelings. When we take an inventory of our mental and emotional reactions to our environment, we will see how these tangible states of our being form our outward experiences of life. In Matthew 8:13, Jesus the Christ exclaimed, "...as thou hast believed, so be it done unto thee." Belief is our mental attitude. *Faith* is a much higher vibrational way of thinking. Faith is an elevated spiritual attitude. It is seeing things past their 3D appearances, as God and the Universe see them. In Hebrews 11:1, faith is "the assurance of things hoped for, the conviction of things not seen." Faith allows us to see past our feelings of inadequacy, doubt, fear, difficulty, and limitation. As we remain patient and keep the High Watch, we maintain our faith and await the Universe's Divine expression to manifest in our life for our Highest Good. Matthew 9:29 states, "According to your faith, it will be done unto us." Keeping our faith by holding the High Watch is powerful beyond measure. To accomplish this, we hold the image and feeling of the desire in our mind without wavering, as though we already have what we are asking for in faith, until it manifests. We take steps in the physical world to show our faith. When our vibration matches in thought, word, and deed, we can manifest as Jesus did. God's power of faith is always within us. It is up to us to use it. We "can" accomplish great things if we have the faith of a tiny mustard seed. We are reminded of this in Matthew 17:20.

In John 2: 1 – 11, Jesus turns water into wine at a wedding in Cana. After Mother Mary informs Jesus that they are out of wine, Jesus responds by asking for six stone jars filled with water. Jesus then requests that one of the servants draw out some of the water and take it to the master of the banquet to taste. When the master samples the water, he remarks that this wine is of the finest quality and asks why they waited to serve it. So, let us look at how this manifestation of wine took place.

Jesus held the highest vibrational thought, word, and deed in his mind and heart so he could manifest the wine in real time. His first Highest Thought was to state his intention through prayer, speaking to God. As Matthew 7:7 reminds us, "Ask and you will receive; seek and you will find; knock and the door will be opened unto you."

Jesus was already filled with the Christ Consciousness. He knew and trusted that God and the Universe would answer his prayer. Faith was all he needed to make the wine. His thoughts/prayer began the manifestation process followed by his faithful word and deed. Keeping his mental, emotional, and physical vibration at his highest and best outcome by holding the High Watch and staying there in heart and mind, Jesus KNEW the Universe would match his vibration in 3D. When our thoughts/words/deeds all match up vibrationally, we too can turn water into wine. And so, it is.

Camp Chesterfield taught me a prayer called The Prayer of Faith written by Hannah More Kohaus. It originally appeared in a Unity School of Christianity publication in August of 1898, as it was a favorite of Myrtle Fillmore, co-founder of Unity.

> God is my help in every need.
> God does my every hunger feed.
> God walks beside me, guides my way,
> Through every moment of the day.
> I now am wise, I now am true,
> Patient, kind, and loving, too.
> All things I am, can do, and be,
> Through Christ, the TRUTH, that is in me.
> God is my health; I can't be sick.
> God is my strength, unfailing, quick.
> God is my ALL; I know no fear.
> Since God, and love, and truth are here.

My favorite prayer in my entire life experience is The White Light of Christ. It is the most POWERFUL energy in the Universe. Why? Because 2000 years ago, the Master Teacher Jesus the Christ incarnated and showed us the way to our heart, to unconditional love, and to our limitless possibilities within through the Christ Consciousness that we all are capable of embodying. Ask and we receive. This prayer is a powerful asking. The Universe has always responded in kind. We alone are responsible for our own Self-growth, and thus for the growth of the world in which we live, collectively.

Here is the prayer that Master Nicodemus gave to Charlotte Bright Daising, in meditation. Charlotte was the Founder of The First Temple of Universal Law in Chicago. This prayer can change our world like it has changed my life and many others:

> Heavenly Father, Mother God, I wish to serve.
> Please surround me with the White Light of Christ for protection.
> I ask for my Highest Good to be served.
> I pray for Divine Order to reign over my life and affairs.
> I am so very grateful.
> Thank you.
> Amen.

We can alter this prayer to our specific situation and need. During a surgery for example, we can surround the operating room, the surgical staff and ourselves with the White Light of Christ. We can ask for the Highest Good of all participants and Divine Order to reign over the entire procedure.

I have many experiences where declaring the White Light of Christ has moved mountains. A profound example is from the 1999 hurricane season in Florida. I had a family member living on the inter-coastal waterway in Miami. That year, the 1999 Atlantic basin hurricane season produced four tropical storms and eight hurricanes. Seven of them hit landfall. We declared the White Light of Christ prayer aloud for each hurricane coming toward Miami. We prayed that my family members' person, home, neighborhood, and belongings be surrounded with the White Light of Christ for protection. We kept the High Watch and held our faith. Every single hurricane meant for Miami shifted. My family members were safe, even though the brutal storms were in their path. Upon the close of hurricane season, I remember my sister staying at a lovely hotel for her 25th high school reunion here in Illinois, a *USA Today* newspaper delivered to her suite. The front page showed the path of all eight hurricanes. Of the six scheduled to hit her area, every single one shifted. Always remember to give thanks to God and the Universe for our fulfilled prayer.

Another powerful example of the White Light of Christ prayer fulfilling its request was with Jeremy. Thank God he was my only child abuse case. In my first book *Dance with an Angel, The True Story of an Eight-year-old Hero,* I declared the White Light of Christ over Juvenile Court, the judge, and all of the participants involved. I know doing so literally saved Jeremy's life. The state of Illinois did gain temporary custody of Jeremy even though there were no founded reports of abuse against the mother. Founded evidence is what allows DCFS to remove a child from their abusive or neglectful home. In this specific case, there were five horrendous incidences of child abuse by the mother of this child dying from AIDS. However, DCFS labeled all five as unfounded. Instead of taking protective custody of Jeremy, DCFS chose to keep him in the custody of his abusive mom, as an intact family, with the hope I could stop her from hurting her dying son. After the fifth incident, which was medical neglect, I was at my wits end. I was doing everything I could to help this mom to stop using violence against her son. Yet her complicated dysfunction continued.

I was ready to threaten the DCFS caseworker that I would go to a local news reporter to blow the whistle on them if they continued to keep this family together. I didn't need to. DCFS finally allowed me to do a preliminary report and take my report to the State's Attorney's office to see if we had a case, even though DCFS did not prove any "founded," evidence against the mother. It was my word against the mother's, which is unheard of in the history of DCFS. Once the mother received a citation for lack of supervision by DCFS, she had to join our brand-new program designed to help her cope, so her family could stay together. DCFS chose to not do anything about the mother's second physically abusive incident against Jeremy and let it go. They hoped the mother would accept our services and work with our program. Their expectation was that I could help her to stop beating her dying child.

Even after the mother physically abused Jeremy while I was chaperoning them on a Make-A-Wish trip, DCFS made the mother attend parenting group instead of finding legal evidence against her and permanently separating her dying son from her abusive hands. Regardless, I declared the White Light of Christ around every judicial proceeding. When I first took this abusive mother to court, two different judges, whose courtrooms we were assigned, failed to hear our request for DCFS to take temporary custody of this child. I refused to give up. I continued praying the White Light of Christ prayer throughout this entire experience.

Our last attempt to have our case heard was successful. A third unfamiliar judge who looked like Santa Claus granted temporary custody to DCFS. Jeremy would no longer live a life of violence from his mother. I gave thanks to the Universe all day long, every day. The White Light of Christ ensured that Divine Order did reign and the boy's Highest Good was served. The White Light of Christ moves mountains!

Pray the White Light of Christ daily for yourself and family for protection. Before driving, I surround my car with it. I also surround my home with it daily. Surround Mother Earth for her healing. The possibilities for the work of the White Light of Christ are infinite. The White Light of Christ works its miracles wherever and whenever it is invoked. And so it is, Amen.

Chapter 23

PRAYER AND MEDITATION

"Oh, then, Soul most beautiful among all the creatures, so anxious to know the dwelling place of your Beloved so you may go in search of Him, and be united with him, now we are telling you that you yourself are his dwelling and his secret inner room and hiding place."
St John of the Cross

Prayer and *meditation* go hand in hand. They are incredibly powerful tools for our life. *Prayer* is talking to God. *Meditation* is listening for answers from within. Being able to meditate is a beautiful gift we give ourselves because it connects us to our Higher Self and directly to Source Energy. We can also set our intention to raise our vibration high enough that we connect with the Spirit World. When we meditate with the intention of communing with Spirit to receive answers, the answers received can be from God, Jesus, Buddha, Quan Yin, Zoroaster, and other Ascended Masters. In addition, our Angels, Spirit Guides, Master Teachers, and our loved ones in Spirit all connect with us during meditation, when we pray and set our intention. Prayer and meditation help us to raise our vibration. I invoke this prayer before I meditate and have taught it to many others:

> Heavenly Father, Mother God,
> I wish to Serve.
> Please surround me with the White Light of Christ for Protection.
> I respectfully call forth my Master Teachers, Spirit Guides,
> Angels, and Loved ones in Spirit
> to be present at this time.
> (Speak their names aloud if possible)
> I ask for only the Highest Thoughts and Truths
> And I, (Speak our name aloud,) respectfully surrender,
> and open my channel to Spirit.
> Thank you.
> Amen.

Meditation is the practice of being able to detach from our thoughts, our body, and our ego, to become no-thing. It is the ability to get out of the way of our thoughts and stinking thinking and intentionally become our Observer. In this space in between our inhalation and our exhalation, we can allow ourselves to let go of our human reality and step into our Higher Self. Here we are WHOLE. We plug in directly to the God Source Energy part of ourselves. Meditation is about getting our ego out of the way and stepping into the real us, a Spirit operating a human body. When we tune in to this higher frequency of our inner being, we learn to communicate with Spirit to receive answers from them for our Highest Good. When we practice for just 15 to 20 minutes each day, we create a space within for our Higher Self to flow through and communicate clearly. With practice, we learn to connect and operate from this vibrational frequency all the time. Spirit always communicates with us. We are also Spirit. As the receivers of their message, we just need to learn their preferred method of communication with us.

It is through our daily practice of quieting our mind during meditation that we work out our transmission methods using our gifts of clairvoyance, clairaudience, clairsentience, claircognizance, clairalience, and clairgustance. Then over time, as we get to know Spirit's vibe, we can commune with them consciously whenever we need to. Whenever we ask, we receive an answer for our Highest Good, or the highest outcome for whatever situation we are dealing with, every single time. We can become the vessel able to receive the answer. We receive when we vibrate high enough to translate it with our spiritual senses. Our unwillingness to forgive ourselves for actual, and even imagined, wrongdoings in our life can limit our ability to meditate and connect with Spirit, as it creates a barrier between us. Healing our trauma and feeling our feelings allows us to open our hearts so we can meditate and open our spiritual senses to Divine Communication.

Over time, as we keep our daily commitment to prayer and meditation, our faith and trust in God, our Spirit Guides, Master Teachers, Angels, and our loved ones in Spirit, grows. As we expand our ability to surrender, what we receive from Spirit begins to evolve. We must be kind and patient with ourselves when learning spiritual meditation. When we set our intention of meeting Spirit in meditation to get answers for our Highest Good, we surrender and receive more of Spirit's love, wisdom, and guidance as a direct result of our efforts. Our commitment to serving God for the Highest Good of Self and others grows, as do the spiritual gifts we begin to uncover and receive.

I will share a beautiful example showing the power of Divine Communication that I received in meditation, which provided a real-life solution to help save an infant's life. His name is Ivan. I began a private practice as a psychiatric social worker and a professional guardian for disabled adults a week after leaving my DCFS AIDS families position in 1991. I continued to help Jeremy on my own time by staying and being a part of his life, while I attended every single juvenile court date. I did not take on more than three guardianship clients at a time, as I was on call 24/7 for all of them, and our two children were young. I often held other part-time positions as a Licensed Clinical Social Worker.

One position I held in the late 1990's was to help my dear friend Leeanne McGrath move her non-profit, Sharing Connections, from her home to a 1,600-foot warehouse and to obtain enough donations to pay the rent. While we were transitioning to the warehouse, Leeanne and I worked from her home and garage. Sharing Connections is a place where folks drop off their gently used items from clothing to furniture and everything in between, and Sharing Connections finds a home for the items locally in our community. The non-profit serves families in distress, transition, and recovery.

One winter morning, I answered Leeanne's telephone, "Sharing Connections, this is Robyn. How may I help you?" A Cook County female deputy sheriff responded and asked who I was and where was Leeanne. I told her that I was the first professional Leanne had hired to help, and that I was a Licensed Clinical Social Worker. The sheriff explained she was at her local bank in Chicago, and her favorite teller was terribly upset, crying and needed our help. She handed the phone to a woman with a strong European accent. She introduced herself as Diana and began to share her need for reaching out to us.

"My husband, Mykola, and I are living in an apartment in Ukrainian Village and are here as legal immigrants. Mykola works as a janitor for Chicago Public Schools, and I am a bank teller. We just got back from New York, and we have our daughter, Anna, son-in-law Dmytro, and our grandson, Ivan, with us. They are here from Ukraine on an emergency medical visa. My grandson was born with a congenital heart defect." Diana was trying hard to catch her breath, sobbing between her words and speaking very quickly.

"Take your time, Diana. It's okay to catch your breath," was all I could muster between her tears.

"Thank you. What did you say your name was?"

"I am Robyn, the new social worker here at Sharing Connections."

"Thank you, Robyn. My family is here with basically the clothes on their back and what they brought in their suitcase. No winter clothes, coats, no crib, or mattress to sleep on, not a thing to help them. My grandson, Ivan, is just six months old. The hospital discharged him; more like threw us out, after he had a stroke during their first catheterization on him. This hospital had promised to fix his heart at no cost, if my family could arrange to get to New York. Now that the procedure had caused a stroke, Ivan was on a ventilator for 10 days. When he awakened, they weaned him off and sent us on our way with zero instructions. We brought everyone home, back to our apartment in Chicago. Thus, the reason for my call. We are desperate."

"Oh my, I am so sorry for the way the hospital treated you all. I am grateful you are here in Chicago, and everyone is safe. We can help with physical needs, such as clothing, baby items including diapers, furniture, and more. I just need to write down your information and sizes for everyone, for starters. So, tell me the size your daughter wears please."

"Anna is a ten petite or a size medium. Dmytro is 6'6" and thin. He takes a 34 extra-long and size large, extra tall shirts. Ivan wears 12 to 18 months. But we need everything." Diana began to sob again.

"Diana, no worries. God is so good. We will make a list of furniture and other items you need and my family will personally deliver them to you at your apartment, if that is permissible." Sharing Connections did not have a truck yet to pick items up. We did not normally make deliveries. Recipients had to get their own transportation for picking up their items.

"My goodness, that would be a gift from heaven, for sure," she said quietly.

"It'd be our pleasure. That's why we're Sharing Connections! I will call you once I pull everything together and make a date for drop off."

She replied, "Thank you with all my heart! I am so grateful. We do not have money to pay for these things."

"We do not charge for these things. We share," I explained.

On that note, I hung up and said a prayer for Diana's family. I got a drink of water and looked out the window. A pick-up truck had just backed into Leeanne's driveway and a male driver got out. He was very tall.

I put on my winter coat and went outside to greet him. "Good morning, Sir. May I ask what you are donating today, please?"

"Why of course. Bags of clothes from myself, my wife, and our baby boy."

"Incredible. I just said a prayer as I hung up from a call with a family in need of clothing for the dad who is 6'6", the mom who is a size ten petite, and baby boy clothing twelve to eighteen months. Be pretty amazing if you are the answer!"

"Swear to God, I am your answered prayer." With that comment and tears in his eyes, the man handed me three bags of clothing. Each bag was marked with the exact sizes I had asked for in prayer.

I burst out in tears of gratitude. By the end of the week, we had loaded my minivan with bags of clothing, a baby crib and mattress, lamps, a chair, a full-sized mattress, and linens. Jim, Kathryn who was six years old, Stephen who was three, and I drove to the Ukrainian Village neighborhood in Chicago to their third-floor walk-up apartment. We delivered an entire van full of needed items. The family had prepared a whole table full of Ukrainian foods and many vodka shots. Such a lovely family. Little Ivan was still quite ill and now he was struggling with having a stroke and being partially paralyzed.

The following week, Diana called and asked for referrals for Ivan, as he was not doing well. Since he did not have the cardiac surgery in New York that he needed to save his life, they needed a pediatric cardiac surgeon who would perform the surgery, pro-bono, here in Chicago. I sent the family first to Shriners Hospital. When they could not help, I referred her to the University of Chicago Children's Hospital. When they were unable to assist, she tried the University of Illinois at Chicago Hospital, Rush University Medical Center, and finally Children's Memorial Hospital, now known as Lurie Children's hospital. Within a few days of seeing the pediatric cardiologist at Children's Memorial, the cardiac surgeon sent the parents a letter, which Diana read to me over the phone, while sobbing.

My heart became incredibly heavy as I learned its contents. The only pediatric cardiac surgeon in Chicago, capable of performing the heart surgery outlined Ivan's serious condition. Then he offered to perform the surgery on Ivan for $250,000. The next sentence stated the possibility that Ivan may have only two more weeks to live with the state of his current heart if he did not receive the surgery. Diana was beside herself and asked what we could do to help raise the monies. She could not imagine life without her beautiful Ivan. I told her for now, we would put out a collection bin at Sharing Connections and at all our local businesses that would allow, and I would get back to her.

I hung up and began to cry. The responsibility for saving Ivan's life came down to money. We put coffee cans out for collection but knew this would not be sufficient without a miracle. So, we prayed for Ivan and for him to have his life-saving surgery in Divine timing. Several days went by with no answer.

The fourth day, I prayed for Ivan and then decided to meditate to see if I would be able to receive any messages from Spirit to help with his situation. During my meditation, I received clairsentiently, that if Anna and Dmytro gave up custody of Ivan to Diana or Mykola, and one or both of the grandparents became temporary guardian, then Ivan would qualify on the grandparent's insurance and have his life-saving surgery. I quickly came out of meditation and called Bob, the owner of Guardianship Services Associates (GSA), where I served as one of their associates. I began a private practice in 1991 to act as guardian of the person for their adjudicated disabled wards. Bob, who was a social worker and a guardianship expert, said the grandparents becoming temporary guardian was possible! He said he could file an emergency order in Cook County Probate Court the following day and had me ask Diana to meet him there with the $50 filing fee at 8 a.m. He also wondered how I came up with the brilliant plan to save Ivan's life. I shared that Spirit gave me the answer in meditation. Bob was thrilled to be a part of the solution.

I called Diana and gave her the miraculous news. I arranged for her to meet Bob the next day at Cook County Probate Court. Diana was crying tears of joy this time. She shared that she knew I would come up with a miracle to save Ivan. I told her I received the information from my Spirit helpers, and she thanked them, too.

The following day, Diana called me, crying hysterically. She shared that she had been robbed on her way to probate court. I took down the number of the pay phone and told her I would call her back. I called Bob. He was already at court. He said to have Diana meet him anyhow. He would pay the $50 filing fee and get an emergency hearing scheduled, and he did.

Less than a week later, the cardiac surgeon from Children's Memorial Hospital performed Ivan's life-saving surgery. My family visited Ivan in the Pediatric Intensive Care Unit the next day. We all said a prayer of Thanksgiving. Ivan's life was indeed saved! Thank you, God. Thank you, Christ. Thank you, Angels. Amen. To this day, our son, Stephen, keeps a photo of Ivan next to his bedside table, where Ivan, six-months of age, has a feeding tube in his nose. Building compassion and empathy by volunteering with our children gives them a powerful foundation for their future and for our world's future.

I have received many more profound answers and teachings through meditation since I began studying Spiritualism in 1989 after finding Camp Chesterfield. My hope is we will all take the time to learn to receive during meditation from God, our Angels, Spirit Guides, Master Teachers, and loved ones in Spirit. Let us embrace the authenticity of who we really are… by become fully human and fully Divine. And so it is, Amen.

Chapter 24

MANIFESTING, THE LAW OF ATTRACTION, AFFIRMATIONS, VISUALIZATION, AND THE PENDULUM

"The whole problem with the world is that fools and fanatics are always so certain of themselves, and wiser people so full of doubts." Bertrand Russell

---

Manifestation is another helpful tool for our spiritual toolbox and our life. When our beliefs and our desires match up, we can manifest our desires into the physical world. If we desire something in our future, but we do not believe we are worthy, then we are not a vibrational match for it. If we are not a vibrational match for it, it would be impossible to manifest the desire on the Earth Plane. However, when we stop our stinking thinking and operate from our Observer, we can experience life more truthfully as the conscious co-creators that we are, instead of from a wounded place.

Other ways we interfere with our manifestation coming to fruition are by being impatient, doubtful, angry, and frustrated. Negative feelings are all indicators of our resistant thoughts, and our trauma-filled hearts, which show us where we are out of alignment with Source Energy. When we do not do our Self-work, we obstruct the receipt of our desire. Our stinking thinking impedes our connection to our Source Energy. When we align with our Source Energy, it flows through us with ease. It is our destiny to feel enthusiastic and passionate about our life. When we keep the High Watch, our vibration changes from belief to standing and staying in our faith. By holding this high vibe, we match the vibe of our desire, and over time, the outcome manifests for all to see.

My husband, Jim, and I manifested the exact home we wanted to purchase in the year 2000 after outgrowing our first home. We wrote down a description of every detail of our heart's desire that we wanted in our new home. We had read our manifestation list aloud many times daily while we acted toward our goal by viewing houses for sale with our realtor. I also carried our list with us as we looked for our new home. Whenever a feeling came up to counteract our desires, I would pull out our list and read it aloud, giving thanks to the Universe for our home already being here ready for us. By the end of the second week, we found our new house. It was not even on the market yet! We wrote our manifestation list as follows:

At the top of the page, we wrote: Thank you, Universe. I am/we are so grateful now that...

- Our new home has three bedrooms
- So grateful for our one and a half bathrooms
- And our two-car garage
- Thankful for continuing in the same school district
- Grateful for our fenced-in yard
- Thankful for our hardwood floors
- Grateful for our fireplace
- Grateful for our basement
- Grateful for our friendly neighbors
- Grateful to pay our top price of $169,000
- Grateful to close the sale on time for the beginning of the new school year

At the bottom, we wrote: Thank you, Universe. We are so grateful for this or something better, for our Highest Good. Amen.

When we searched for houses with our realtor in that price range, some of the homes were not even livable. One had raccoons and a condemned sign on the front door. Most houses with 3 bedrooms, a garage, basement, and 1.5 baths listed at $189,900. On my husband's full time LCSW salary and my part-time LCSW private practice income, we were unable to afford a mortgage to cover that amount.

The house had everything we had asked the Universe for on our list. It had three bedrooms, one and a half baths, hardwood floors, a basement with a fireplace, a fenced in yard, was within our desired school district for our two children, had great neighbors, and we paid exactly $169,000 for it. The Universe is amazing, and so are we as co-creators. When our beliefs and desires match up, voila! We manifest our heart's desires right here on earth.

There are many great books out there today to help us learn how to manifest our heart's desire and learn to utilize The Law of Attraction. Some of my favorites are *Creative Visualization* by Shakti Gawain, *The Secret* by Rhonda Byrne and *Ask and It Is Given* by Esther and Jerry Hicks. Esther channels the non-physical entity called Abraham who teaches us how to manifest our heart's desire through the Law of Attraction and the science of deliberate creation. Dr. Joe Dispenza is another favorite. He was in a bicycling accident with a truck and became paralyzed when he broke six vertebrae in his spine. While in the hospital he visualized daily for many hours that his spine was healed. When he was able to hold the High Watch and merge his belief that he could walk again with his desire to walk again, he healed from paralysis and walked out of the hospital in 10 and a half weeks!

The Law of Attraction is a Universal Law. Universal laws are Natural laws that govern our Universe. Universal Laws regulate the unseen world and rely upon our experience to show themselves. They are fundamental principles that describe the relationship between things under a certain set of conditions, which apply equally throughout the Universe. Newton's law of gravity is one example. Many Universal Laws are metaphysical and provide laws governing the unseen world of Spirit. The Law of Attraction specifically states that like attracts a like vibration. Another way to define it is that which is like itself is attracted to itself. That is why when meditating with the intention of reaching our Spirit Guides and loved ones in Spirit, we use the White Light of Christ prayer of protection. Only Spirit that comes with the highest and best vibration may enter the White Light of Christ to come close to us. Period.

Tools for putting the Law of Attraction into motion include stating our intention to the Universe of what we want, writing affirmations to support our desires, and visualizing and feeling the outcome of our desire as if it has already happened in the now. Our unconscious mind does not know if what we are practicing is real or imagined. Therefore, it is important to imagine it and picture us already achieving our goal in order to create a feeling within that what we want to manifest is already here. I read a book called *Small Miracles* that shared the story of a man who survived each day during the Holocaust, while living in Auschwitz, by visualizing himself golfing a perfect game every waking minute. When he was rescued from the concentration camp, one of the first things he did was to play 18 holes of golf. He scored a perfect game! The power of our imagination is infinite.

"The brighter the Light, the darker the shadow," is a quote from Carl Jung. Jung even described a place called the Collective Unconscious, which contains our collective thoughts, knowledge, and imagery that we all share, even with our ancestors. Jung described it as shared wisdom inherited from our ancestors in the form of archetypes, including the shadow, which we discussed in *mirroring*. I like to think of the Collective Unconscious as a place where like thoughts congregate. Since our thoughts eventually become things, I see it as the place where the collective energy of our combined thoughts live.

What about God's Divine Ideas? How do they manifest here on Earth? The Archangel Jophiel coordinates a team of seven Angels who see each of God's ideas through until they manifest physically here on the Earth Plane. Through whom do God's ideas manifest? Through us! We are the instruments of Spirit through which these ideas manifest here on Earth. Each Angel on Jophiel's team has a role in making the manifestation happen. From receiving God's vision to ensuring clear communication, we have help from the Angelic Realm. God wants us to join in co-creation of directing energy into form.

Christianity calls God a triune God, meaning Father, Son, and Holy Spirit. Spirit told me years ago it is more of a four-part connection, Father, Son, Holy Spirit, and us. We are the instruments who carry out God's Divine Ideas here on Earth. We each have the potential to complete this connection and become the instrument through which the Divine Idea happens, here and now.

Personally, I have been coming to terms with the power of my Inner Light since before my prophetic dreams began in 1987. Even when I was 17, I felt and witnessed God's presence literally as a white blinding light when I drank psilocybin tea at a party with the abuser. Since 1987, I have received so many nudges that the knowledge I was receiving was from the Divine. But my feelings of unworthiness and self-judgement held me back from going public. I still used the knowledge to walk my talk, serving God through my clients, friends, family, and my community daily. But it was not until 2019 that I got the idea it was time to begin authoring this book, which Spirit gave me the title to over 25 years ago, when our kids were small. I guess I was the Reluctant Messiah long enough. I will share in the last couple of chapters how I received the courage in the fall of 2021 to finally share my experiences as this book.

The next spiritual tool in our toolbox is *affirmations*. An affirmation is a statement affirming or making firm, the desire or image we wish to manifest. It is a powerfully effective tool for helping us to create a more positive life for ourselves. They also help us to achieve our goals more easily. In Job 22:28, we learn, "Thou shalt also decree a thing, and it shall be established unto thee, and the Light shall shine upon thy ways." Writing affirmations and placing them on sticky notes all around our home helps to remind us of what we want to move toward instead of what we lack. They remind us to stop our stinking thinking. Speaking affirmations aloud grounds us in knowing that we speak our power into the words of what we want and not what we do not want. Remember that like attracts like vibration. Affirmations are like a prayer to our Higher Self and to the Universe, affirming and putting out there what we desire. When I was working my job with DCFS families with AIDS, my husband Jim got me two powerful affirmations cards. The first was, "I am powerful, beautiful, and creative, and I can handle it." The second one was, "All details take care of themselves; it is safe to let go!" I have been sharing these two powerful affirmations for the past 32 years, and I still use them myself. Other good ones include:

- I love standing in my Light.
- Everything is working out for my Highest Good.
- I am blessed.
- I am abundant and have enough to share.
- I am worthy of my heart's desires.
- I am healed and whole.
- I love and accept myself completely.
- Only good will come from this experience.

Thoughts become things, so let us speak our way into what we want to manifest.

Visualization is another powerful spiritual technique for us to use. When we create a physical picture of our desire, we are creating a blueprint to show the Universe what we want. Visualizing helps put the energy of our desire into motion to help us attract our goal. Creating a vision board is a great way to show the Universe exactly what we want to manifest. By making a collage using pictures, words, drawings, and more from magazines, books, cards, photos, etc., we are creating a literal treasure map for the Universe to follow in order to manifest our heart's desire. Upon awakening and before sleeping take a few minutes to focus on our treasure map and thank the Universe for it coming to fruition.

Another important spiritual tool I use is the *Chevreul Pendulum*. In 1835 a French scientist named Michel Eugene Chevreul found that when a pendulum, which can be as simple as a washer tied to a string, is held by our dominant hand between our index finger and our thumb, it elicits our ideomotor response. An ideomotor response is a small unconscious movement created in response to our thoughts. When you ask yes or no questions, the pendulum swings in different directions depending upon the answer. Our unconscious mind responds by moving the pendulum while our finger, thumb, hand, wrist, and elbow remain steady.

I learned how to use the pendulum, to speak directly to my unconscious mind, when I took a self-hypnosis class in 1985 before returning to college after my six-year hiatus during the domestic violence I experienced. This was two years before my prophetic dreams began and even before I met Jim. When the self-hypnosis teacher taught that we could get answers from our unconscious mind, I had no experience or knowledge of the Spirit World yet. Thus, I had no clue that I was opening my channel to Spirit through the pendulum, and that I could speak directly to Spirit by setting my intention through prayer and asking. Once Jim and I began to attend classes at Camp Chesterfield, I figured out quickly that using the pendulum was a direct route to Spirit communication. As such, I needed to say my White Light of Christ prayer of protection, as the pendulum had become a powerful spiritual tool.

When using the pendulum for spiritual discernment, we need to find out which way the pendulum will swing if the answer to the question asked is yes or no. My yes, since 1985, has been the same. The pendulum swings away from me diagonally then back toward my right hand. My no has always been a horizontal swing. My answers have remained constant. For the first year or so, I tested the pendulum to confirm which direction it would swing for each answer.

Using the pendulum as a divination tool can sometimes be inaccurate. If we are asking about another person or animal who has free will, timing is key. The moment we ask, the answer may be correct. However, the free will of the person or animal can change their actions, thus changing the answer received. Another inaccuracy is if we do not ask an exact question. For example, if we misplaced our keys, and we ask if our keys are in THE living room, the pendulum may answer yes. Yet we search and still cannot find the lost keys. What if our friend accidentally picked up our keys and placed them in their coat pocket and returned home to THEIR living room? Timing and exact wording are key to receiving a correct answer from the pendulum. The pendulum cannot elaborate. It can only answer direct yes or no questions. Our clairvoyance often kicks in to elaborate on the answer received once we know how to connect with Spirit.

First, we need to obtain a pendulum. I have even tied a rock onto a piece of dental floss and used that as my pendulum. One can purchase a pendulum at a metaphysical bookstore, a crystal, or a rock shop. To discern our answers, we begin by placing the pendulum in our dominant hand. Next, we say our meditation prayer of intention and protection and open our channel to Spirit as shared earlier in this chapter. Once we state our intention through prayer, simply ask, "I am asking my Higher Self, which way the pendulum will move if my answer to the question is yes." Then concentrate on the pendulum and it will start to move. For some, it moves immediately. For others, it takes practice. Repeat that practice to discern how our no answer swings the pendulum. Once we know which way the pendulum swings, we are ready to ask Spirit direct questions, not open-ended ones. We can call forth and ask specifically for our Spirit Guides, Master Teachers, and our loved one(s) in Spirit to be present with us right now to answer our question(s). We can verify which specific loved one is present and accounted for by asking the pendulum exactly that. Once the connection is established, we can ask Spirit a question about ourselves or another person or situation. Our loved one in Spirit will answer us using the pendulum. The White Light of Christ Prayer sets our spiritual boundaries to only allow Spirit of the same vibration to enter.

I will share an experience that taught me to use a note of caution when operating the pendulum. Since the pendulum can only answer direct yes or no questions and not open-ended ones, we may receive an incorrect answer by not asking the right question. Here is the experience that taught me this. I am not a physician nor do I give medical advice. My friends know this about me yet often call me for spiritual support. A friend had called and requested I ask the pendulum a question about their child's healing from a specific acute condition. The pendulum answered yes, the child was indeed healing from this acute condition. My friend called back a few days later to say her child was now in the hospital and the pendulum was wrong. However, the next day the child received a diagnosis of another acute condition. The pendulum was not wrong. The child had healed from the first condition. But another health challenge was lurking underneath. Thus, the pendulum is a powerful divination tool but it can require further spiritual discernment.

Chapter 25

THE IMPORTANCE OF COLOR VIBRATION AS A SPIRITUAL TOOL

"Christ has no body now but mine. He prays in me, looks through my eyes, speaks through my words, works through my hands, walks with my feet, and loves with me here." St. Teresa of Avila

---

Utilizing *color* is another particularly important tool we have at our fingertips, in our spiritual tool chest, to help others and ourselves. We may see colors in our meditation that are stationary. They can also be moving and pulsing as Spirit uses color as one of their ways of communicating. Every color has a specific vibration. Seeing things in meditation is our spiritual gift of clairvoyance. The meaning and symbolism of each color is important to know both in a spiritual and physical sense. Colors have universal meaning. Feel free to ask Spirit specifically for the meaning of the color they are showing us in meditation. Then add it to our spiritual tool chest. The meanings here are a culmination of classes I have taken and personal experience. The book *The Mystical, Magical, Marvelous World of Dreams*, by Wilda B. Tanner also informed much of my color interpretation.

Gold is a color representing high spiritual wisdom and vibration. Gold can represent spiritual refinement and attainment as well as God's love. Gold has the capability of penetrating and dissolving dark negativity as well as ignorance within a person or situation when used with intention. More on this shortly.

White is all colors in one. White works well for healing and for protection. White can represent purity, perfection, and holiness. I have experienced the White Light of Christ as the highest and purest vibrational energy in the Universe. I invoke its power daily.

Wearing *black* helps us to block or alleviate the energy of others and contain energy. Black has many everyday uses. It can be symbolic for death, or the ending of an old condition. The color in this instance does not have to indicate physical death. Black can symbolize the unknown, darkness, grief, negativity, confusion, depression, and other negative human mental states. If we see black in meditation as part of a message from Spirit, depending upon the feeling Spirit sends with the color, it can have a positive implication as well, such as the harboring of hidden spiritual gifts, personality traits, or qualities.

Brown represents earth energy such as the trunk of a tree. It may mean worldly or practical. It is a great color to use to ground our energy if we visualize it like roots connecting us to the center of the earth.

Red is the color of our root chakra and symbolizes us using our willpower. Red gives us physical energy and power. It can also symbolize anger or rage as in "seeing red."

Buddhist and Hindu monks often wear robes of *orange*. Orange can represent illumination, or the highest state of being, as well as fire, which cleanses impurities. It is the color of the spleen chakra. Orange creates a warm, peaceful feeling and signifies achieving balance. It can also symbolize an outgoing nature and friendliness.

Yellow is the color of wisdom, especially spiritual knowledge, or gnosis. It can represent intellectual involvement. It can also symbolize well-being. Our solar-plexus chakra is yellow.

Green is an earthy color and represents healing energy, hope, victory, balance, peacefulness and more. It is the color of our heart chakra. It is a great color to visualize and ground others, or ourselves, to the earth.

Blue is the color of the throat chakra, which symbolizes communication and speaking our truth. Blue can represent Mother Mary and Archangel Michael. It also is a powerful calming, healing energy.

Indigo is the color of our third eye chakra. It is a shade of blue violet. It can represent high spiritual qualities, inspiration, and richness of spiritual truths, trustworthiness, and a deep spiritual presence.

Violet is the color of our crown chakra. It is one of the highest spiritual colors, as are white and gold. Violet can represent higher spiritual wisdom, love, compassion, goodness, and power. It can signify royal energy and oneness with Source Energy.

Pink is the universal color of love. Specifically, Pepto-Bismol pink is the highest vibration of unconditional love which is Divine Love. Its vibration can penetrate even the most hateful of hearts. It may also represent the color of the heart chakra.

Our knowledge of colors can be applied to our own or another's life to elicit positive change. My favorite exercise using colors is what I call the *Bubble Tool*. It has worked every single time I have used it. First, visualize the person/situation needing positive change, and place them/it inside of a Pepto-Bismol pink bubble. This is to surround and cover them, or it, with Divine Love. Surround that pink bubble with a larger gold bubble. Gold dissolves negativity. Then release the bubble with the person or situation in it to the Universe and let go of the string. Set your intention through prayer and pray for Divine Order to reign and for the Highest Good of the person/situation to be served. Remember to give thanks. Moreover, every time we feel anything but the Divine Love surrounding the perpetrator/situation in the bubble, instead of feeling triggered, (angry, frustrated it has not happened yet, fearful, and so on,) we need to plug into our Spirit and hold the High Watch. Visualize the bubble, send it love from our heart, and give thanks to the Universe for the outcome we desire.

Increasing our vibration to love and sending that love to the bubble assists with dissolving all negativity. If we curse or hate the person/situation, we are taking control of the string again. Doing this prevents our desired outcome, which will not be in Divine Order or from Divine Love. Our stinking thinking is interfering with the outcome of what we surrendered for the Highest Good into our bubble. For this exercise to work, we must shift our ego from wanting revenge and being hateful, to coming from our Spirit and unconditional love. Thus, Divine Love and Divine Order will be served. Releasing the bubble filled with color vibrations to the Universe is a powerful action. It resolves the negativity and changes the outcome to a positive one. Every second we feel fear, anger, or anything but love toward the bubble and its contents, we are negating our intended outcome. The more we can fill our hearts with love and send that love to the bubble and its contents, the faster the Universe will provide our desire.

My most profound example comes from my experience with Jeremy, the six-year-old boy with AIDS, who suffered abuse by his mom with borderline personality disorder. I had come home from chaperoning Jeremy and his abusive mom from a Make-A-Wish trip to Give Kids the World in Kissimmee, Florida, after staying in a villa with them. Jeremy's physicians had urgently arranged for the trip as Jeremy's T cells had dropped to such an all-time low, they were not sure how much time he had left to live. If I did not chaperone them, Jeremy would not get his wish. So, against my good judgement, I accompanied them on a trip to Disney World. Without giving too much away I will share that while we were outside Space Mountain, in the bathroom, the mother was physically violent with Jeremy inside his bathroom stall. I had been keeping a watchful eye on her, but I never expected this. When we returned to Chicago, I felt utterly drained. I had never experienced such exhaustion on all levels of my being. My boss had promised me a week off as comp time for the time I spent with Jeremy and his mom in Florida. However, when we came home, my supervisor had changed her mind. After all, as she reminded me, I was in Florida a whole week.

Are you kidding me? I felt devastated. It was not a Florida vacation! I had experienced the mother's violence firsthand while I was completely helpless to intervene in a bathroom stall with Jeremy. My supervisor had promised me before I agreed to even go on the trip that I could have equal days off when we returned home from Florida. Honestly, I could not stand to even look at her once she reneged on her promise.

Therefore, I used my spiritual bubble technique on my supervisor. With as much disdain as I felt toward my supervisor, I did my best to send her love. I prayed for Divine Order to reign over her life and affairs and that her Highest Good be served. I prayed that Divine Love would change her heart. To do this, here are the exact steps I took. I placed my supervisor inside a Pepto-Bismol pink bubble. I surrounded that pink bubble with a gold bubble, and I let go of the string. Every single time I saw her, had to interact with her, felt angry, hurt, and other heavy emotions, I visualized her inside the bubble and kept the High Watch. I prayed for her and sent her love many times a day. The Universe worked its magic in only 10 days! My supervisor called me in her office and shared that I could take a week off with full pay as comp time for chaperoning Jeremy on his Make-A-Wish trip. Thank you, Universe! The bubble technique is an immensely powerful tool to dissolve negativity and to implement positive change for others and for ourselves.

Another powerful exercise using color is to send all the colors of the rainbow for healing someone or something. I taught a professional class for continuing education credits at a nonprofit school near Chicago. My class was entitled: *Learning to Communicate with Your Angels and Guides: Understanding and Using your Clairvoyance.* We would end each class with a healing circle. The participants would form a circle and we would visualize Mother Earth in the center of our circle. We would rub our hands together, placing our palms outward toward the circle's center. We would state our intention of sending all the colors of the rainbow to surround the Earth and its inhabitants for their healing. Anyone who needed healing could also step into the center of the circle, and we would send all the colors of the rainbow to heal them as well. All the colors of the rainbow coincide with our chakra colors. It is a beautiful thing. Colors can help our mood and energy, too. When we wrestle with changing our clothes, for example, it may be due to the energy of the color of our clothing we had picked out the night before. We are responding to the colors vibration when we put the clothes on the next day and decide to wear something else. Colors hold powerful vibrations and meaning. Wearing or surrounding ourselves with color can help us to balance our energy. When we intentionally use them as spiritual tools, they help us to improve our lives and the lives of others.

Chapter 26

ESSENTIAL/ANOINTING OILS AND DIVINATION CARDS

"We don't even know how strong we are until we are forced to bring that hidden strength forward." Isabel Allende

---

Essential oils support our physical, mental, emotional, and spiritual health. They have been used medicinally for thousands of years and for a multitude of reasons. From killing bacteria, fungi, and viruses to treating bug bites, balancing our mood, and stimulating nerve regeneration, many essential oils have antimicrobial, antibacterial, and anti-infectious properties. The Bible contains over 200 references to essential oils in the form of aromatics, incense, and oils. Frankincense, myrrh, cinnamon, cassia, rosemary, hyssop, and more were used for anointing and healing those who were ill. Moses receives a specific recipe to make holy anointing oil in Exodus 30: 22-31. Proverbs 7:17 states "I have perfumed my bed with myrrh, aloes, and cinnamon." James 5:14 also mentions oils when the question comes up, "Is anyone among you sick? Let them call the elders of the church to pray over them and anoint them with oil in the name of the Lord." Personally, I use Young Living's Essential Oils. I find them to be powerful and they continue to support my healing journey. I use them as anointing oil during all my healing sessions, including Reiki healing. Combining prayer with anointing oil is a most powerful form of healing.

Since childhood, our children Kathryn and Stephen became a part of our ministry through their great listening skills and their big empathic hearts. In 2003, a friend, Priya, who my daughter knew from school and Girl Scouts passed away of a peanut allergy in her own home. Priya was in 6th grade. Her siblings ages 10, eight, and three watched helplessly as Priya's EpiPen failed to work, after taking a bite from an eggroll.

A week later, at a school assembly for the entire second grade, which both our son and Priya's sister Vaniya were in, Priya's family attended and sat in the front row of the event. After it was over and we drove home, Stephen asked me not to get out of the car. He asked his dad and sister to go in the house because he wanted to speak to me privately. They did.

I remained silent and allowed Stephen to speak when he was ready. "Hey Mom?" he began.

"Hey Stephen. What's going on, Sweetie?"

He began cautiously, "Priya isn't dead. She was at school with her family. You saw her, too, right?"

"What do you mean, I saw her, too? Did you see her, Stephen?"

"Of course, I saw her. She was right there chasing her little brother! That's why he was running around acting silly."

"So, you saw Priya like she was solid like us, three-dimensional?"

"Don't you, Mom?" he responded.

"No, Sweetie. Not very often. It's a little scary for me, so, I asked Spirit to show me only in my mind's eye. That means inside my headspace like when I'm meditating. Or when I'm intentionally connecting to Spirit like at church when I'm giving clairvoyant messages. Then I see Spirit line up on my left side in my mind's eye in my head with my eyes closed. Were you scared, Sweetie?"

"No. What was there to be scared of? It was Priya playing with her little brother. She had on a long purple dress with beads all around on it and there was bright white light coming out from under her dress."

"Wow, Stephen, that's amazing! Such a beautiful spiritual gift you have. How long have you been seeing Spirit? And why didn't you say anything before this?"

"Since I was little, Mom. I thought you knew. That's why I can't go to sleep until you say my prayers and sing our songs." Every night, Stephen would have me recite The Lord's Prayer and the 23rd Psalm. Then I would have to sing "How Great Thou Art" and "In the Garden" to Stephen or he could not go to sleep. Never did I imagine it was because he saw Spirit as if they were real solid people. I am so grateful he did not shy away from his gifts. I know I was frightened at first, for sure. Going public with these gifts has not been easy for me, either.

"I had no idea, Stephen. I am so glad you told me though. Now, we have to come up with a plan to tell Priya's family."

"Tell her family? No way, mom. We can't tell anyone. I just wanted you to know."

"Hmm…"

"Hmm…what does that mean?" asked Stephen.

"Well, how would you feel if we went to church, and a medium had a clairvoyant message for you from Jeremy, but they chose not to give it to you," I asked.

"I'd be really mad!"

"I'm sure you would be. You would want to receive a message from your loved ones in Spirit, correct?"

"Yep," Stephen stated emphatically.

"Well, if you choose to keep this message from Priya to yourself, how do you think Priya's mom might feel if you don't share it with her?"

"Let me think a minute."

"Take your time, Stephen. This is an important decision." I placed my hand on Stephen's shoulder.

Stephen took a few minutes to make his decision. "Okay. I've decided what to do. Can you tell her that your son got this message from Priya that she is okay but please do not tell her my name?"

"That would be a great way to handle it, Stephen, thank you. That way the family will know Priya is okay. They will be so happy to receive your message. Thanks, Stephen! You are amazing! Such an awesome message!"

"Okay Mom. You're welcome. Now you got to figure out how to tell her. You'll be great, Mom."

"Thanks, Stephen. I will figure out how to approach her. Not sure how open she will be or how she will receive it though. It is our responsibility to deliver the message to the receiver. It's not our responsibility how well they receive it."

"Can we go in the house now?" Before I could answer, Stephen opened the car door and darted toward the house.

I had to chuckle at my son's innocence in asking that I share his clairvoyant message to Priya's family without divulging his name. I felt so proud of him.

A few days later, I approached Priya's parents through Priya's Girl Scout troop leader, my friend and neighbor, Kim. Her troop wanted to plant a tree in our town's community park in Priya's memory. Kim set up our meeting to share about the tree planting and to introduce me to Priya's parents. I accompanied Kim to Priya's home, with a copy of my manuscript, *Dance with an Angel: The True Story of an 8-year-old Hero*, in hand. I brought it to legitimize my and my son's clairvoyant gifts, as this book shows mine in action.

As soon as we met the parents, I felt an instant connection to Priya's mom. Even though I had only met her once during a Girl Scout troop service project I had organized 5 years earlier, I swear I knew her from somewhere. Once I was introduced, I shared that I had some information for her from Priya that had been delivered by my son. Anju, the mom, was also a physician. After I introduced my manuscript to show my legitimacy, Anju asked where I had worked with my DCFS/AIDS families. When I answered, she responded with enthusiasm, "I think we have met before, Robyn, and I know where. Did you have a pregnant mom with AIDS on your caseload? Her first baby was born addicted to cocaine."

Feeling extra excited, I blurted aloud, "Yes, I did! I went to Cook County Hospital every Friday and met with a bunch of professionals from four universities who were all part of the WITS Program."

"That's it; I was your client's MD from the Women and Infants Transmission Study. I headed all of those Friday Interdisciplinary meetings. I thought you looked familiar. I was pregnant with Priya at the same time!"

"Oh, my goodness, I remember you. What a small world. It's so powerful that the Universe put us so close in proximity all these years." Before Anju and I knew each other, we both lived and worked in Chicago. Eventually we both moved to the same suburb west of Chicago, and our children attended the exact same schools since kindergarten.

"That is amazing," responded Anju. "Obviously, we are destined to be connected for some reason. What is the message from Priya that came through your son?"

"Well, most importantly, he said Priya is not dead. He saw her like she was three-dimensional playing with your son during the 2nd grade assembly the other day. My son described the dress Priya was wearing. He said it was a long, purple velvet dress, with long strands of beads cascading down. He saw blinding white light coming from underneath her skirt. He thought she was alive, and we all could see her! He said she looked very happy, but she was concerned about you all."

"That's amazing. How old is your son?"

"Seven years old. He's in second grade but has a different teacher than your daughter, Vaniya."

"Second grade?! I thought you would say he is in college or something! I figured he was there with you watching the assembly and not a student!"

"Stephen is currently seven years old. He is clairvoyant, as am I."

"I am so grateful you had the courage to approach us. Priya also reached out to another friend, and the friend told us Priya was okay and that she is a powerful Spirit. It seems Priya has brought us together, as well as the little boy you wrote your book about. Did you say his name was Jeremy?"

"That's not his real name. It's his name in the book."

"I would like to buy a copy please," responded Anju.

"I can allow you to read my manuscript if you'd like. My book is not published just yet."

"That'd be great, thanks."

Anju and I realized we had come full circle and that the Universe indeed had brought us together, again. This time to stay. We have become and remain close friends.

Nearly two years after Priya had passed away in spring of 2003, I was outside meditating in our backyard before heading to Stephen's elementary school for their end of year assembly. Stephen and Vaniya were now in fourth grade. While deep in meditation, I felt an entity approach me on my left side. Suddenly, I smelled a strong scent of Lilies of the Valley and was startled when, in my mind's eye, Jesus the Christ spoke to me while standing on my left side. He stated, "I love the scent of Lilies of the Valley, don't you? It is my favorite flower." With that, Christ took a very deep breath and walked away the same way he came. His Light was so very bright; I had to avert my eyes when he was next to me. This was not my first visit from Jesus the Christ in my meditation or in a dream. I immediately stopped meditating and opened my eyes. I began to cry as Christ left my heart filled with the most beautiful and powerful unconditional love.

I went in the house to digest what had just occurred and to get ready for the school assembly. When I walked out to our minivan and opened the door, I was surprised to find a glass vial right in the center of the driver's seat. I picked it up and was intrigued when the top of the vial had a menorah on it with Hebrew letters written at the bottom. I unscrewed the lid and when it opened, I felt overcome with emotion. The vial smelled heavenly. The label on the bottom said it was Lilies of the Valley anointing balm.

I immediately called Jim at work to ask if he had placed the vial on the driver's seat. His response was, "No, however, my sister gave the healing balm to me over three years ago, but I misplaced it. Literally, I have not seen it since the day she gave it to me. A friend of hers brought it back from her visit to Israel. It is for sale and can be purchased there. Frankly, it literally disappeared until today. I put it in my jacket pocket when she gave it to me three years ago on Thanksgiving Day. Pretty amazing it appeared today. What's on your agenda for the rest of the day?"

"I'm headed to the fourth-grade assembly now. Dinner is in the crock-pot. Stephen is going to a friend's house after school, and I am not working today. So, I will see you later. Love you. Thanks for the information."

"Love you, too! Tell Stephen great job this year in fourth grade. Dad is really proud of him. Love his digeridoo!"

The assembly was to share with parents the results of an art grant project the school received. The students got to work with professional artists and made musical instruments from recycled materials. They put on a beautiful show with these highly decorated instruments, including playing a digeridoo they made. Incredible experience.

When I left afterward, Anju's receptionist from her clinic, Eileen, whose children also attended the same school, called to me. She walked over, handed me a note, and asked me to read it and then call Anju as soon as possible. I went to my car, sat down, and read the note. It shared that Nika, Anju's 2nd oldest daughter who watched the EpiPen fail on her sister at the top of the stairs, was in the Pediatric Intensive Care Unit (PICU) of a Chicago hospital, the same exact place her sister Priya had passed away two years prior. Nika had been on a ventilator for 12 days now, and the doctors did not know what to do anymore to get her oxygen levels to rise. They were deciding later that day about whether or not they were removing Nika from the ventilator. I called Anju who communicated that she told the doctors not to make any decisions until I came to help. She asked me to come to the PICU and do the prayers I did for Jeremy on Nika. She added she could not handle losing another daughter and asked me to hurry.

I drove home, grabbed my Angel Divination Cards, and made sure I had the Lilies of the Valley anointing balm given earlier to me by Christ. I arranged for Stephen to stay later at his playdate. Then I drove to the hospital. When I arrived, Anju and her husband, Pradeep, were waiting for me. I had to gown up and wear a mask. Anju drew the curtains. We hugged. We began by holding hands and reciting The Lord's Prayer and then the 23rd Psalm. Then I said my prayer of intention and protection and we got started with our healing session. Anju pulled two Angel cards on Nika's behalf to start us off: the Archangel Chamuel and the Seraphim Sandalphon.

Archangel Chamuel fills our hearts with love and heals our relationships. Chamuel is the Angel of Peace and Divine Justice who guards all innocent children and gives great strength to overcome difficult situations.

Sandalphon is a mighty celestial being who oversees the many abilities given to the powerful Seraphim. Seraphim have immense strength, the authority to heal others, the power to direct the forces of nature, and more. Sandalphon gathers and receives our prayers and sends them onward directly to God. Sandalphon may also use music to achieve these goals.

Based upon these two cards, Spirit helped me to discern that our prayers were most definitely received directly by God and delivered on the wings of Sandalphon for Nika's behalf. Archangel Chamuel was also present and accounted for, assisting in lending strength to Nika to overcome her difficulty being on the ventilator. Anju, Pradeep, and I gave thanks.

Next, I shared my meditation with Priya's parents. I told them about Jesus telling me Lilies of the Valley are his favorite flower. I showed them the anointing balm and asked their permission to use it on Nika. Of course, their answer was yes.

We went over to Nika, and I began by placing my palms together and spoke aloud, addressing Father and Mother God.

"Heavenly Father Mother God, I wish to Serve.
Please surround me, Nika, Anju, Pradeep, this entire room,
all of Nika's physicians and medical personnel, and
the entire hospital with the White Light of Christ for Protection.
I respectfully call forth Nika's Spirit Guides, Angels, and loved ones
in Spirit and my own to be present at this time.
I ask for only the Highest Thoughts and Truths to be given.
I pray for DIVINE ORDER to reign over Nika's life and affairs.
I ask for Nika's Highest Good to be Served.

> I am so very grateful.
> I ask this in the name of Jesus the Christ. And so it is, Amen.
> Thank You God. Thank You Christ. Thank You Angels.
> Thank you Spirit Guides and Ancestors.
> Thank you, Universe. Thank you, Nika."

Then I opened the anointing balm, placed some on my right index finger and thumb, and stepped close to Nika. I made the sign of the cross on Nika's forehead. I took a deep breath and again prayed for Divine Order and for Nika's Highest Good to be served. I gave thanks aloud. Then I took my time as I repeated the same on her throat, her heart, the tops of her hands and feet, and the soles of her feet. Each time I prayed for Divine Order to reign over Nika's life and affairs, and for her Highest Good to be served. I gave thanks at each turn. Amen was my last statement. I hugged Anju and Pradeep and left for home.

Anju contacted me that evening. A miracle had happened. Exactly four hours after I left the PICU, Nika's oxygen began to rise, and eventually she came off the ventilator the following day. Nika recovered fully and left the hospital a few days later. Thank you, God. Thank you, Christ. Thank you Angels. Thank you all helpers seen and unseen who were instrumental in Nika's healing. Thank you, Universe!

A year later, nearly the same date, Anju called me to share they had just admitted Nika to the hospital for the exact same reason as the year prior, when she spent 12 days on the ventilator. Anju took her to a different hospital than the one Priya passed away in. Anju said she could not handle another repeat of last year and asked me to please come to the hospital and do my prayers on Nika again.

This time I only brought the lilies of the valley anointing balm and myself. I began Nika's healing session with the Lord's Prayer and the 23rd Psalm. I spoke aloud my prayer for the White Light of Christ, Divine Order and Nika's Highest Good to be served. I performed the exact same prayers while using the anointing balm and giving thanks at each sign of the cross I made on Nika's body. Afterward, we all hugged, and I returned home.

Within four hours, Nika stats began returning to normal. She did not need to be airlifted to the Chicago trauma hospital or be placed on a ventilator. In fact, Nika was discharged from the hospital a few days later. She has not ever again been on a ventilator. Thank you, God. Thank you, Angels. Thank you, Christ Energy. Thank you Spirit Guides. Thank you Ancestors. Thank you anointing oil and Angel cards for your help.

Angel, Tarot, and Oracle cards are divination tools. Divination is a way to connect to God, our Angels, Master Teachers, and Spirit Guides so we can obtain knowledge to help us make the best choices for our Highest Good. Divination cards assist us in expanding our awareness by allowing us an opening to seek understanding and answers from the spiritual realm. Tarot has been around since 1200 A.D. In the Tarot, the Death card represents the end of an old condition, followed by a new beginning. Spirit gives this same interpretation to us in meditation as a clairvoyant message. Another example is the Devil card. It represents our shadow self. It can also mean addictions or restrictions, limiting beliefs, and even detachment. When working with these cards, always use the White Light of Christ prayer of protection before opening. As I shared earlier, when I went to the PICU to help Nika on the ventilator, her mom pulled the Angel cards of Chamuel and Sandalphon. Both cards told us that the Angels were working for Nika's Highest Good for healing to occur, and it did. Amen.

Chapter 27

CLAIRVOYANT READINGS, ASTROLOGY, AND CRYSTALS

"Out of your vulnerabilities will come your strength." Sigmund Freud

---

Clairvoyant Readings are another powerful life-changing spiritual tool. When a total stranger communicates information directly to us from our deceased loved one, there is no doubt what we are receiving is from Spirit! After my very first clairvoyant reading, I wanted to rent an airplane and write in the sky, "There is no such thing as death." When we experience the energetic presence of our deceased loved one during a clairvoyant reading, their communication gives us peace that surpasses all human understanding. I know of few other experiences that offer this level of comfort and life-altering wisdom. A psychic reader may give an accurate reading of our vibes. Clairvoyant readings allow us to receive guidance from our Spirit helpers and our loved ones in Spirit. Once we do, there is no turning back!

Astrology provides powerful information about our Soul's purpose. It can provide past life information that connects us to our current lifetime. It can also shine Light on our destiny and our agreement for this specific incarnation. Astrology seeks to give us understanding about the influence of the position of the sun, moon, and planets that occupied the sky at the exact moment of our birth. Just like the star of Bethlehem showed the birth of the Christ child, the sky at the exact time and place of our birth foretells much about our personal character and potential. It can even explain specific happenings at exact times in our life. Astrological markings have been recorded on cave walls over 25,000 years ago showing the moon, the constellations, and the nighttime sky changes.

I had my first astrological chart, called a Natal Chart, completed on January 31, 2023, after finishing my first draft of this book. I wanted to treat myself, and I am so grateful I did. The reading of my chart was incredibly affirming for me, and exceptionally accurate. I have been the Reluctant Messiah for too long now. So saddened that my astrologer, Rick DiClemente, passed away in January 2025. Rick was also clairvoyant. He not only shared my natal chart, but he also received messages intuitively to help me breakthrough some barriers holding me back. Rick provided Soul knowledge from the cosmos that helped me to know I am absolutely on track with who I am and what I am here to accomplish.

During my Zoom call to read my chart, Rick asked for my mom's birth date. The information he gave was mind-blowing. It first showed my mom was born a rebel and meant to shine. When describing her, Rick shared that she was for women's rights, desegregation, the underdog and more. She taught her children that we could accomplish anything we want to in life if we give it our all. Her chart showed she became alcoholic to dim her own light of being a rebel. Why? Because my dad was Jewish and did not want to stand out for fear of prejudice against us. I was not born yet, but my Jewish grandmother had asked my mom to return to Ireland so she could raise my older siblings herself. On top of that, in 1967 when desegregation came to my elementary school, my dad became furious with my mom when she was on the front cover of our local newspaper as a "Ni--er lover" in 1967, for sticking up for the busloads of Black kids forced to desegregate my grade school as a pilot project in Chicago. She put out the American flag that another white parent had started on fire. She literally tried to stop people from throwing rocks at the Black kids as they exited the busses. My family got death threats over the phone beginning that fateful night. Two years later, in 1969, my mom became an alcoholic before my 10th birthday. My dad wanted her to dim her light. Alcohol certainly did the trick. This information from Rick helped me to see my mom in a much bigger radiance.

Rick also looked at my chart during the time my prophetic dreams began in 1987. He found that the planet Chiron, discovered in 1977, was 180 degrees opposite Neptune. Apparently, this is an unusually powerful spiritual opening. He shared that it was like a new vine of a plant coming up through the center of my being, pushing its way to the Light. Others who shared this same Chiron/Neptune activity that year had experienced psychotic breaks with their spiritual experiences and ended up with a mental illness diagnosis. Rick asked why I did not have a psychotic break. My answer was because I sought knowledge to give me insight into this powerful spiritual opening I experienced. I found my answers at a Spiritualist center, Camp Chesterfield. After my experience with psilocybin when I was 17 where Jesus baptized me in the bathroom of the Shell station, the experience felt so real and so loving, it changed my life. I knew I was mentally stable and opening spiritually. I was not experiencing mental illness.

Rick's explanation of my destiny chart made me cry tears of relief and delight. Without me telling him anything about the contents of this book, Rick said I was here to teach the masses about their emotions and how they lead us to Spirit. This knowledge confirmed that I was indeed born to be the Reluctant Messiah and to share my experiences with the world. And so it is, Amen. Thanks for the confirmation, Rick. I am forever grateful.

Crystals are powerful tools for working with our energy. Computer chips and micro-electronic circuits come from a single crystal of silicon. Crystals also allow for precise energy control that gave rise to the electronic oscillators found in radio, television, and radar. Different crystals can control and direct energy, even energy in our body. Our body is a network of powerful computers connected to our master computer, our brain. When our lines are crossed or circuits break, our resulting messages are blocked and even cut off from our energetic network, resulting in dis-ease. Just as a crystal quartz in a watch is reliable to keep exact time, the constant frequency of energy from crystals helps to bring coherence to our body's mixed-up energies.

In 1989, Jim and I went to our first and only vacation to Mexico. We took a boat to Cozumel for one of the days we were there. Jim purchased a silver and lapis lazuli cross for me, as lapis is a favorite of mine. He bought a silver chain, which I placed the cross on and wore daily without removing. The cross was close to my thyroid gland. Two years later, in 1991, during month six of my pregnancy with Kathryn, my obstetrician noticed symptoms that she thought were preeclampsia. My pulse rose, my blood pressure began to climb, I had trouble sleeping, and I was hungry all the time. Turns out even though I did not have preeclampsia, she had me on bed rest much of the time for these exact symptoms. Three years later, I was pregnant with Stephen. By six months the same symptoms began, but more amplified. This obstetrician placed me on bed rest as she was convinced that I had preeclampsia. Yet, my ultrasound was normal. My symptoms grew stronger as the days continued, even on bed rest.

Near the end of week two, while on total bed rest, I received a catalog in the mail for crystals. As I looked it over while resting, I was stunned when I read the healing properties of lapis lazuli. It helps with many body processes including activating the thyroid gland, among others. I had Graves' disease in 1989 in graduate school and drank radioactive iodine to shut my thyroid down. A piece survived, and I began treatment of thyroid hormone replacement. Could it be that the lapis was causing my symptoms? Only one way to find out. I took my lapis cross off and told Jim. I had an appointment with my obstetrician in one week. I stayed on bed rest the entire week and began to feel better. When I saw my M.D., she asked what I was doing differently, as all my symptoms had disappeared. My pulse and blood pressure were back to normal, and I was sleeping and eating more normally. I shared about my lapis lazuli cross I had worn throughout both pregnancies and the receipt of the crystal catalog showing the properties of lapis. I took the necklace off for exactly one week, and all my symptoms disappeared. My obstetrician was ecstatic and said if she had more time, she would write a journal article about my experience. That taught me that indeed crystals and gemstones impact our bodies and our health. Thank you, Universe, for sending me that catalog in Divine time.

Chapter 28

REIKI HEALING

"When you go through deep waters, I will be with you." Isaiah 43:2

Reiki Healing is a profound spiritual tool. A Reiki Master has been spiritually attuned and initiated into Reiki levels I, II, and III and has demonstrated their attunement and practice of performing Reiki with palpable outcomes. Rei means "Divinely guided" and Ki is the same as Chi or "Life Force Energy." Reiki is a Japanese term, which translates into "Divinely guided life force energy." We can take classes to learn Reiki and perform it on ourselves and others. We can even do distant healing. Dr. Mikao Usui, born in 1865, is the founder of Reiki. He is now known as Master Usui or Usui Sensei. He was Soul-searching for answers to find a method of healing unaffiliated with any religion, with the intention that his healing method would be available to all people, so they could learn to heal themselves and others. Alone, he retreated into a cave on Mount Kurama in Japan. Mount Kurama is known for its high, sacred energy.

Through fasting, meditation, and prayer while in the cave, at dawn, on the 21st-day of his experience, Master Usui received his answer. It was life changing. The answer came in the form of Sanskrit based

Japanese symbols which he received as Light. On the way down to the monastery to share his incredible breakthrough, Master Usui took a fall and injured his leg. He used his hands to direct the Reiki energy to his injury. He drew different Sanskrit symbols in his mind while sending Reiki to himself. His pain dissipated, and his injury healed. Master Usui practiced and taught Reiki until he founded his first Reiki clinic and school in Tokyo in 1922. Reiki is finely tuned life force energy that is Divinely directed throughout the body by a Reiki practitioner. Reiki restores our physical, mental, emotional, and spiritual bodies back to balance and wholeness. When I perform Reiki, it amplifies my clairvoyant senses. Often the person receiving the treatment also feels and sees an expansion of their spiritual gifts, as well. I highly recommend we all become Reiki practitioners. Healing the world and ourselves through Reiki is possible.

One profound experience comes to mind where Jesus also participated in part of my Reiki session. While performing my Reiki breathing and working over a returning client's heart chakra, I experienced a powerful vision in my mind's eye, which I shared aloud with her. I saw the woman and me sitting in a rowboat during a powerfully scary storm. The sky was very dark. The waves crashed all around us, even into our boat. We sat, drenched from the rain. I remember looking over on my left. I saw Jesus the Christ walking on the water, headed straight toward us.

When he arrived, Jesus stepped into our boat and sat down. He looked at the woman, put her hands in his, and stated, "Everything is going to be all right. You have nothing to worry about." Then Jesus stood up, stepped out of the boat, and walked on water right back from whence he came. No other information was given. When the client and I processed the Reiki session afterward, neither of us had any idea what Jesus was specifically referring to, until the following day.

I received a call from the sister of my client, who shared that a miracle had taken place the previous day, after her sister's Reiki session. Several hours after our session ended, my client had a cerebral aneurysm and survived! Statistics show that 25% of individuals do not survive within the first 24 hours of an aneurysm, and there is a 25% chance they will pass away from complications within the next six months. As of now, it has been more than 20 years since her aneurysm, and there have been zero complications.

Many months later, when this same client came for her next Reiki session, I saw another clairvoyant vision while working over her heart chakra. I saw the two of us in a rowboat. This time, the water was like glass which reflected exquisite orange, pink, and purple light as the setting sun was shining upon the still water. Jesus walked toward us on the water, stepped into our boat, and sat down. He took my client's hand in his, looked her in the eyes, and said, "I knew there was nothing to be afraid of the last time I visited you. So glad things turned out for the best." Then he stood, stepped out of the boat, and walked away. My client sat up and began to cry happy tears. I soon joined in her celebration. Thank you, God. Thank you, Jesus the Christ. Thank you, Angels. Thank you Master Usui and all the Reiki Master Healers. And so it is, Amen.

Chapter 29

NUMEROLOGY, MEDICAL QIGONG, SOUND HEALING, MASARU EMOTO, AND CHAKRAS

"You are a child of God. Your playing small does not serve the world. There is nothing enlightened about shrinking so that other people won't feel insecure about you. We were born to make manifest the glory of God that is within us." Marianne Williamson

---

Numerology is the ancient study of the mystical significance of numbers. One key to understanding ourselves more deeply lies in the numerology of one's birthdate, name, and more. Numbers, number combinations, and letters provide insight into our Soul. We have 26 letters to our alphabet. Each letter corresponds to a number, with the letter A being number 1 and the letter Z being number 26. All numbers in numerology break down to a primary number when added together. For example, Z is the 26th letter of the alphabet; 2 + 6 = 8. Z has the number vibration of an 8. There is evidence of numerology used by ancient civilizations including Rome, China, Greece, and Japan. Numerology gives us details about ourselves, including our life path, our personality expression, our Soul's urge, and more. Our given name at birth, date of our birth, and other important numbers in our life influences our life's journey. Numerology provides incredible insights into who we are and influences our life's journey. Many of us look at the clock and see 1:11, 2:22, 3:33, 4:44 and 5:55. Eleven and 22 are the highest spiritual numbers in numerology. The Universe supports us with the power of numbers.

One powerful example in my life is the number 624. When my parents moved to a suburb of Chicago when I was nine years old, the number of our new address was 624. My husband's address growing up was 3624. When I learned of Jeremy's birthdate, the boy with AIDS whom my husband and I were going to adopt, was 6/24, I knew my connection with him was a Sacred Contract created by God prior to us meeting one another. Our children were both born at UIC hospital in Chicago after Jeremy passed away, without us being able to adopt him. The hospital room I was assigned for the birth of our daughter, of course, was 624. Three years later, I was again assigned to room 624 for the birth of our son. Thanks Universe!

Medical Qigong is another powerful spiritual tool for our use. Developed over 2,000 years ago, its fundamental principles work on restoring us to energetic balance by breaking through the deeply stagnant energy within us. This allows us to have unobstructed circulation and energy flow back to our body, mind, and Spirit. The practitioner can access the individual's bio-energetic field even at a distance. They use their intention, visualization tools, Qigong energy techniques, and prescription medications to help restore the body to balance. Homework is often given in the form of Qigong exercises and meditations, as well. I love Medical Qigong. It has been a beautiful tool for me to help release physical and emotional pain.

There are many types of *Vibrational Sound Healing*. The ancient Greeks used music to cure mental disorders. King Solomon helped lift his depression with David's harp music. Native Americans know music has mystical powers. Sound vibration helps us to relax our body, mind, and Spirit through shifting our vibrational frequency from low to high.

Our body is made of 75% water. Water is a fabulous conductor for vibrational sound healing. Sound vibrations encourage improved circulation and energy flow in the body, which help to lower our stress, improve sleep, and treat certain dis-ease conditions in the body.

Music, tuning forks, gongs, singing bowls, binaural beats (a perception of sound that our brain creates,) vocal toning, and *Solfeggio frequencies* are all forms of beneficial sound healing. Even a cat's purr registers between 20 to 50 hertz. The optimal frequency for bone stimulation is 50 hertz. A cat's purr is the optimal frequency for bone growth and fracture healing. My cat, Sally, is very intuitive. Since the day I adopted her from a rescue shelter, she has been a little healer kitty. Her favorite place to sleep and purr is while lying across my heart and leaning into my neck. I know she is aware of my thyroid issues, which also affect my heart, and she does her best to support me.

YouTube has many offerings of Solfeggio frequencies. Solfeggio frequencies are ancient scales that are part of a six-tone sequence of electro-magnetic frequencies. They align us with the rhythm and tones that form the basis of the Universe. These frequencies use specific patterns of sound meant to synchronize our brain waves and help us to heal by restoring the normal vibrational frequencies of our cells. Vibrational sound healing is great support to achieving our inner balance.

There are seven commonly used Solfeggio frequencies:

> 396 Hz – Freeing guilt and fear
> 417 Hz – Undoing situations and facilitating change
> 528 Hz – Transformation and miracles
> 639 Hz – Connecting relationships
> 741 Hz – Awakening intuition
> 852 Hz – Returning to spiritual order
> 963 Hz – Divine consciousness or enlightenment

I love to listen to vibrational sound healing on YouTube, especially to meditate and to write. They are easy to listen to and absorb.

Masaru Emoto, a Japanese researcher who dedicated his life to understanding the language of water, published his book, *The Hidden Messages in Water,* in 2004. His work demonstrates the impact our human consciousness has on water. Our thoughts, words, music and more literally change the molecular structure of water. Dr. Emoto's experiments began when he became aware of the ability to measure the vibration and frequency of water by freezing it and examining the ice crystals with microscopic photography. He began by preparing tap water, polluted water, and fresh clean flowing water from nature, froze the samples, and photographed their frozen crystal structures. There is a huge difference in the appearance of each sample of frozen water crystals. The photos of the crystals from tap and polluted water are messy, discolored, and asymmetrical. The photos of the water crystals from nature's clean flowing water are symmetrical, bright, and succinct. The water crystals show that the water is reacting to its environment and responds by literally creating harmonious crystal structures.

Dr. Emoto expanded his experiment further. He placed containers of water and directed different types of music, including classical and hard rock, at them. Again, the results were astounding. The crystals became more harmonious and symmetrical when they heard classical music versus hard rock. He went further and wrote words on the containers of water. The containers written with positive words like "love" and "gratitude" showed harmonious beautifully formed crystals. The containers written with negative words including "hate" and "I will kill you" formed asymmetrical, discolored, and disorganized crystal structures.

This incredible information shows us that our thoughts and feelings produce such powerful energetic vibrations that they can change our biology! How? Because our body is made up of 70% water. The way we speak to ourselves is especially important. When we continuously believe our stinking thinking, we are causing harm to ourselves. When we speak and behave in loving ways to ourselves, we are helping. Our words, thoughts, and emotions literally cause this structural change in the biology of our cells. Knowing this, please choose more wisely and lovingly toward Self and toward others!

The word *Chakra* comes from ancient Sanskrit and literally translates to "wheel of light." It originated in India more than 25,000 years ago. Chakras describe the subtle energies of our human energy system that drive our life force energy. Chakras are our conductors of energy. They are based upon the knowing that all of life is both energetic (vibrational) and spiritual in origin. Humans have seven major chakras and 21 minor chakras. Plants, animals, rocks, minerals, and all inanimate objects have chakras because everything is energy. This even includes Mother Earth and celestial bodies. Each chakra, or energy center, is a spinning vortex of energy created when the molten core of the center of the Earth rises to meet the electrical energy coming from the cosmos and Universe. When these two energies meet and merge into our wheels of light, our chakras, they propel our life force energy.

Each chakra within our human body is an energy center that is associated with a specific part of our body and our life. The lower three chakras take in magnetic energy from the Earth. These are the root, spleen, and solar plexus chakras, also known as the feminine chakras, as they are the receiving ones. They take in energy and information from our environment. They tie us to family, our ancestors, and community. They assist us in mastering our physical life. The upper four chakras – our heart, throat, third eye and crown are masculine chakras. They give out energy in the form of love, communication, and spirituality. As we grow more attuned with ourselves as spiritual beings operating human bodies, those chakras are strengthened and connect to the continuity of life. Our chakras are like a ladder that connects us from the physical plane to our higher mind and then to the Divine. Each chakra has a corresponding color, sound, and purpose.

Our *Root Chakra* is at the base of our spine, at our perineum, between our tailbone and our genitals. It is red in color and represents our basic physical needs and survival. It draws magnetic energy from the core of the Earth. It helps us to receive pure life force energy. When we feel safe and secure deep within, we trust the flow of life. Our root chakra helps us to feel safe and grounded to the Earth. It gives us a sense of belonging and trust and helps us lead a more fulfilling life.

Our *Sacral Chakra* is located near our spleen and coincides with the color orange. It represents our sexuality, sensuality, and pleasure. It houses our ability to find pleasure, health, and joy through our physical presence. It represents our ability to connect with others. It also anchors our overall well-being and abundance. The more we feel life is joyful and that the Universe is conspiring for our best and highest outcome, the more open our sacral chakra becomes, and helps us to walk our journey with ease and flow. Our sacral chakra helps us to feel playful, passionate, and friendly.

Our *Solar Plexus Chakra* is located over the stomach above our navel. It is yellow. It aids us in our physical digestion and our mental discernment, giving us good judgement and a sense of who we are. Our solar plexus chakra governs our ability to filter toxic environments, food, and people. We each have a right to be ourselves and live our unique individual lives. This chakra gives us a sense of belonging. This is where our emotional memories are stored. Thus, our gut feeling comes from here. When it is strong, we have a sense of knowing our worth and who we are. It is also the seat of our clairsentience, our inner knowing. When we can connect with our worthiness as a way of being and allow it just because of the fact we are a Spirit operating a human body, our life force energy grows through this chakra. Our solar plexus chakra helps us to feel confident and calm and hold our integrity and our respect for Self and others.

Our fourth chakra is our *Heart Chakra,* which is at the center of our human energy system. Its color is green. It operates both physically and emotionally, energy in motion, to keep our life force energy thriving. Unconditional love is its highest vibration. It is the seat of the Divine within. This chakra can receive and give love, compassion, and healing. We are love itself. The more we open our heart chakra and allow our innate unconditional love to be seen and felt through our being and our actions, the more the Christ Consciousness flows in and through us. The world needs us to open our heart chakra fully and invite Source Energy inside. It is through this chakra that we align our body, mind, and Spirit, and we walk our talk. Our heart chakra helps us to have empathy, to feel loved and to love. It makes us have a contagiously good vibe.

The fifth chakra is our *Throat Chakra,* which is blue in color. It represents our personal expression of our will and our Soul's expression of who we are. It is our chakra for communication and clear perception. It holds the ability for us to speak our truth and ask for what we need. Attitudes and behaviors that suppress our truth such as being too polite, allowing others to control us, and even repressing our negative feelings can clog our throat chakra and weaken our flow of life force energy. Our throat chakra helps us to express our Self and our creativity. Our throat chakra experiences harm from emotional and physical abuse, and injuries we have experienced. Many of our coping behaviors can harm our throat chakra. Gossip, lying, excessive alcohol and drug consumption disrupt the flow of our energy to our throat chakra. It can shut down from repressed feelings. When we do not express our feelings in a healthy output of our 4-stroke cycle, it stops us from receiving our own vital life force energy. Saying what we mean and meaning what we say is an integral part of who we are. When we consciously stand in our personal power and speak our innermost truths, we are aligned with our throat chakra and our purpose for this incarnation. This distinguishes us from all other living things.

Our sixth chakra is our *Third Eye*. It represents our spiritual wisdom and knowledge. It is in the center of our brow, and is the color indigo, a bluish purple. It is our chakra for understanding our vastness. It helps us to see our past, present, and future with vision, knowledge, and spiritual clarity. This chakra aids us in developing right thinking versus stinking thinking and supports us in knowing what people and situations in our life are there to nurture our Highest Good using our spiritual discernment. It is the seat of our clairvoyance or seeing clearly with our spiritual eyes. When this chakra is in balance, we feel charismatic. We are intuitive, know our purpose, and exude wisdom.

Our *Crown Chakra* is the opening for our Spirit to enter our body at the time of our birth into human form and leave our body at the time of our death when we return to the Spirit World. It is violet in color and located at the crown of our head. It is our chakra for connecting with our spiritual understanding and knowing we are One Spiritual Community. It is where we can directly connect and align with Source Energy. When we can connect this chakra and use it consciously in our life, we can see each experience as an opportunity for our Soul's growth, even the toughest ones, thus strengthening our connection to Spirit. When this chakra is in balance, we feel joyful, wise, compassionate, and connected to Source Energy.

We can manifest dis-ease when we are out of balance in our chakras. For me personally, I see directly how my throat chakra had been blocked in my alcoholic family and from six years of domestic violence. I developed Graves' disease, an autoimmune thyroid disease in 1989 during graduate school, two years after my first prophetic dreams, and seven years after fleeing domestic violence. My resting pulse was 220 and I was covered in hives and raised welts for over six weeks as I reacted to the only two medicines to treat Graves' disease. My thyroid has been difficult to treat ever since. I drank radioactive iodine to shut down my thyroid completely, but a small piece survived and is still working. Why then since 2010 have my symptoms worsened? Well, dear reader, I will share this experience in my very last chapter entitled, *My Beloved James Accetturo*. Until then, it is time I shared some more powerful experiences of healings and Divine Interventions that occurred through me.

When we heal our own instrument of as much trauma as possible and become a vessel for the Christ Consciousness to work through us, miracles happen, just as Jesus the Christ told us when he walked this Earth. In John 14:12, Jesus the Christ tells us. "Verily, verily, I say unto you, He that believeth on me, the works that I do shall he do also; and greater works than these shall he do; because I go unto my Father." Jesus the Christ did not ask for us to worship him and put him on a pedestal. He became an example of how to embody the Christ Consciousness and asked us to do the same. When we do, the Christ Consciousness works through us, also. And so it is, Amen.

It took me many years of practicing my gifts over time to learn to stand in my spiritual power. I preferred to hide. In my social work practice and in my everyday life, I did help freely using my gifts when people needed or asked for my help though. I prayed daily to serve God. God, Source Energy, and the Christ Consciousness have literally healed many people and experiences using me as the instrument through which the healing occurred. I have never shared these truths publicly, until now. I do my best to be a humble servant.

The week before Thanksgiving of 2021, I won a scholarship to a writing retreat in Vermont. It was at that retreat, that the host and two other women participants confronted me on my writing. They said they could tell I was holding back. When asked why I was not sharing my whole truth, I revealed that the power of my experiences was too much, and that it frightened me. The host pushed further and broke me open, for which I will always be grateful. I shared several of the experiences where the person experienced healing through my instrument including Nika's experience of getting off the ventilator. Through my experience of that fateful evening at the writing retreat, I made a commitment to stop hiding, and to share my gifts through authoring this book. I have known since Jim and I went to Camp Chesterfield back in 1989 that I am meant to share my knowledge and experience publicly with the world. I know now is the Divine time.

Chapter 30

JEREMY'S HEALING

"You must fulfill the way that is in you." Carl Jung

The first time I became aware of the Christ Consciousness working through me to heal someone was when I picked Jeremy up from school one fall day in 1990. As I have shared earlier, Jeremy was my only abuse case from my AIDS/DCFS families, the job I took after resigning from the psychiatric inpatient unit, where I met Billy in person.

That day, I had driven to Jeremy's school to take him to our next therapy session at the foster care agency. They were allowing me to provide therapy for Jeremy at their local office. I was transitioning him from one agency to another with a new therapist. When I went to the principal's office to sign him out, the principal got up from her desk in her office and raced toward me.

"We've been trying to get a hold of Jeremy's foster mom all day today, but she hasn't been answering her phone. Her emergency contact was not available either. Jeremy has been sick all day. His temperature climbed to 104. He's asleep in the nurse's office right now. The nurse wasn't in today, so I had an aide sit with him all day. I called his hospital, and they told me to give him two Tylenol every four hours. His last dose was at one. I'm glad you're here. I'm very concerned about him."

"I don't know where Lindsey has been. You can call me if this ever happens again, and I can pick him up earlier," I said.

"That'd be great. Come with me." She led me to where Jeremy was sleeping. When I looked in on him, my heart sank. He looked awful. He woke up as soon as I entered the room.

"Robyn..." He reached out his hand from under the covers. He shivered. His lips were slightly bluish in color.

"Hi, Buddy. I'll take you home and sit with you until Lindsey gets there, okay?"

I grabbed his coat and put it on him. I quickly scooped him up and carried him, as fast as I could, to my car. My heart raced as I thought, *Oh Dear God, please let him be all right.*

I managed to buckle him in his seat belt, as limp as his body was, blasted the heater, and drove like a mad woman to Lindsey's. I carried Jeremy up the stairs, found the hiding place for the key, and opened the door. Suzy, the cat, scooted out of the way, as I ran with Jeremy up to his room. Jeremy's teeth were chattering by then, and his lips were now blue. His extremities felt ice cold.

As we passed the spare bedroom, I grabbed three quilts from the foot of the bed and piled them on top of Jeremy. I hurried into his room, placed him on his bed, pulled both of our coats off, and without even thinking, pulled down his covers and jumped into his bed. With his back resting against my solar plexus, I pulled Jeremy onto my lap and covered us both up with his bed linens. I piled the three heavy knit quilts on top of us. I snuggled him in as close to me as I could get him, wrapped my arms tightly around his upper body, placing the palms of my hands on his tummy and my legs gently over his.

I soon began rubbing my hands up and down his arms and legs trying to warm him up. I placed the soles of my feet over the tops of his feet. It took a good ten minutes for his teeth to stop chattering and for him to stop shivering. When he finally started to warm up, I began rocking us back and forth for comfort. I prayed silently.

Dear God, please heal Jeremy. Please do not let him die. I am not ready.

I continued rocking, placed the palms of my hands over Jeremy's solar plexus, and began to sing "In the Garden," a favorite hymn of mine. I sang it repeatedly, even after Jeremy fell asleep in my arms.

After about an hour, as my prayers, placing my hands over Jeremy's solar plexus, and singing continued, I heard Lindsey come home. She walked upstairs and found us. I told her what had happened. The sound of our voices awakened Jeremy.

She said, "I'm sorry I wasn't home today, Jeremy. You're not feeling good, huh?" Jeremy looked at her glassy eyed. "I'll get you two Tylenol and come right back. Do you want something to drink?" Jeremy shook his head in the affirmative.

Lindsey quickly came back. Jeremy chewed two Tylenol and took a sip of 7-Up. Lindsey walked out to get a thermometer. Jeremy, still in my arms, suddenly sat upright and projectile vomited across the room. I screamed, "Lindsey!"

Lindsey came running back in. "Oh boy!" She helped Jeremy climb out of bed, and I jumped up and ran out of the room, gagging, and apologizing. "I don't handle vomit well, sorry." Lindsey laughed. She calmly carried Jeremy into the bathroom as I stood in the spare bedroom watching from afar, feeling somewhat embarrassed, hoping I would not add to the mess. I folded my arms and suddenly realized my clothes were soaking wet from perspiration. I walked downstairs to collect myself. I sat in the kitchen until Lindsey called me back upstairs.

When I returned to Jeremy's room, Lindsey, clad in disposable gloves, had just finished bleaching everything down and had stripped the bed linens. She began putting clean sheets on his bed. Jeremy sat at his child-sized table and chairs, playing with Legos. The color had come back to his face. "Hi," he said meekly.

I smiled. "Hi! Feeling better?"

"Yeah, I'm feeling much better. Want to draw some pictures with me?"

"Sure, I'd love to," I responded.

Jeremy ran to his closet and took down a pad of sketch paper and some crayons. "How 'bout I draw a picture of you, and you draw a picture of me?"

"Sounds good," I said.

"Hey, Lindsey," Jeremy yelled.

Lindsey yelled back, "What?" She was in the bathroom emptying her cleaning bucket.

"I'm hungry. Can I have some bologna and cheese, please?"

Lindsey came rushing into Jeremy's room. "Did I hear you correctly? Did you say you want a bologna and cheese sandwich?"

"Yep!"

"Let me take your temperature first, okay?"

Lindsey slid the thermometer under Jeremy's tongue and left the room. She came back shortly and read it. "Oh my, normal. It's 98.6. Bologna and cheese coming right up!"

That night, I prayed hard for Jeremy to stay well enough to attend a field trip to see Santa Claus the next day with his class. He had been looking forward to this outing with his classmates. Sure enough, Jeremy's fever and other symptoms stayed away long enough for his wish to come true. Jeremy went to school, attended his field trip, and got to see Santa. Thank you, Universe.

But that evening, his fever spiked again to 104.3, and nothing would bring it down. Jeremy was admitted to the hospital for treatment.

A friend pointed out that Jeremy was healed during our prayer time, enough to receive his wish of seeing Santa Claus on his field trip the next day. This was my first experience of someone being physically healed through my spiritual efforts and intention. It was 1990, three years after my prophetic dreams began. Thank you, God, Jesus the Christ, the Angels, and both my and Jeremy's Spirit Guides. And so it is, Amen.

Chapter 31

CAROLYN'S DIAGNOSIS AND PROOF OF HER HEALING

"Faith is the strength by which a shattered world shall emerge into the Light." Helen Keller

---

Carolyn was an elderly Black woman whose title was Community Worker for the DCFS Intact Families with AIDS program I ran in the early 1990s. She was also a Unity School of Christianity teacher working toward her ordination papers. Although we had both stopped working with our AIDS families, we remained friends. Carolyn knew Jeremy personally, as he was the only abuse case on our caseload.

Carolyn was a part of the Southside Unity Church in Chicago. Often, Jim, our two kids, and I would attend. My kids had participated in several different Unity churches in the suburbs and especially loved Carolyn's church.

Carolyn had called me one summer day and invited our family to attend their barbecue for the church's anniversary after their Sunday service. She shared that she had a huge favor to ask of me. "I was diagnosed with a cancerous tumor in my neck, Robyn, and I am having surgery the Monday following our barbecue. Would you please come to the chapel with me when our service is finished to pray for me like you did Jeremy? I would be so grateful. God is so good. You know that. You were the instrument through which Jeremy was healed a couple of times. And you know I have a lot of Faith."

"Of course, Carolyn, I would be happy to help. And I will bring this anointing balm I have that Jesus put on the front seat of my car one day a couple of summers ago. It is quite powerful. I am honored to pray with and for you on Sunday in your chapel. See you then. Thanks for asking."

"Girl, you will have to tell me more about how you came to possess this anointing balm when Wes and I see you. That is amazing! See you Sunday at 2 sharp when we begin our service. Don't be late. I am preaching. Love you."

"Love you, Carolyn. See ya Sunday." And we hung up. Sunday came along quickly. We attended Carolyn's church service and sang our hearts out to "Let There Be Peace on Earth" and more after Carolyn's sermon. Once the service was completed, we all entered the courtyard for the barbecue. When my family settled, Carolyn and I slipped away unnoticed, although Jim knew where we were headed.

Carolyn took me to a smaller chapel. It had a beautiful life-size statue of Christ. I pulled out my Lilies of the Valley anointing balm and shared the story of how it came to be on my car seat before we got started with our prayers. Carolyn was grateful that I brought it. She also knew that before I received the anointing balm, Jeremy was healed through my instrument without it. Carolyn was always my rock and kept the High Watch for our AIDS families and my own family. She was quite open and Faith filled before I even began. I started out by placing my palms together while speaking aloud, addressing Father and Mother God, just like with Jeremy and with Nika.

> "Heavenly Father Mother God, I wish to Serve.
> Please surround Carolyn, myself, this chapel,
> and the entire Southside Unity Church building
> with the White Light of Christ for Protection.
> I respectfully call forth Carolyn's Spirit guides, Angels,
> and loved ones in Spirit to be present along with my own.

I ask for only the Highest Thoughts and Truths to be given.
I pray for Divine Order to reign over Carolyn's life and affairs.
I ask for Carolyn's Highest Good to be served.
I am so very grateful.
I ask this in Jesus' name, and so it is, Amen.
Thank You God. Thank You Jesus the Christ.
Thank You Angels, Ancestors, and Spirit guides.
Thank you, Universe. Thank You Carolyn.
Amen."

Then I opened the anointing balm, placed some on my right index finger, and stepped close to Carolyn. I made the sign of the cross on her forehead. I took a deep breath and again prayed for Divine Order and for Carolyn's Highest Good to be served. Then, I gave thanks. I made the sign of the cross and repeated our prayer on her throat, her heart, the tops of her hands and feet, and the soles of her feet. Each time I prayed for Divine Order to reign in Carolyn's life and affairs, and for her Highest Good to be served. I gave thanks at each turn. "And so it is, Amen" was my last statement. I hugged Carolyn and we walked outside to join our families.

The following morning, Carolyn had to be at UIC Hospital for her cancerous tumor removal at 6 a.m. She called me later that morning to share her news. "Robyn, a miracle happened! My surgery was cancelled!"

"What do you mean, Carolyn?"

"I mean that when the tech did my ultrasound of the tumor on my neck to mark the exact spot for the surgery, IT WAS GONE! THE TUMOR DISAPPEARED! They called the surgeon in and he was aghast. I told him God healed me through you. He looked rather shocked, but he cancelled the surgery. What else could he do, it was gone! Oh, my God, Robyn, thank you, thank you, thank you! And thank you, God! I am HEALED!" Carolyn was beside herself with joy, and so was I. Thank you God. Thank you Jesus the Christ. Thank you Angels. Thank you Spirit Guides and Ancestors.

And so it is, Amen.

Chapter 32

MY BELOVED JAMES ACCETTURO

"Be yourself. Everybody else is already taken." Oscar Wilde

Standing in our inner Light as a Spirit operating a human body, being the best we can be by being ourselves and sharing our Light, is where I stand today. Dear reader, this is the most challenging chapter for me to share. My beloved James Accetturo passed away to higher ground in 2019 after a nine-year traumatic battle with systemic scleroderma. It is only with his support from the other side of life that I have decided to be totally vulnerable and share my life's work and experiences publicly. I am ready to acknowledge that indeed, I am the Reluctant Messiah. Guess what? So are YOU! We all are works in progress, filling with enough love that our Light shines in not only who we are, but in all that we do. Whatever it is we each have come here to do, my reason for sharing my heart and Soul as I have here is to show, by example, how to heal our trauma and unexpressed emotions. Why? Because it is time. The world is awaiting our arrival as Spirits inhabiting human bodies. We must step into our personal spiritual power and begin to operate as we are meant to as fully present humans standing in our Light. Jim is an immensely powerful Spirit. He is literally helping me from the other side of the veil. He has been sharing his Spirit with me since the day after he passed away.

Systemic scleroderma is a devastating, rare autoimmune disease wherein our immune system attacks the connective tissue in the body causing diffuse fibrosis. Fibrosis, or the hardening and tightening of our connective tissue, is the main symptom. Most times, this manifests as fibrosis of the skin. Connective tissue runs throughout our entire body, including our vital organs. With systemic scleroderma, the skin, lungs, and other organs become tightened and severely compromised. Jim began to get very ill with a systemic yeast infection in 2010 that lasted for several years and he went to many physicians to find out why. Systemic scleroderma is a difficult disease to diagnose, as it affects so many different body parts. They say it can take years to diagnose, and once given this diagnosis, many folks pass away by year seven. It literally took us four years to get a diagnosis as Jim had such severe symptoms in so many areas.

Systemic scleroderma affected all of Jim's connective tissue and his organs including his esophagus, heart, lungs, skin, muscles, gut and more. Our daughter, Kathryn, was in her last year of high school, and our son, Stephen, was a freshman in high school when Jim's mysterious symptoms began. When Kathryn went away to college, Jim did not want Kathryn to know how his symptoms were progressing or how difficult our lives had become. Stephen and I had to hide our experience, for the most part, from Kathryn to respect Jim's wishes. He knew that Kathryn would quit college and come home to help if she knew how scary and challenging things had become.

Jim saw numerous specialist groups including cardiology, gastroenterology, pulmonology, neurology, and more. None of the physicians communicated with one another. Nor were they able to look at the whole picture of what was happening inside of Jim's body to connect his mysterious symptoms. After four years of tests, appointments, and specialists, we still did not have a diagnosis. Despite having great health insurance, we had put over $100,000 on credit cards trying to get answers. Alternative medicine practitioners do not accept insurance. Jim was no longer able to work, so we had to declare bankruptcy.

This decision was devastating and led us to losing our beautiful home of 14 years, which we had manifested when our kids were young.

After four years of devastating symptoms, Jim finally received the correct diagnosis of systemic scleroderma. At that time, he was in and out of the hospital several times for various complications. He was admitted to inpatient rehabilitation twice, staying for weeks at a time, in order to be strong enough to walk and manage at home. Jim had a feeding tube inserted for over a year. He also had to have a pacemaker/defibrillator surgically implanted as the scleroderma had damaged much of his heart. He took a blood thinner, which he eventually had to go off as it caused internal bleeding on two occasions. This led to him coding both times. They prescribed Jim a large dose of liquid Prednisone daily, which he took for years. While this was necessary to save his life, it brutally changed his personality. I called his prescribing physician and told her of his behavior changes, and she eventually lowered his dose drastically.

My beloved husband coded seven times during his nine-year illness. I was with him through every single code. My heart breaks now as I write this. So much loss, jammed into nine years of our lives. Spirit always told me that family comes first when one has children and a spouse. I pulled back from my own life during these years to be there as much as possible for my family. It was dreadful to see him go through such a devastating disease.

In May of 2018, the day before Kathryn graduated from the University of Pittsburgh with her Doctorate in Physical Therapy, she, and Alan, our now son-in-law, were responsible for saving Jim's life. As the ER physician told us, "Had you arrived five minutes later, your husband wouldn't have made it." This was Jim's sixth code. On graduation day, Stephen helped his dad watch it on a Facebook livestream from the ICU.

In 2017, Jim joined a support group from the National Scleroderma Foundation. One of the men in the group shared that he saw a warning on the back of a bag of cement. The warning said that cement can cause several rare autoimmune diseases, including scleroderma, dermatomyositis, and polymyositis. Jim had all of them. They come from inhaling too much silica, a key ingredient in cement. Jim worked in a cement factory for only three months, between high school and college. Nearly 30 years later, he became severely ill out of the blue. We had him genetically tested to make sure our kids were okay. Scleroderma was not genetic for him. We suspect it was from his exposure to cement dust. Jim also developed Raynaud's disease and Sjogren's syndrome as a result.

In August of 2019, Jim and I drove to Wichita, Kansas to visit Stephen who had recently moved there for a new job. Stephen and his dad had become distant during Jim's years on Prednisone and after. The large doses of Prednisone may have been saving Jim's life, but it was also stealing him away from us in other ways. My beloved Jim, never unkind, was now struggling with a drastically altered personality. He was angry and aggressive due to the prescribes steroids. Stephen and Jim had barely spoken in a year. At times, it was difficult to separate who we knew Jim was from the behaviors the steroids caused. Our visit to Wichita began healing their broken relationship. We stayed a week and had a lovely visit. Healing had begun.

While we were out for lunch one afternoon and Jim and Stephen were sitting across from me at the restaurant, I looked at Jim and felt an incredible rush of sadness. Spirit impressed upon me using my clairsentience, that Jim would pass away within the next three months. I refused to allow myself to accept that message. Nevertheless, I remembered it and how it felt. On our last day visiting, Jim woke up to share with me his dream about a phoenix. It was a long and detailed dream that brought Jim feelings of transformation and new beginnings. I literally felt his excitement like a fresh start was ahead for Jim. It felt hopeful! When we left to load the car and say goodbye to Stephen at work before driving back to Illinois, the construction fence erected overnight across the street from Stephen's apartment complex stunned us. Yep, Phoenix Construction Company. We saw many enormous red phoenixes draped across a large city block. Jim and I were both astounded. We both felt excited to receive confirmation of his dream of transformation. A phoenix is a mythical bird that can burn into ashes and then create itself anew, arising from its own ashes to begin life again.

In October of 2019, two months after Jim's dream, we drove to Pittsburgh to visit Kathryn and Alan, now engaged, who had just bought their first home together. Their wedding date was set for June of 2020, and it was to take place in Chicago. Jim was ecstatic to be able to walk Kathryn down the aisle. Earlier that year in June of 2019, Kathryn, Jim, Kathryn's maid of honor, Melissa, and I shopped for Kathryn's wedding dress. Jim broke down in tears when he saw Kathryn in the beautiful wedding gown she had picked out. During our visit to Pittsburgh, Jim intentionally began preparing his muscles for next year's wedding by proudly walking up and down the stairs in Kathryn and Alan's backyard. Just a few years earlier, his muscles had become so weak that he had difficulty even walking. Climbing stairs had become impossible for his weakened muscles.

After a beautiful week's visit and much excitement over the next year's wedding festivities, we drove back home to Chicago. Three days later, I was shopping at our local farmer's market. As I was carrying bags of fruit and vegetables up the hill to our apartment, Jim came out to help me. I went to the car for a second load. When I walked up the hill for the second time, Jim came out of the house, unable to speak. He looked panicked pointing to his throat and lungs. I quickly responded by asking if he needed the Heimlich maneuver, assuming he was choking. He nodded yes. We stepped into the apartment through the sliding glass patio door, so I could perform abdominal thrusts on him. Jim had lost so much weight; he weighed less than I did. As I began to perform the Heimlich maneuver on him, Jim literally flopped over like a ragdoll in my arms. With all his dead weight literally pulling us, we both fell to the ground. Unfortunately, we were standing near the sliding glass door rail, and I fell to the floor while still holding onto Jim. He fell on top of me, and my back landed on the raised metal rail of the sliding glass door. I blacked out briefly.

When I awakened, I felt excruciating pain in my back. Jim was still on the ground and not responding, so I rushed to call 911. I did CPR on him until the police and ambulance arrived. I was in shock. My back pain was a 10. Everything felt like a blur. EMTs continued to work to stabilize Jim. As the ambulance took Jim to the emergency room, two police officers stayed to help me find my car keys and pick up the groceries from the lawn, which I had dropped in all the chaos.

It was just shy of three months since Spirit told me Jim would pass away during that period. The ambulance rushed Jim to the hospital, and before I could get there, they placed him on a ventilator and started a procedure to lower his body temperature to see if it would help him. I called our children, and they flew in from Wichita and Pittsburgh. Jim had little to no brain activity and his organs were all shutting down from lack of oxygen. Over the next two days, we placed Jim in hospice and additional family came to say their goodbyes.

After Jim was taken off the ventilator, a powerful miracle happened! Kathryn and Alan were standing on Jim's right side and Kathryn was holding his hand. Stephen was standing on his left holding his other hand. I was at Jim's head, stroking his hair and forehead. The hospice chaplain and nurse were both at his feet. As his blood pressure slowly dropped, Jim literally picked up his head, turned his face toward Kathryn, smiled and squeezed her hand. We all witnessed it! Then he turned his head toward Stephen, smiled at him, and squeezed his hand! Then his head came back to center, he relaxed, closed his eyes, and passed away. The hospice chaplain and nurse were stunned. I always knew James Accetturo was a powerful Spirit operating a human body. That day we began to learn just how powerful of a Spirit he is.

The following day, as the kids returned from printing photos for their dad's memorial dinner and celebration, Jim began to communicate from the world of Spirit! And he is still here, helping me from the other side of the veil to this day. Jim's first communication was through Kathryn's cell phone. As soon as the kids walked in with the enlarged photos, Kathryn's cell phone rang. She was startled as she always keeps her cell phone on vibrate. We were all shocked when her phone said I was calling her. My cell phone was on the kitchen counter. Indeed, I was not calling her. Then we looked at Kathryn's phone while it was ringing. She gasped when she noticed the time of the call was Jim's birthdate. Wow!

That same day, I began to hear the song "Waterloo" by Abba playing repeatedly in my head. I went into our bedroom and looked up the lyrics to "Waterloo." Abba, by the way, was Jim's favorite band. As I listened to the song and read the words, I was in awe. Jim was communicating to me directly with every lyric. I kept replaying the scene of Jim slumped over in my arms and us falling to the floor. I was still in shock. I did not want to believe it was real. How could he have coded right then? Why did it have to happen that way? We deserved more time. The lyrics explained that indeed it was the right time. His battle was over as he finally faced his Waterloo. Oh my! I felt such comfort that Jim was watching over me and communicating from Spirit. He continues to do so to this day, and I am so incredibly grateful.

I went out and told the kids about the lyrics. We were amazed. I had been singing "Waterloo" all day and, once I acknowledged its meaning, it stopped playing. It felt like the scene in the movie, *Ghost*, where Patrick Swayze sings, "I'm Henry, the VIII, I Am" to Whoopi Goldberg until she acknowledges him. I cried myself to sleep that night, still having back pain of a 10 and still in shock that my beloved was now in Spirit. I finally fell asleep at 2 a.m. I awakened at 3 a.m. with the song "Who Loves You" by Frankie Valli and The Four Seasons playing in my head. It asks, "Who's gonna help you through the night?" Thanks Jim!

The next day I received two powerful telephone calls. One was from my brother-in-law, Michael, Jim's brother. My mother-in-law was holding a conversation with someone at her kitchen table. Michael joined her to see if he could figure out what his mom was doing. He quickly realized she was conversing with Jim. My friend, Justine, called the next morning and said Jim had just visited her in her kitchen to say he was okay! Jim knew Justine was a medium. Jim also knew his mom had spiritual gifts, as she had given us many clairvoyant messages over the 32 years we were married.

Kathryn and Stephen also felt Jim's energy around the first three days. Then the day after his memorial family celebration, I could no longer feel his energy. When the kids awakened, I shared my experience. They checked in and agreed, their dad's energy was gone. That morning as I was preparing breakfast, I was humming a song that I could not put my finger on just yet. I was still humming when Kathryn came up and asked, "Mom, why are you humming a Kelly Clarkson song?" I asked her for the title. Her response was, "Breakaway." Again, Jim to the rescue. He was telling me he was at his Life's Review and had to spread his wings and learn how to fly. I had no idea Jim would be able to communicate so quickly as a Spirit. Many new Spirits take a year or more to come through with a message. As of today, as I am writing this page, Jim has been gone for over four years. My deceased husband has selected, thus far, 181 songs, which are exact matches to what was going on with me at the time I received them. Sometimes they play in my head and other times I hear the song outside of myself like on a radio or overhead sound system for example. I look up the lyrics, which show me just how close my beloved husband really is here and now.

Stephen flew back home, and Kathryn took six weeks off work to clean out our apartment and move me to Pittsburgh to live with her and Alan. During this time, Kathryn had driven me to urgent care for my back where my x-rays showed two compression fractures of my L4 and L5 vertebrae. My prescription was a lumbar back brace and pain medicine that barely made a dent in the pain. Kathryn was an absolute Angel who worked her tail off for the next six weeks. She even drove the packed U-Haul the entire way to Pittsburgh while towing my car behind. I am so incredibly grateful to and proud of our children, Kathryn and Stephen, and our son-in-law, Alan.

A life-changing moment happened while Kathryn was going through all our things. She discovered the paper I had written and copyrighted on January 11, 1990, entitled "The Coming of New Humanity." It was my theory of the 4-stroke cycle combustion engine that I created with Billy on the psychiatric unit. I had written it after Billy passed away in 1989. Back in 1990, I had asked the head of clinical psychology, who was my favorite undergraduate professor at UIC, Chris Keys, to read it. I then presented it at the UIC Crises Intervention Hotline Convention hosted by the UIC student counselling service at a hotel in downtown Chicago. There were 150 people present for my talk, and I received a standing ovation when I finished presenting. Professor Keys wrote one statement on the back of my paper. "What do you plan to do with this, Robyn? Are you the next Carl Jung? Or will this be a best-selling self-help book?" Instead, I filed the paper in my filing cabinet. I used the 4-stroke cycle with my clients and myself over the next 30 years of my practicing social work, but I never did anything to publish it.

I began to receive a strong impression (clairsentience) that it was time to begin to write about my life experience as the Reluctant Messiah, which Spirit gave me the title of more than 25 years earlier. Unfortunately, trying to concentrate while I was still in excruciating back pain made it difficult to write. So, Kathryn got me an appointment with an Orthopedic surgeon at the hospital where she worked in Pittsburgh. The physician ordered an MRI of my entire spine. The results showed that I had six fractured vertebrae from falling on the sliding glass door rail with Jim in my arms; four lumbar and two thoracic compression fractures. Ugh, no wonder the pain was a 10+. I wore two back braces, which completely immobilized me. I could only take them off to sleep. One large Velcro immobilizer supported me from the back and another metal brace helped me to stand straight in the front with what looked like the underneath of a turtle's shell. When I finally went to physical therapy, my back would not bend. I felt like my spine had become a concrete pillar.

By then, Covid had hit and we were on lockdown. Both Kathryn and Alan are physical therapists, so they continued working. I was in therapy with a wonderful holistic grief counselor in person, which transitioned to Zoom sessions once the pandemic hit. I spent my days committed to writing, meditating, cooking healthy meals for my family, doing my physical therapy exercises at home, and taking good care of myself so I could heal more quickly. Jim continued communicating with me through songs he played in my head and through the radio. It was a powerful feeling when I would read the lyrics to a song that I heard on repeat in my head and realize it was Jim telling me he was watching over me, knowing exactly what I was going through mentally and emotionally.

In June of 2020, I performed Kathryn and Alan's official wedding ceremony. By the week of their wedding, the state of Pennsylvania had lifted the ban of no group gatherings and allowed 10 people to gather at a time. They got married in a beautiful state park called McConnell's Mill. It is about 30 miles from Pittsburgh. They have whitewater kayaking, a famous covered bridge, beautiful hiking trails, waterfalls, and more. Stephen drove Kathryn and me to the park. We were fully dressed for the wedding. The plan was that at exactly noon, the professional photographer would take the first photos of Kathryn and

Alan's "first look." This is when the bride and groom see each other in their bridal wear prior to the wedding ceremony.

Stephen had driven Kathryn and me to McConnell's Mill in my car. He put his playlist on shuffle, and randomly the first song that came on was "Daughters" by John Mayer. We knew instantly that Jim was with us and did our best not to cry and ruin our makeup. When we arrived at the park, we saw people hiking and enjoying the beautiful weather after being in lockdown for several months. Stephen got a handicapped parking space with my placard right next to the covered bridge. He then helped me to put on my minister's robe while Kathryn, fully dressed in her gorgeous wedding gown, met the photographer by the covered bridge and mill for her and Alan's first look photo.

Then Stephen took my arm, and we all walked to the site where Kathryn had chosen as their wedding altar. It was right alongside the riverbank where kayaks were floating by. Stephen, who was a groomsman, helped me step up onto the large square rock that the bride, groom, and I stood on for the beautiful custom wedding ceremony I had written with Kathryn and Alan's input. It was a magnificent wedding. We ended up with an audience of hikers up on the trail. Some stood and watched the entire wedding ceremony. I noticed during the ceremony that Stephen was pacing on my left, his eyes filled with tears. I knew if I made eye contact with him, I would lose it and start crying. But when the ceremony was completed, I later asked him what was happening with him during the ceremony. He shared that he saw clairvoyantly, a brilliant white light coming straight up from under the rock we were standing upon during the ceremony. He described it as the brightest white light he had ever seen. It ceased once the ceremony was over.

The next day when we began to look through photos taken at the wedding, one photo caught our attention. Alan's mom captured it with her cell phone. It shows a brilliant white light shining down on Kathryn during the first look. Since the photo was staged at noon, and they were standing under a large tree in the shade, we knew the light was not sunlight. It was Kathryn's dad, my beloved James Accetturo, showing up to give his blessing to our daughter and son-in-law. Let me explain. First, at noon, the sunlight would be directly overhead. This photo was taken at noon, yet the light shines at a 45-degree angle. The bright shining ray of light stops at Kathryn's waist. It does not shine through to the ground. There is shade on the ground. Physically, if this were a sun's ray, it would be impossible for the light to stop and not shine onto the ground. The photo preceding this one shows the rays of light are only about 25% formed. Then this white light photo appears next. In the last photo taken at the first look, the light disappears as soon as Alan turns around to see his beautiful bride. Kathryn's dad, my beloved James, has proven to us repeatedly that he is still here, watching us and participating from the world of Spirit. Our hope is that our photo will show all that we simply leave our physical body at the time of our death, and we continue to exist as pure Spirit, pure energy, and pure unconditional love.

© Ruth Kuminkoski

Chapter 33

EPILOGUE

"Stop acting so small. You are the Universe in ecstatic motion." Rumi

———•••———

I have done my best to serve God and the Universe throughout my life. "Knowing" God and Spirit and "believing" in God and Spirit are vastly different. We are co-creators with Source Energy. In John 14:12 Christ tells us, "Truly, truly, I sat unto you, whoever believes in me will also do the works that I do: and greater works than these will he do, because I go unto the Father." Over time, we have forgotten we are Spirits operating human bodies. Only relating to our physical body and mind sets us up for a much tougher life. We are missing the bigger picture of our purpose here on the Earth Plane. We have denied feeling our feelings for too long now. Their energy awaits our attention. My hope is that my life's experience will give courage and proof that we are a Spirit operating a human body. Our feelings hold the KEY to our creating HEAVEN ON EARTH RIGHT HERE, RIGHT NOW. By each of us taking responsibility and doing our inner work to become free from the energetic hold of our swallowed feelings, we will uncover our Light within to usher in the fifth dimension.

In the fall of 2020, while I was meditating at a park on the Allegheny River in Oakmont, Pennsylvania, my beloved Jim spoke to me through my clairaudience. He shared that he was meditating with me. When I opened my eyes, I saw my husband as Light, meditating with me! He is sitting with his legs crossed. Thank you James Accetturo for continuing to be by my side. I am forever grateful. Here is the photo from my camera on my cell phone.

© Robyn Accetturo

In 2017, while visiting Pittsburgh, Jim and I went with Kathryn and Alan to Phipps Conservatory. Kathryn took our photo sitting on a bench near the brick walkway where families can purchase a brick in someone's honor. In 2021, two years after Jim passed away, I returned to Phipps Conservatory with Alan's mother, Ruth. When we passed the same area, I immediately remembered my photo with Jim. I asked Ruth to take my picture there. In my mind, I asked Jim to join me in the photo. After Ruth took the photo, I could not believe it! Here are the two photos. The original photo was taken in 2017, and the one on the left was taken in 2021. ©Ruth Kuminkoski

Inside the highlighted circle, I see my husband plain as day! His widow's peak, his goatee, his eyes, and his arm and shoulder are clear to me inside the yellow circle. I hope he is visible to all. James Accetturo is a powerful Spirit. We all are. Please, let us acknowledge we are Spirits

operating human bodies, and let us create Heaven on Earth. The shift to 5D begins with each of us taking action to heal our broken hearts and become responsible for stepping into our Higher Self. Both Jim and I hope that these photos will show the world proof that Spirit is REAL, here, and NOW. Thanks, Jim, for continuing to love me from the other side of the veil. I will always love you. I am so very grateful.

The 100th Monkey is a theory that shows us how a message becomes truth to the masses. Back in 1952, on a remote island in Japan, scientists followed the behavior of a young female monkey. She began to wash her sand-covered sweet potato in a stream of water before eating it. Soon her family, her playmates, and their families began to do the same. One by one, her behavior spread and became the norm. The monkey had achieved *Critical mass.* This is the tipping point where all others follow the same truth.

When enough of us do our inner work to feel and heal the traumas of our past, and we shift internally to behave responsibly in our ways of being and doing, we become open-hearted Spirits operating human bodies. When enough of us take accountability for our feelings, which allows us to naturally step into our spiritual power, we will reach critical mass. Together we will shift the energy of our entire planet to achieve spiritual ascension by creating Heaven on Earth, one heart at a time. We are so worth our own efforts. Let us allow ourselves to "become" unconditional love by doing our inner work to heal our heart of our trapped feelings. Then let us share our love and inner Light with the world.

Spirit is real. The Spirit World is real and operates right here, right now. It is simply unseen by our physical eyes. My husband communicates with me sometimes daily from the Spirit World. Together, we continue our journey. Ours is a true love story. I know it is Divine Order that our life together has unfolded perfectly, traumas and all. Each trauma is an opportunity for our Soul's growth. It is through the loving wisdom of our healed heart that we open the door to fulfilling our Divine and highest destiny. We are each the Reluctant Messiah. The world awaits our special gifts and talents. The best is yet to come. Honoring ourselves by feeling our feelings and communicating with Spirit are both essential to bringing heaven here on Earth. Now is the time. Let's do this!

I want to thank you dear reader from the bottom of my heart for joining me in our Spiritual Revolution to bring Unconditional Love and Light back to the Earth Plane. Let us call on God, Spirit, the Angels, and our Ancestors to help us live a more fulfilled life right here, right now. We can do this. We are One Spiritual Community.

I want to leave us with a favorite Bible verse of mine, Philippians 4: 4-9. "Finally, brothers, whatever is true, whatever is noble, whatever is right, whatever is pure, whatever is lovely, whatever is admirable – if anything is excellent or praiseworthy – think about such things."

And so it is, Amen.

ABOUT THE AUTHOR

A 1989 master's graduate of Jane Addams College of Social Work, Robyn V. Accetturo became a Licensed Clinical Social Worker in 1991. For more than 3 decades, she has been in practice as a private guardian for disabled adults as both a psychiatric and medical social worker. Robyn began having prophetic dreams in 1987 during graduate school at the age of 27, two years after leaving a relationship filled with domestic violence. She worked hard in counselling to ascertain the reason she allowed herself to be in that violent situation which led her to becoming a social worker. In 2008, Robyn pledged her vows and became an Ordained Spiritualist Minister and Healer. Her passion and courage give us strength and hope in these difficult times.

Website: www.revrobyn.com

www.ingramcontent.com/pod-product-compliance
Lightning Source LLC
Chambersburg PA
CBHW060519080526
44586CB00012B/541